Disease and Distinctiveness
in the
American South

Disease and Distinctiveness
in the
American South

EDITED BY

TODD L. SAVITT

AND

JAMES HARVEY YOUNG

THE UNIVERSITY OF TENNESSEE PRESS

KNOXVILLE

Cloth: 1st printing, 1988; 2nd printing, 1991.
Paper: 1st printing, 1991.

The paper in this book meets the minimum requirements of the
American National Standard for Permanence of Paper for
Printed Library Materials. ∞   The binding materials have been
chosen for strength and durability.

Library of Congress Cataloging-in-Publication Data

Disease and distinctiveness in the American South / edited by
Todd L. Savitt and James Harvey Young.—1st ed.
     p.   cm.
   Bibliography: p.
   Includes index.
   ISBN 0-87049-572-0 (cloth: alk. paper)
   ISBN 0-87049-685-9 (pbk.: alk. paper)
   1. Diseases—Southern States—History. 2. Public health—
Southern States—History. 3. Southern States—Civilization.
I. Savitt, Todd Lee, 1943–   . II. Young, James Harvey.
   [DNLM: 1. Disease Outbreaks—history—United States.
2. Public Health—history—United States. WA 11 AA1 D6]
RA650. 5. D57 1988
362.1'0975—dc19
DNLM/DLC
for Library of Congress   87–30238
                                                          CIP

DEDICATION

To the memory of
RICHARD HARRISON SHRYOCK
Pioneer social historian of
American medicine,
who was concerned with the
theme of diseases in the South

Contents

·

Illustrations

·

Contributors

.

JAMES O. BREEDEN, professor of history at Southern Methodist University, received his Ph.D. from Tulane University. His published works include *Joseph Jones, M.D.: Scientist of the Old South*, *Advice Among Masters: The Ideal in Slave Management in the Old South*, and articles on the social history of the South with an emphasis on science and medicine. Breeden is now completing a study of science in the southern context.

JO ANN CARRIGAN is professor of history at the University of Nebraska at Omaha and adjunct professor of the history of medicine at the University of Nebraska Medical Center. She received her Ph.D. from Louisiana State University. She has edited and written commentaries for an edition of Alcee Fortier's *History of Louisiana* and has published articles on southern medical and public health history. Carrigan is currently studying the career of Dr. Oscar Dowling, progressive president of the Louisiana State Board of Health, 1910-28, as part of a broader project on health promotion strategies in the early twentieth-century South.

JOHN DUFFY, Priscilla Alden Burke Professor of History Emeritus at the University of Maryland in College Park, received his Ph.D. from the University of California in Los Angeles. He is the author of ten books, including a two-volume history of medicine in Louisiana, a two-volume history of public health in New York City, works on the history of epidemics, and a history of American medicine entitled *The Healers: The Rise of the Medical Estab-lishment*. Duffy is currently writing a history of American public health.

ELIZABETH W. ETHERIDGE, professor of history at Longwood College, during 1987 held a visiting appointment as historian at the Centers for Disease Control in Atlanta. She received her Ph.D. from the University of Georgia. Her writing has concerned southern health and cultural history, including *The Butterfly Caste: A Social History of Pellagra in the South*, and, as coauthor, *The Neighborhood Mint: Dahlonega in the Age of Jackson*. Etheridge recently completed a study of American summer vacations from 1870 to 1920.

ALAN I MARCUS, director of the Center for Historical Studies of Technology and Science and professor in the Program in the History of Technology and Science, Department of History, Iowa State University, received his Ph.D. from the University of Cincinnati. He is author of *Agricultural Science and the Quest for Legitimacy: Farmers, Agricultural Colleges, and Experiment Stations, 1870–1890* and articles on American public health. A second book, coauthored with Howard Segal, entitled *Technology in America: Brief History*, is scheduled for publication in 1988. Marcus is presently writing about the history of and controversy over diethylstilbestrol (DES) as an animal feed additive and component in human food.

TODD L. SAVITT, professor of medical humanities in the School of Medicine and professor of history at East Carolina University, received his Ph.D. from the University of Virginia and engaged in postdoctoral study of the history of medicine and science at Duke University. He has written primarily on the history of black health and blacks in medicine, including *Medicine and Slavery: The Diseases and Health Care of Blacks in Antebellum Virginia*. He coedited the *Dictionary of American Medical Biography*. Savitt's most recent works are a history of the discovery of sickle cell anemia and a history of medical education for blacks in the United States.

JAMES HARVEY YOUNG, Charles Howard Candler Professor of American Social History Emeritus at Emory University, received his Ph.D. from the University of Illinois. His books, *The Toadstool Millionaires* and *The Medical Messiahs*, together trace the theme of health quackery through the American experience, and *American Self-Dosage Medicines: An Historical Perspective* describes the slow emergence from quackery of reputable over-the-counter medicines. Young, who is working on a history of food and drug regulation in America, is now completing a first volume on the roots and legislative history of the Federal Food and Drugs Act of 1906.

Preface

.

In 1926 a southern medical school professor noted a "mad rush southward" of people from the North and East and, with great optimism, predicted eventual Sunbelt prosperity. Granting that other reasons might be involved, C.C. Bass, professor of experimental medicine at Tulane University School of Medicine, asserted that the fundamental factor making the migration "really . . . possible" could be stated simply in the title of his article, "Tropical Diseases Are on the Wane in the South."[1]

The conquering of yellow fever, the "progressive decline" in malaria, and the rapid reduction of the hookworm plague, Bass wrote, brightened immensely the region's future prospects. These diseases "formerly gave to all the South an unfavorable reputation as to security and health." But the afflictions "no longer stand in the way, and it is now quite natural that the people should emigrate to regions where it costs less in energy and effort to live comfortably and where now the promise of health and longevity is as good as anywhere else, if not, indeed, better than in other less favored parts of the country."

In 1982, half a century after Bass published his article, a panel at the Southern Historical Association annual meeting in Memphis addressed anew the question whose answer Bass had taken quite for granted: "Was disease a factor in southern distinctiveness?" At the session Jo Ann Carrigan, Elizabeth Etheridge, and Alan I Marcus presented papers, while James O. Breeden served as commentator and John Duffy as chair. All the participants were medical historians who have focused their research on the South. In the audience that afternoon sat the editors of the present volume. More than a year earlier, the convention program chair, Robert W. Johannsen, had asked the medical historian on his committee (Savitt) to develop a session at the annual meeting acknowledging the special research interests of the association's president (Young); the session on disease and southern distinctiveness resulted. Listening to the three papers on yellow fever, hookworm, and pellagra, and to the ensuing commentary and discussion, we would-be editors recognized immediately that the panel's contributions were worthy of developing into a book. No volume existed containing profiles of disease entities especially associated with the South, or wrestling with the relation of diseases to an issue of perennial concern to southern historians, that of southern distinctiveness. We hoped and believed that such a book might interest southern historians, medical historians, and, indeed, readers concerned with history more generally.

So we persuaded commentator Breeden to broaden his convention commentary into an overview of the theme of southern distinctiveness, which here appears as the introductory essay to our volume. Panelists Carrigan, Marcus, and Etheridge have revised and expanded their Memphis papers on yellow fever, hookworm, and pellagra, while chairman Duffy has specially prepared an essay on malaria. These chapters on diseases, along with essays by the editors themselves, compose the book. Savitt studies the health of slaves. Young, after a brief discussion of physician therapy, considers both the taking and the making of patent medicines, paying special heed to those diseases discussed by his fellow authors. Each essay in our book, though rooted in its author's previous work, embodies new research.

As James Breeden's introductory chapter shows, the notion of southern "otherness" has had a long and embattled history. A growing body of scholarship also has concerned itself with southern health and disease. Our goal in the present volume is to bring these two themes together and so to elucidate more directly and searchingly than has yet been done in such commentary as that by Professor Bass, the disease and therapy aspects of southern distinctiveness. Our authors have handled distinctiveness in varying ways, while still remaining faithful to the book's basic theme. As John Harley Warner has recently pointed out, claims of distinctiveness were not unique to the South, for a sense of regional medical differences existed in all parts of the country, especially in the nineteenth century.[2]

Whereas the diseases discussed are certainly the major maladies that afflicted the South, we realize that other facets of our theme warrant exploration, for example, black health after 1865, Native American health, overall demographic patterns in the region, and the reflection of southern health in literature. The opportunity for research on these and related topics stands invitingly open. We hope that our essays, reviving an environmentalist consideration of southern distinctiveness, somewhat neglected recently, and focusing on a special aspect of that approach, may prompt other scholars to join us in assessing distinctive circumstances relating to health in the South and the impact of those factors on the section.

> Todd L. Savitt, East Carolina University
> James Harvey Young, Emory University
> September 27, 1987

NOTES

1. C.C. Bass, "Tropical Diseases Are On the Wane in the South," *The Nation's Health* 8 (1926), 75, 76, 144. On Bass, see John Duffy, *The Tulane University Medical Center: One Hundred and Fifty Years* (Baton Rouge: Louisiana Univ. Press, 1984), 126–27, 149–56, 164–65.

2. John Harley Warner, "The Idea of Southern Medical Distinctiveness: Medical Knowledge and Practice in the Old South," in *Sickness and Health in America*, ed. Judith Walzer Leavitt and Ronald L. Numbers, 2d ed. (Madison: Univ. of Wisconsin Press, 1985), 53–70.

Disease and Distinctiveness
in the
American South

"An Infected Family: A Typical Group of Hookworm People." From *World's Work* 24 (1912), 515.

1

Disease as a Factor in Southern Distinctiveness

·

JAMES O. BREEDEN

"Tell me about the South. What's it like there?
What do they do there? Why do they live at all?"

· · ·

"You can't understand it. You would have to
be born there."

William Faulkner, *Absalom, Absalom!*

Because of the importance of region in the nation's history, regional studies have abounded in American historical scholarship.
And the South has clearly dominated such studies. Indeed, an
astounding number and variety of authors, ranging from serious
students to popular interpreters, have subjected the South to
portrayal and analysis. "The result of this intense sectional
scrutiny," Dewey W. Grantham, Jr., observes, "is that the South
has probably become the most thoroughly interpreted part of the
country." "So numerous are the books on the Southern region,"
he adds, "that even the matter of selecting a title has become a
problem." Grantham suggests two principal reasons for this remarkable show of interest: "the region's own self-consciousness
and its recognizable identity in the nation as a whole."[1]

The two—regional self-consciousness and the idea of a separate southern identity—are intimately interrelated and mutually
reinforcing. John Shelton Reed, a sociologist, has written exten-
sively on the persistence of a southern subculture within American mass society. "For many—perhaps most—white residents of

the South," he holds, " 'Southerners' is not merely a descriptive label for a category which includes them, but the name of a group to which they feel they belong." In fact, so strong is this feeling of group identity, he argues, that "Southern regional subsociety may be thought of as roughly coterminous with a Southern ethnic subsociety, and that it differs in this respect from most other regional subsocieties."[2] Accompanying and bolstering the South's self-consciousness is the idea of southern distinctiveness, or "the axiomatic acceptance of the belief that there was in fact an American South and that it possessed clearly defined traits which set it apart from the rest of the nation."[3] Expanding upon this theme, Frank Vandiver, in his introduction to the published proceedings of a Rice University symposium on the idea of the South, exclaimed: "Surely there lurks somewhere a South, a tangible, knowable, living South, with traditions and meanings and ideals to serve the present and future as well as the past. . . . "The South," he elaborated, "must be . . . self-defining, self-contained, self-reliant, a section more than a section, a province, or a realm."[4] It was, however, Wilbur J. Cash, the iconoclastic interpreter of the South, who most memorably stated the case for southern distinctiveness, when at the outset of his controversial classic, *The Mind of the South*, he asserted: "The peculiar history of the South has so greatly modified it from the general American norm that, when viewed as a whole, it decisively justifies the notion that the country is—not quite a nation within a nation, but the next thing to it."[5]

The idea of southern distinctiveness has been one of the most irresistible themes in the region's history. It is, I.A. Newby contends, "one of the nation's great riddles." Reducing the issue to its simplest form, he queries: "What is it that makes, has always made, the South distinctive?"[6] This question has evoked an enormous body of literature. Much of this literature is devoted to a quest for one central theme in southern history, in the belief that the South "has had, historically, a unifying focus at its center" which, if found, will yield a coherent understanding of the exotic character, mystery, and mystique of America's most distinctive region.[7] Indeed, so absorbed have historians been in this quest that it has been called "the central theme of southern historiography."[8]

The search for a central theme in southern history has been characterized by great activity but little agreement. While various theories have had their day, none has stood the test of time. This state of affairs has led some historians to conclude that the American South, as David L. Smiley put it, "defies either location or analysis." Rather, it is "an enigma challenging comprehension."[9] More expressively, David Potter likened the South to "a kind of Sphinx on the American land."[10] "Southernism," Francis B. Simkins wrote in agreement, "is a reality too elusive to be explained in objective terms. It is something like a song or an emotion, more easily felt than recorded."[11] To Cash, it was a state of mind.[12] If such is the case, then perhaps James G. Randall was correct when he observed: "Poets have done better in expressing this oneness of the South than historians in explaining it."[13] But the elusiveness of the central theme of southern history, as Newby notes, should not be a cause for despair; rather, it should serve as a stimulus to further study. This will-o'-the-wisp quest casts light not only on the history of the South, but, since in all likelihood without American nationality there would have been no southern consciousness, on that of the nation as well.[14]

An awareness of the growing divergence of the South from the rest of the country and speculations on the reasons for this phenomenon appeared early in the region's history, well in advance of the emergence of a southern sectional consciousness. In 1778, William Henry Drayton, the chief justice of South Carolina and a delegate to the Continental Congress, while voicing his concerns to the South Carolina Assembly regarding the prospects of the South under the proposed Articles of Confederation, contended that "from the nature of the climate, soil and produce of the several southern states, a northern and southern interest naturally and unavoidably arise."[15] Better known is Thomas Jefferson's 1785 letter to the Marquis de Chatellux discussing the traits of Americans. Jefferson detected clear distinctions between northerners and southerners, pointing out:

In the North they are	In the South they are
cool	fiery
sober	voluptuary
laborious	indolent
persevering	unsteady
independant [sic]	independant [sic]
jealous of their own liberties, and just to those of others	zealous for their own liberties, but trampling on those of others

interested	generous
chicaning	candid
superstitous and hypo-critical in their religion	without attachment or pre-tentions to any religion but that of the heart

So pronounced were these regional differences, Jefferson held, "that an observing traveller, without the aid of the quadrant may always know his latitude by the character of the people among whom he finds himself." While not ruling out the influence of other factors, he attributed the peculiar character traits of southerners chiefly to climate, or in his words, "to that warmth of their climate which unnerves and unmans both body and mind."[16]

The modern search for the roots of southern distinctiveness dates from the 1920s and the work of Ulrich B. Phillips, the first great historian of the South. Perhaps influenced by the turn-of-the-century debate over American nationality which pointed up southern deviations from national norms, Phillips, within a matter of months, articulated the two related streams of thought which subsequently have dominated the quest for the central theme in southern history. These are, as Smiley explains them, "the causal effects of environment" (the environmental theory) and "the development of certain acquired characteristics of the people called Southern" (the inheritance theory).[17]

Initially, Phillips, in one of the most famous articles in American history, stressed the acquired characteristic of racism. Considered by Newby to be—in spite of its disturbing and, to many, unsatisfactory thesis—"the most enduring statement of sectional identity as well as the most important interpretation of southern history ever offered," this study pinpointed the essence of southernness in white supremacy.[18] The South, Phillips asserted, "is a land with a unity despite its diversity, with a people having common joys and common sorrows, and, above all, as to the white folk a people with a common resolve indomitably maintained—that it shall be and remain a white man's country." "The consciousness of a function in these premises, whether expressed with the frenzy of a demagogue or maintained with a patrician's quietude," he continued, "is the cardinal test of a Southerner and the central theme of Southern history."[19] A few months later, in his equally well-known *Life and Labor in the Old South*, Phillips attributed southern distinctiveness to environmental causation.

"Let us begin by discussing the weather," he wrote at the outset, "for that has been the chief agency in making the South distinctive."[20]

Although subsequent scholars have called into question the credibility of Phillips' work, and his preoccupation with the issue of race in particular, "the twin trails he blazed," Smiley maintains, continue to furnish the methodological framework for students of southern distinctiveness.[21] Some have sought to document the environmental theory; others have pursued the inheritance model; a few have attempted to combine them.

The notion that the impersonal forces of geography and climate deterministically shaped the South and its institutions has been advocated by a number of respected students of the region, including, in addition to Phillips, Avery O. Craven, Francis B. Simkins, John R. Alden, and Clarence Casson. Advocates of this viewpoint have attributed a variety of perceived southern peculiarities and characteristics to the effects of environment. These range from a slower pace of life and an aversion to manual labor, to the purification of the region's Anglo-Saxon blood lines and the evolution of a superior race, the Southron. But perhaps the best known environmental argument is the contention of Phillips and others that the warmth of the southern climate dictated the region's staple crop–slave labor–plantation system, a development which, it is argued, not only set the South apart from the rest of the nation but also gave rise to southern distinctiveness.

The "plantation legend," as this thesis is commonly called, set off one of the liveliest debates in southern history. The thesis has been resolutely defended and roundly assailed. Supporters, while admitting that the plantation system did not characterize the entire South, nevertheless insist that it was "general enough to serve as an archetype . . . of a recognizable Southern society."[22] It was the plantation that, more than anything else, defined the South by setting standards for the entire region and serving as the source of much of its romantic tradition. In short, the great estate was the ideal image of the South. Sheldon Van Auken perhaps best captured the essence of this argument, asserting: "The plantation is central to any understanding of the South."[23]

Opponents of the plantation legend have attacked it on numerous grounds. Especially damaging has been the charge,

made by such figures as Frank L. and Harriet C. Owsley, Avery
O. Craven, Thomas P. Abernethy, and Richard H. Shryock, that
the plantation was characteristic of southern life only in isolated
areas such as tidewater Virginia and the South Carolina low
country, and did not dominate it anywhere. The issue was hotly
contested, but today few students of the South view the plantation as the central theme in southern history. Rather, most believe that in focusing on the planter elite, the plantation legend
created "a warped picture of southern society."[24]

Interest in the environmental approach to southern distinctiveness has declined sharply in recent years. There are a number
of reasons for this decline, chief among which are the theory's
indisputable inaccuracies (for example, the South is uniform in
neither geography nor climate), its deterministic orientation, and
the disappearance of most of the things that it was said to have
explained.[25] Edgar T. Thompson and William A. Foran typify
contemporary reactions to the environmental theory. In a
reevaluation of the role of climate in the evolution of the antebellum plantation, Thompson repudiated the older contention of a
direct cause-and-effect relationship. He found human factors
more compelling than environmental ones, observing: "A theory
which makes the plantation depend upon something outside the
process of human interaction, that is, a theory which makes the
plantation depend upon a fixed and static something like climate,
is a theory which operates to justify an existing social order and
the vested interests connected with that order."[26] On his part,
Foran claimed that climate of opinion was more important than
climate in shaping the southern experience.[27]

When climate was discredited as a causal agent, acquired
characteristics came to be emphasized in the quest for the central
theme in southern history. Charles S. Sydnor is probably most
responsible for the focus on social patterns, calling attention at an
early date to the importance of social history in understanding the
South and compiling one of the first lists of distinctively southern
cultural traits.[28] Others quickly followed suit.

The resulting criteria proposed for defining and measuring
southernness have grown to enormous proportions and range
from the serious through the seriocomic to the comic. The following is a sampling of the best-known and most enduring contributions to the social origins of southern distinctiveness.[29] Avery O.
Craven and Frank L. Owsley pioneered the popular school of

thought that attributes southern ethnicity to perceived outside attacks during the antebellum period. In defending its interests, the South became a conscious minority. This was a development of great import. "Opposition," Smiley explains, "drew people together in defense of their peculiarities when their natural course would have been to fight among themselves."[30] Moreover, the South's response to external criticism was often militancy, a behavior pattern that, as Frank E. Vandiver and John Hope Franklin point out, affixed the characteristics of extremism and violence to the region.[31]

Defensiveness is but one of many social characteristics that have been linked to southern distinctiveness. The southern agrarian tradition and its influence on the life of the region have been subjects of great interest. There is no better example of this tradition than the Vanderbilt Agrarians, who, in their famous manifesto, *I'll Take My Stand* (1930), contended that the southern way of life rested on an agrarian base and bemoaned the transforming effects of industrialism.[32] The South's unique religious experience—the predominance of Protestant evangelical fundamentalism—has often been singled out as a major factor shaping and sustaining regional identity.[33] C. Vann Woodward attributed the endurance of the South to its peoples' remembrance of their unique history. While other Americans celebrated abundance, success, and innocence, southerners shared a tradition of poverty, failure, and guilt. This collective historical experience, "the burden of Southern history," was a common bond that underlay their special identity.[34] T. Harry Williams stressed the significance of romanticism in southern distinctiveness. The quality that made the southerner "unique among other Americans," he held, was his tendency to create "mind-pictures of his world or of the larger world around him—images that he wants to believe, that are real to him, and that he will insist others accept."[35] David Potter postulated that the nostalgic persistence of a regional folk culture explained the South: "The culture of the folk survived in the South long after it succumbed to the onslaught of urban-industrial culture elsewhere."[36] And George B. Tindall, noting the relative lack of attention to social myth in a region steeped in mythology, called for a bold new approach to the question of southern identity. "Perhaps by turning to different and untrodden paths," he provocatively suggested, "we shall encounter the central theme of Southern history at last on the new frontier of mythology."[37] Tindall's seminal essay sparked an impressive renewal of interest in myth and southern history, but mythology failed to resolve the riddle of the South.

Another of the paths that remain untrodden is disease. The South's long history of poor health is well documented. Yet poor health has figured little in the debate over southern distinctiveness. This is not to imply that students of the South's separate identity have ignored the issue of health; such has certainly not been the case. Rather, they have tended to look upon a high incidence of disease as a characteristic of the distinctive South and not as a major factor contributing to its evolution and perpetuation. But as such works as Henry E. Sigerist's *Civilization and Disease* (1943), Frederick F. Cartwright's *Disease and History* (1972), and William H. McNeill's *Plagues and Peoples* (1976) convincingly argue, disease has been a powerful force shaping the histories of peoples and nations. The sectionalization of the American South was no exception. Indeed, while it would be foolhardy to contend that disease was the central theme in southern history, the South's unique health history undoubtedly contributed to making the region a distinctive national subculture in two principal ways. First, a reputation for poor health helped perpetuate a negative image of the South that retarded regional development by discouraging immigration and investment. Second, to many, a high rate of disease symbolized the distinctive South, a region of poverty, ignorance, backwardness, and insularity. Without doubt, the high incidence of disease and its effects retarded social and economic development and contributed to the national image of southern backwardness. Moreover, regional health problems served as a lens through which some southern shortcomings were projected and magnified, reinforcing the notion of regional inferiority. In turn, charges of a flawed way of life, including poor health, were viewed by southerners as unfair and unwarranted and responded to with hypersensitivity and defensiveness. In making this response, southerners banded together in a common cause, growing increasingly aware and protective of their separateness. In addition, in denying or explaining away criticisms of their region, southerners forestalled long-overdue social and economic reform. The consequent persistence of the causes of backwardness, such as excessive morbidity and mortality, was a powerful factor sustaining southern distinctiveness.

The notion of regional diseases is an old one. In the Western world it can be traced back as far as Hippocrates' *Airs, Places, Waters.* Moreover, from the earliest days of colonization the explorers and settlers of America had been struck by the area's distinctive flora and fauna, prompting them to assume that new types of disease would also be encountered. The colonial experience seemed to bear out the validity of this assumption, as familiar European disorders soon took on strange and more virulent forms. The preoccupation with regional climate and disease is evident in a perusal of the titles of medical treatises of the eighteenth and nineteenth centuries. These range from Lionel Chalmers' standard work on South Carolina, *An Account of the Weather and Diseases of South Carolina* (London, 1776), through William Currie's more general volume, *An Historical Account of the Climates and Diseases of the United States of America* (Philadelphia, 1792), to Daniel Drake's classic study of the Mississippi Valley, *A Systematic Treatise . . . on the Principal Diseases of the Interior Valley of North America* (Cincinnati, 1850–55). In addition, medical journals frequently printed observations on regional meteorology and medical topography.

Initially the product of differences in climate and geography, regional health patterns, then, began with colonization. And while health hazards—ranging from endemic "ague" (chills and fever) and "flux" (dysentery) to epidemic outbreaks of smallpox and yellow fever—endangered the lives of colonists everywhere, the southern colonies, it is generally agreed, were the most unhealthy. "Seasoning," or becoming acclimated to the South's semitropical climate, was a source of great morbidity and mortality. In addition, owing to the inviting physical environment for insect life, the general disregard for draining swamps and marshes, and the steady influx of blacks with the rise of slavery, in the eighteenth century malaria tightened its hold on the South just as the disease began to disappear from New England. And southern forms of the disease were more debilitating and deadly than those that prevailed elsewhere in the colonies.[38]

By the emergence of the Old South in the opening decades of the nineteenth century, a distinctive southern health picture was evident. It was the worst in the nation. So poor was the state of health in the region considered to be that northern life insurance companies charged their southern policyholders higher premiums. Examples of the South's unhealthiness are plentiful.

Malaria remained endemic and was the principal cause of disabil-
ity and death. Residents of the southern port cities and the
surrounding countryside lived in fear of yellow fever, which
became a southern disease in the nineteenth century. New Orleans, the Old South's largest city, was popularly known as "the
graveyard of the Southwest" because of its frightful mortality rate
(nearly three times that of Philadelphia and New York, the principal urban centers of the middle and northern states). Infant
mortality rates were the highest in the nation. In addition, it is
estimated that as many as half of all southern children may have
suffered from hookworm infection, a condition not diagnosed
until the opening years of the twentieth century. Finally, inadequate diets, poor housing, unhealthy quarters, and hazardous
working conditions exacted a heavy toll on the health of the
South's large slave population.

The Old South's health problems were the result of environmental and cultural factors. Climate and frontier conditions in the
developing region, in conjunction with slavery, combined to
account for the continued presence of malaria. The insect vectors
of a number of other disorders that threatened southern health
—yellow fever and typhoid fever, for example—also thrived.
In addition to fostering insect life, the long, hot summers
made the preservation of food difficult, exacerbated sanitary
problems, and encouraged going barefooted, a habit associated
with the spread of hookworm. The cultural lag that increasingly
set the South apart from the more progressive North contributed
significantly to regional health problems. For instance, the level
of southern education, lowest in the nation, complicated the
health picture. Nationwide, during the first half of the nineteenth
century the "heroic" procedures of physicians were questioned,
encouraging the reliance on irregular practitioners and self-
dosage with patent medicines. Rural and undereducated southerners were particularly prone to resort to these sometimes
health-threatening practices. The absence of a social conscience
on the part of the dominant planter class further mired the region
in poor health. And the late antebellum period witnessed the rise
of what has been called "states-rights medicine," the high point
of southern interest in a distinctive health experience. The product of longstanding belief in regional diseases and the sectional
tensions of the era, states-rights medicine stressed the uniqueness of the South's medical problems and the crucial need for

southern-trained physicians and a southern medical literature. Southern medical nationalism adversely affected health in the region in important ways, principally by discouraging southern youths from attending the nation's best medical schools in Philadelphia and New York and encouraging the proliferation of inferior regional schools.[39]

By the end of the antebellum period, the South's reputation for poor health was well established. The region's experience with malaria and yellow fever, its chief endemic and epidemic disorders respectively, suggest that this poor health was a significant source of southern distinctiveness. Malaria was the first of the South's so-called "diseases of laziness," and played a leading role in the popular image of the "lazy southerner." Indeed, malaria's enervating effects, along with its discouragement of immigration, incalculably retarded regional social and economic development. The South's resulting failure to conform to national patterns and norms produced growing charges of backwardness from outside the region. Yellow fever unquestionably deserved the epithet "scourge of the South." This much-feared killer was clearly sectional in character. Its frightful outbreaks, which threw entire populations into blind panic and disrupted commerce, were widely publicized, focusing national attention on the South. As in the case of malaria, such attention was often critical. Already hypersensitive because of the slavery question, southerners responded to charges of poor health with feelings of grievance and alienation and put aside personal differences to band together in defense of their way of life, thereby strengthening their regional self-consciousness and group identity.

The Civil War and its aftermath had a disastrous effect on health in the South. On the one hand, the hostilities left untold thousands of southerners, noncombatants as well as combatants, in precarious or weakened health. On the other, the conflict's legacy of poverty exacerbated the region's tradition of poor health.[40] The much ballyhooed New South movement did little to reverse this frightful trend. If anything, the tendency of its leaders and spokesmen either to ignore or play down southern shortcomings and problems worsened the situation. Not until the twentieth century would significant steps be taken to improve regional health conditions, and even then much of the impetus for reform came from the outside.

In the dark days after Appomattox, old diseases increased in incidence and virulence, and new health problems arose. Malaria, the leading cause of debility and loss of efficiency in the antebellum South, had showed signs of declining in the decade preceding the Civil War. In the postwar period, however, it soared to record levels and reappeared in areas where it had previously been brought under control.[41] Yellow fever, another old and distinctively southern disease, was a recurrent source of terror, death, and economic blight. The epidemic of 1878–79, which swept through the Gulf states and up the Mississippi as far as Missouri, was the most widespread and virulent in the nation's history, claiming 16,000 lives.[42] Tuberculosis was more prevalent in the South than elsewhere. Blacks were especially hard hit. A higher incidence of tuberculosis was only one indication of the deteriorating health of the former slaves. Left to fend for themselves after the collapse of Reconstruction, the freedmen experienced excessively high rates of sickness and death.[43] Black health problems, as well as those of growing numbers of whites, were in large part the result of the rise and spread of tenancy, the cruel backbone of postwar southern agriculture. The proliferation of the mill town, the chief symbol of the New South, further eroded the health of the poor whites.[44] The principal diseases of poverty were hookworm and pellagra. The former, although undetected, was an old health hazard. In the antebellum period, however, it had been limited to slaves and the relatively small class of poor whites. Postwar poverty exposed growing numbers of southerners to hookworm infection, making it a major threat to regional health. Pellagra was the most spectacular and deadly of a number of dietary deficiency disorders that plagued the swelling ranks of the southern poor who were reduced to the nutritionally inadequate "three M" (meat, meal, and molasses) diet of the frontier. Almost exclusively southern in incidence, hookworm and pellagra were widespread in the South by the time they were diagnosed at the turn of the century. A prominent symptom of both was lassitude. Along with malaria, which also sapped the strength of its victims, hookworm and pellagra made up what Tindall calls the "Southern trilogy of 'lazy diseases.' "[45]

Urbanization was largely a postbellum phenomenon in the South, and New South cities were notoriously unhealthy. Chief among the health hazards were unpaved and poorly drained streets, inadequate or nonexistent sewage arrangements, public garbage heaps, and contaminated water supplies. Conditions were the worst in the segregated quarters into which urban blacks were crowded. With growth came the multiplication of health hazards.[46] And since health administrations were virtually nonexistent before the last two decades of the century, little could be done to improve conditions. Endemic disorders were attributed to climate and tolerated as a fact of life; epidemic outbreaks triggered panic and flight, disrupting commerce and reducing industrial output.

After the war as before it, the South's health woes set the region apart from the rest of the nation and promoted regional ethnicity. The unremitting ravages of malaria and yellow fever continued to wreak havoc with social and economic development and revived charges of inferiority and backwardness. Pellagra and hookworm only served to exacerbate this situation. Each came to be viewed as largely southern in incidence and as the result of the region's poverty and colonial economy. National attention accorded these diseases was interpreted as unwarranted outside criticism aimed at embarrassing the South, causing southerners to band together once more in defense of their way of life. Prominent in the region's response to its perceived detractors was the tragic refusal to admit that serious health problems existed. To do so would have entailed an admission of inferiority. Consequently the blighting effects of disease continued, prolonging the backwardness and misery that underpinned southern distinctiveness.

The inhibiting influence of disease on regional life did not go unnoticed in the South, but poverty and the inability of the medical profession to combat the principal causes of morbidity and mortality stymied would-be reformers. Toward the end of the century, however, improvement in the southern economy and the practical implications of the new germ theory of disease provided the opportunity for health reform. The result was the genesis of the southern public health movement. Following Louisiana's lead, several southern states established boards of health and empowered them to investigate and combat health problems. Although the effectiveness of these agencies was limited by inadequate budgets, legislative interference, suspicion and hostility on the part of businessmen, and the ignorance of the masses, they pushed health reform on a broad front. The state boards of health uncovered and attacked a host of health hazards, inspected water supplies, sought to impose quarantines during outbreaks of epidemic disease, supervised vaccines, published reports, and strove to educate the public on health matters.[47]

A series of medical discoveries around the turn of the century propelled the southern public health movement into a new stage of activity and accomplishment. Between 1898 and 1906, the insect carriers of malaria (1898) and yellow fever (1899) were identified, and hookworm (1902) and pellagra (1906) were diagnosed as endemic among the southern poor. On the one hand, these developments vividly underscored the South's unique and stigmatizing health problems and focused national attention on them. On the other, they paved the way for the eventual conquest or control of the region's principal causes of sickness and death and promoted increased interest in public health reform.

The campaigns against malaria, yellow fever, hookworm, and pellagra, although hindered by regional poverty and the resistance of business and political leaders who were outraged over the embarrassing exposure of the South's myriad and frightful health problems, were landmark victories for southern health, as by the end of World War II these scourges had become relics of the region's benighted past. Their eradication, or control in the case of pellagra, was in large part the result of the national discovery after 1900 of the South's health plight. While publicizing the shocking state of southern health reinforced the stigma of regional inferiority, it also led to crucial assistance from northern philanthropies and the federal government. The indispensable role of the Rockefeller Foundation in the control of hookworm and of the U.S. Public Health Service in the fight against pellagra are informative cases in point.[48]

The nascent southern public health movement was a major beneficiary of the late nineteenth- and early-twentieth-century medical advances that had stripped the region's principal diseases of their mystery. As increasing numbers of southerners became aware of the modern concept of disease, and of the lifesaving potential of laboratory medicine, the longstanding belief that an unhealthy climate was the cause of disease was toppled, the importance of sanitation and drainage was recognized, the popular image of the poor white as by choice shiftless and lazy declined, opposition to the recognition of regional health problems lessened, and a greater willingness to confront those problems evolved. These developments coincided with and were influenced by the southern Progressive movement. Chagrined by the South's backward image, the Progressives, and urban ones especially, sought to rid the region of the principal causes of backwardness. Health reform was high on their agenda.[49]

Disease was attacked on a broadening front. The crusades against malaria, yellow fever, hookworm, and pellagra touched off similar campaigns against tuberculosis and syphilis. Sanitaria and hospitals were built. Beginning with Florida in 1903, bacterial laboratories sprang up. Boards of health were set up in those states that had not already established them, until by 1913 every southern state had some kind of state health agency. Responding to the stimulus of the Rockefeller Sanitary Commission for the Eradication of Hookworm Disease, which combatted this disease at the local level, county health departments mushroomed, propelling the South into the lead in this area. Health department expenditures increased, despite the region's ongoing economic woes. They grew by 81 percent between 1910 and 1914, and continued to expand. Additional funding for health reform came from philanthropic organizations and federal agencies. During the twenty-year period 1913–32, the Rockefeller Foundation's International Health Board, the principal source of private funds for the improvement of southern health, spent more than $1,000,000 for the support of local health departments. Federal health expenditures in the South, largely grants-in-aid from the U.S. Public Health Service, increased from $230,496 in 1902 to $4,217,997 in 1930. The Frontier Nursing Service, established in 1925 by Mary Breckinridge in the mountains of Kentucky, illustrated the awakening of concern for the health of the isolated poor of the southern Appalachia. Southern senators and congressmen also began to take a greater interest in health legislation. Politicians from the region, for example, were instrumental in the passage of the Sheppard-Towner Act (1921), which provided federal aid for state studies in maternal and infant mortality, and the creation of a National Institute of Health (1930) to promote scientific research on disease. The cumulative effect of these developments was the gradual improvement of southern health. The narrowing of mortality rate differences between the regions attests to the gains made.[50]

But as revolutionary as the progress in health reform was, at the onset of the Depression the South remained the nation's sickliest section. Familiar disease forms continued to plague the region. For example, malaria had not been brought under con-

trol, and plummeting cotton prices in the 1920s led to a resurgence of pellagra. As before, southern cities were unhealthy.
Statistics further illuminate the South's continuing health problems. The region's colonial economy and modest share of the
nation's wealth (a mere 12 percent on the eve of the Depression)
severely limited funds for public health. As late as 1940, only
Louisiana exceeded the national average per capita expenditure
in this area. The South lagged badly in the construction of hospitals and the training of physicians. In 1930 hospital beds per 1,000
population numbered less than six in twelve southern states, a
level surpassed by all but three states outside the region. The
national average for physicians per 1,000 population at this time
was 125.2; in the states of the Southeast the average was 95.1. The
continuing precarious condition of southern health is reflected in
comparative mortality. During the decade of the twenties only
four states in the region—Arkansas, Oklahoma, North Carolina,
and Kentucky—recorded death rates consistently below the national average.[51]

As improvements in health attest, one of the major accomplishments of the southern Progressive movement was a
quickening in the pace of Americanization, the return of the
region to the national mainstream from which it had withdrawn
during the antebellum period. This development is largely attrib-
utable to the Progressives' desire to remove the stigma of regional
inferiority. But for all their efforts, southern distinctiveness persisted. Misery widened with the collapse of the South's cotton
economy in the twenties. This misery, and the bitter battle for
control of the mind of the region that raged between fundamen-
talists and modernists throughout this decade, reinforced the
national image of southern differences and benightedness and
revived sectionalism.[52]

To be sure, there was much about the South to criticize—
economic stagnation, poverty, racism, violence, ignorance, and
the like. Moreover, with such things as the resurgence of the Ku
Klux Klan, the fundamentalist crusade, and the Scopes "monkey
trial," the region invited ridicule. And it was forthcoming. No
one was harsher on the section than H.L. Mencken, the vitriolic
Baltimore journalist and social critic, who, as Tindall puts it,
"developed the game of South-baiting into a national pastime at
which he had no peer."[53] To Mencken, the South was "the
Sahara of the Bozart [i.e., *Beaux-arts*]." "For all its size and all the

'progress' it babbles of," he reviled, "it is almost as sterile, art-
istically, intellectually, culturally, as the Sahara Desert."[54] While
cultural and intellectual barrenness was a favorite focus of the
South's critics, its sickliness did not go unnoticed. For example,
the continued presence of hookworm and pellagra, disorders
clearly associated with regional economic plight, ideally suited
the purposes of those who, like Frank Tannenbaum, called for the
reform of the southern economy.[55]

True to form, in the twenties the South reacted to its critics with
outrage and denial. In fact, so sensitive to criticism did southerners become that even the most well-meaning concerns about
regional problems provoked fury. Such was the case in 1921 when
Joseph Goldberger, who had discovered the link between the
southern diet and pellagra, warned the U.S. Public Health Service that the drastically reduced wages of textile workers, the result
of falling cotton prices, were producing widespread famine and
renewing the threat of rampant pellagra in the South. The publicizing of Goldberger's warning evoked national concern for the
southern poor and offers of assistance. But to the mystification of
solicitous outsiders, the region's leaders and spokesmen angrily
denied that hunger existed in the South and brusquely rejected
philanthropic overtures.[56] To have done otherwise would have
been to admit a flawed way of life.

Cotton was the chief cause of the South's problems. This staple
had long been a dominant factor in southern history, but never so
much as after the Civil War. Cotton increasingly dominated the
region's predominantly agricultural economy, and its manufacture lay at the heart of the New South movement. But no matter
how understandable, even natural, the South's decision to build
its future on cotton may have been, the choice was a tragic error.
A "white plague," in the words of one critic, slowly spread over
the southern landscape, exacerbating old social and economic ills
and creating myriad new ones. Blinded by their own version of
King Cotton, regional leaders either denied or explained away
problems of all kinds, especially during periods of popular unrest
or outside criticism. Consequently, the long overdue reform of
southern society was forestalled.[57]

But the South was being transformed, as the result of developments that, although frequently distrusted or opposed,
drew southerners back into the national mainstream. Chief
among these were the Depression and New Deal, and World War

II and its aftermath.[58] As unwelcome as these trends often were to southerners, the people reaped immense social and economic benefits from the decline of the sectional South. Improved health was one of the most important of these.

The first attempts at a national health program, according to John Duffy, were made during the New Deal. "Almost every New Deal agency, temporary or permanent," he writes, "made some contribution to health."[59] The South was a major beneficiary of the New Dealers' concern for health. Numerous examples point up the vital role of the New Deal in the improvement of southern health. Funds for medical care were provided by the Federal Emergency Relief Administration. Civilian Conservation Corps members received medical attention. The draining of two million acres of swamp by the Civil Works Administration, the Federal Emergency Relief Administration, and the Works Progress Administration and studies of the breeding habits of mosquitoes by the Tennessee Valley Authority expedited efforts to eradicate malaria. The control of typhoid fever and dysentery was advanced through the federally sponsored construction of 2.3 million sanitary privies by 1939. Crusades against tuberculosis and venereal disease were launched. The Works Progress Administration built hospitals and sewage plants. The Federal Housing Administration's slum clearance program, with half its projects in the South, promoted urban health reform. The Bankhead-Jones Farm Tenant Act of 1937, aimed at ending tenancy and sharecropping, pointed to improved rural health. Of far-reaching significance was the Social Security Act of 1935. This historic piece of social welfare legislation provided federal funds for health purposes and created a permanent machinery for distributing them.

Although overshadowed by the massive New Deal programs, important public health activity occurred at the local level. The southern public health movement had lost its momentum during the economically troubled and socially stressful twenties. The New Deal and the era's growing concern for public welfare revitalized it. The result was a new period of expansion and accomplishment. Illustrative of the gains made were the proliferation of county health departments and increased health expenditures. After a period of slow growth in the early thirties, the number of county health departments soared between 1935 and 1941, rising from 396 to 747. Expenditures for health care also increased dramatically. Funds for these increases came largely from federal assistance programs and new forms of taxation.

Improvements in southern health during the thirties were reflected in the region's declining death rate, especially for infants. As before, however, the economically hardpressed South, aptly labeled "the Nation's No. 1 economic problem" by Franklin D. Roosevelt, retained its degrading distinction as the unhealthiest region in the country. Indeed, while considerable progress had been made, serious problems remained to be solved if the South was to shed its pestilential image. Southern stillbirths and maternity and infant death rates were the highest in the nation. The region either led in the incidence of, or exceeded the national average for, tuberculosis, venereal disease, malaria, hookworm, hypertension, and heart ailments. It still lagged behind the rest of the nation in funding for health services. The South also continued to fall below the national averages for the number of hospital beds and physicians proportionate to population. And its practice of racial segregation necessitated a costly dual system of health care that condemned blacks to poor health. Indeed, in every meaningful area of comparison—infant mortality, the incidence of disease (and tuberculosis and syphilis most notably), life expectancy, the availability of health care personnel and facilities—the plight of the southern blacks is all too apparent.[60]

World War II had major uplifting effects on southern health. With large numbers of troops stationed in the region, resources of the federal government were brought to bear in the fight against disease on an unprecedented scale. As the conquest of malaria illustrates, public health was greatly advanced. The health screenings and medical attention that accompanied military service led to vastly improved health for thousands of southerners. And military instruction in hygiene inculcated in them the importance of good health and taught them how to achieve it. The wartime appearance of enriched flour and bread, containing synthetic vitamins, considerably curtailed the threat of pellagra and other dietary deficiency disorders. Above all, however, the war reinvigorated the southern economy. With growing prosperity came a greater concern for health and increased means, personal and public, to combat health problems.[61]

But World War II did more than pump new life into the southern economy. It also accelerated the regional transformation that had begun during the New Deal. This historical evolution carried over into the postwar period, where social change became the chief characteristic of southern life. With the exception of the 1960s and 1970s, Newby contends, more fundamental change occurred in the years after World War II than at any time in the region's history. The result, he observes, was the movement toward national socioeconomic patterns, signaling the demise of the "sectional South" and the rebirth of the "American South." The changes in southern life extended across a broad front. Prominent among them, Newby points out, were the triumph of industry, the transformation of agriculture, burgeoning urbanization, the breaking of the hold of ruralism, the end of physical and cultural isolation, the dismantling of the Jim Crow system, the disintegration of the Solid South, and a revitalized role in national politics.[62] Although accomplished at the expense of regional distinctiveness and at times, as in the case of race relations, vigorously opposed, the Americanization of the South has led to unprecedented prosperity, dramatic improvements in the quality of life, and growing opportunities for southerners.

With the postwar transformation of the South has also come unparalleled improvement in health. Indeed, the "sickly South" is steadily becoming a thing of the past, as the region moves toward national patterns and norms in health matters. Problems, however, remain to be overcome before it can be said that southerners as a group enjoy good health. Representative of such problems are an elevated rate of postnatal mortality, the lowest life expectancy rate in the country, the nation's highest rate of work-related medical problems, a high incidence of poverty-related disease, the fewest number of doctors and medical professionals per capita, a lack of adequate outpatient service and preventive care departments, and the substandard state of health care delivery systems in rural areas. As before, ethnic minorities and the economically troubled are the least healthy southerners. But in contrast to former times, the South's health problems are now attributed not to backwardness but to residual economic lag.[63]

For students of the region, one of the major consequences of the post–World War II Americanization of the South has been a growing tendency to recast the debate over southern identity, away from the search for the central theme in southern history to the question of the enduring South. Two significant recent studies—both appearing in 1979—dramatically frame the present debate. The opposing positions are represented by Michael O'Brien, a promising English-born historian of ideas, and Dewey W. Grantham, a southern-born senior historian of the South. O'Brien, in a provocative study of the idea of the South between the World Wars, rejects any notion that the South as an entity is a meaningful concept. Rather, he contends, "the South is centrally an intellectual perception, closely tied to the survival of the organicist tradition of Romantic social theory, which has served to comprehend and weld an unintegrated social reality."[64] But Grantham, in a collection of his essays on southern political history, reaffirms the continuity of southern distinctiveness. "The South," he asserts, "has been and continues to be measurably different from other parts of the country."[65] As before, each side has its advocates.[66] While it is too early to predict what will come of this new debate over southern identity, one thing seems clear: if the distinctive South is disappearing, a major factor in its demise will be the eradication of the blighting and benighting effects of disease.

NOTES

1. Dewey W. Grantham, Jr., "The South to Posterity!", *Midwest Quarterly* 8 (1966):59 (first quotation); 62 (second quotation); 64 (third quotation).

2. John Shelton Reed, *The Enduring South: Subcultural Persistence in Mass Society* (Lexington, Mass.: D.C. Heath, 1972), 9 (first quotation); 10 (second quotation).

3. David L. Smiley, "The Quest for the Central Theme in Southern History," *South Atlantic Quarterly* 71 (Summer 1972):308. This study is the best survey and analysis of the quest for the central theme in southern history, and one to which I am deeply indebted.

4. Frank E. Vandiver, ed., *The Idea of the South: Pursuit of a Central Theme* (Chicago: Published for William Marsh Rice University by the Univ. of Chicago Press, 1964), viii.

5. Wilbur J. Cash, *The Mind of the South* (New York: Knopf, 1941), viii.

6. I.A. Newby, *The South: A History* (New York: Holt, Rinehart and Winston, 1978), xiv.

7. Smiley, "The Quest for the Central Theme," 307; Newby, *The South: A History*, xiv.

8. Newby, *The South: A History*, xiv–xv.

9. Smiley, "The Quest for the Central Theme," 324.

10. David M. Potter, *The South and the Sectional Conflict* (Baton Rouge: Louisiana State Univ. Press, 1968), 4.

11. Francis Butler Simkins, *The Everlasting South* (Baton Rouge: Louisiana State Univ. Press, 1963), 36.

12. Cash, *The Mind of the South*, viii.

13. J.G. Randall, *The Civil War and Reconstruction* (Boston: D.C. Heath, 1953), 3–4.

14. Newby, *The South: A History*, xiv–xv.

15. William M. Dabney and Marion Dargan, *William Henry Drayton and the American Revolution* (Albuquerque: Univ. of New Mexico Press, 1962), 206.

16. Merrill D. Peterson, ed., *The Portable Thomas Jefferson* (New York: Viking, 1975), 386–88.

17. Smiley, "The Quest for the Central Theme," 309.

18. Newby, *The South: A History*, 11.

19. Ulrich B. Phillips, "The Central Theme of Southern History," *American Historical Review* 34 (1928):30–43.

20. Ulrich B. Phillips, *Life and Labor in the Old South* (Boston: Little, Brown, 1929), 3.

21. Smiley, "The Quest for the Central Theme," 310. For a perceptive analysis of historians and the Phillips thesis, see Newby, *The South: A History*, 15–17.

22. Smiley, "The Quest for the Central Theme," 314.

23. Sheldon Van Auken, "A Century of the Southern Plantation," *Virginia Magazine of History and Biography* 58 (1950):356; also see Francis Pendleton Gaines, *The Southern Plantation: A Study in the Development and the Accuracy of a Tradition* (New York: Columbia Univ. Press, 1924).

24. Smiley, "The Quest for the Central Theme," 315.

25. Newby, *The South: A History*, 25–27.

26. Edgar T. Thompson, "The Climatic Theory of the Plantation," *Agricultural History* 15 (1941):60.

27. William A. Foran, "Southern Legend: Climate or Climate of Opinion?", *Proceedings of the South Carolina Historical Association* (1956):6–22.

28. Charles S. Sydnor, "The Southern Experiment in Writing Social History," *Journal of Southern History* 11 (1945):455–68. Sydnor, "The Southerner and the Laws," ibid. 6 (1940):3–23.

29. This sampling, while representative, is highly selective. For a fuller account and analysis of the myriad social traits associated with southern distinctiveness, see Smiley, "The Quest for the Central Theme," 318–24.

30. Ibid., 322.

31. Frank E. Vandiver, "The Southerner as Extremist," in *The Idea of the South*, ed. Vandiver, 43–55; John Hope Franklin, *The Militant South, 1800–1861* (Cambridge, Mass.: Harvard Univ. Press, 1956).

32. Twelve Southerners, *I'll Take My Stand: The South and the Agrarian Tradition* (New York: Harper & Brothers, 1930), ix–xx.

33. See, for example, Edwin McNeill Poteat, Jr., "Religion in the South," in *Culture in the South*, ed. W.T. Couch, 248–69. (Chapel Hill:

Univ. of North Carolina Press, 1934). See also Smiley, "The Quest for the Central Theme," 319.

34. C. Vann Woodward, *The Burden of Southern History*, rev. ed. (Baton Rouge: Louisiana State Univ. Press, 1968), 3–25.

35. T. Harry Williams, *Romance and Realism in Southern Politics* (Athens: Univ. of Georgia Press, 1961), 4.

36. Potter, *The South and the Sectional Conflict*, 15.

37. George B. Tindall, "Mythology: A New Frontier in Southern History," in *The Idea of the South*, ed. Vandiver, 1–15, 15 (quotation).

38. For an overview of medicine and health in the early South, see John B. Blake, "Diseases and Medical Practice in Colonial America," in *History of American Medicine: A Symposium*, ed. Félix Martí-Ibáñez (New York: MD Publications, 1958), 34–47; Richard Beale Davis, *Intellectual Life in the Colonial South, 1585–1763*, 3 vols. (Knoxville: Univ. of Tennessee Press, 1978), vol. II, 906–36; Wyndham B. Blanton, *Medicine in Virginia in the Seventeenth Century* (Richmond: William Byrd Press, 1930); Blanton, *Medicine in Virginia in the Eighteenth Century* (Richmond: Garrett & Massie, 1931); Gerald L. Cates, " 'The Seasoning': Disease and Death Among the First Colonists of Georgia," *Georgia Historical Quarterly* 64 (1980): 146–58; John Duffy, "Eighteenth-Century Carolina Health Conditions," *Journal of Southern History* 18 (1952):289–302; Joseph Ioor Waring, *A History of Medicine in South Carolina, 1670–1825* (Charleston: South Carolina Medical Association, 1964); John Duffy, *Epidemics in Colonial America* (Baton Rouge: Louisiana State Univ. Press, 1953); St. Julien Ravenel Childs, *Malaria and Colonization in the Carolina Low Country, 1526–1696* (Baltimore: Johns Hopkins Univ. Press, 1940); H. Roy Merrens and George D. Terry, "Dying in Paradise: Malaria, Mortality, and the Perceptual Environment in Colonial South Carolina," *Journal of Southern History* 50 (1984):533–50; Darrett B. Rutman and Anita H. Rutman, "Of Agues and Fevers: Malaria in the Early Chesapeake," *William and Mary Quarterly* 33 (1976):31–60.

39. General accounts of medicine in the Old South include Richard H. Shryock, "Medical Practice in the Old South," *South Atlantic Quarterly* 29 (1930):160–78; William Dosité Postell, "The Doctor in the Old South," ibid. 51 (1952):393–400; John Duffy, "Medical Practice in the Ante Bellum South," *Journal of Southern History* 25 (1959):53–72; David R. Goldfield, "The Business of Health Planning: Disease Prevention in the Old South," ibid. 42 (1976):557–70; Martha Carolyn Mitchell, "Health and the Medical Profession in the Lower South, 1845–1860," ibid. 10 (1944):424–46; Ronald L. Numbers and Todd L. Savitt, eds., *Science and Medicine in the Old South: Essays from the First and Second Barnard-Millington Symposia on Southern Science and Medicine* (Baton Rouge: Louisiana State Univ. Press, forthcoming). Representative state studies are Lucie Robertson Bridgforth, "Medicine in Antebellum Mississippi," *Journal of Mississippi History* 46 (1984):82–107; Wyndham B. Blanton, *Medicine in*

Virginia in the Nineteenth Century (Richmond: Garrett & Massie, 1933); John Duffy, ed., *The Rudolph Matas History of Medicine in Louisiana*, 2 vols. (Baton Rouge: Louisiana State Univ. Press, 1958–1962), vol. 1, pt. 3; vol. II, pt. 1; Howard L. Holley, *A History of Medicine in Alabama* (University, Ala.: Univ. of Alabama School of Medicine, 1982; produced and distributed by the Univ. of Alabama Press), passim; Joseph Ioor Waring, *A History of Medicine in South Carolina, 1825–1900* (Charleston: South Carolina Medical Association, 1967), pt. 1; Waring, "Charleston Medicine, 1800–1860," *Journal of the History of Medicine and Allied Sciences* 31 (1976):320–42; John Harley Warner, *The Therapeutic Perspective: Medical Practice, Knowledge, and Identity in America, 1820–1885* (Cambridge, Mass.: Harvard Univ. Press, 1986). Slave health has been the subject of considerable attention; see, for example, Victor H. Bassett, "Plantation Medicine," *Journal of the Medical Association of Georgia* 29 (1940):112–22; Weymouth T. Jordan, "Plantation Medicine in the Old South," *Alabama Review* 3 (1950):83–107; Mary Louise Marshall, "Plantation Medicine," *Bulletin of the Medical Library Association* 26 (1938):115–28; Felice Swados, "Negro Health on the Ante Bellum Plantations," *Bulletin of the History of Medicine* 10 (1941):460–72; William Dosité Postell, *The Health of Slaves on Southern Plantations* (Baton Rouge: Louisiana State Univ. Press, 1951); Todd L. Savitt, *Medicine and Slavery: The Diseases and Health Care of Blacks in Antebellum Virginia* (Urbana: Univ. of Illinois Press, 1978); Kenneth F. Kiple and Virginia Himmelsteib King, *Another Dimension to the Black Diaspora: Diet, Disease, and Racism* (Cambridge, England: Cambridge Univ. Press, 1981); David O. Whitten, "Medical Care of Slaves: Louisiana Sugar Region and South Carolina Rice District," *Southern Studies* 16 (1977):153–80. For an account and analysis of states-rights medicine, see John Duffy, "A Note on Ante-Bellum Southern Nationalism and Medical Practice," *Journal of Southern History* 34 (1968):266–76; James O. Breeden, "States-Rights Medicine in the Old South," *Bulletin of the New York Academy of Medicine* 52 (1976):348–72; John Harley Warner, "A Southern Medical Reform: The Meaning of the Antebellum Argument for Southern Medical Education," *Bulletin of the History of Medicine* 57 (1983):364–81.

40. The medical history of the South during the Civil War era is chronicled and analyzed in an extensive literature. See, for example, H.H. Cunningham, *Doctors in Gray: The Confederate Medical Service* (Baton Rouge: Louisiana State Univ. Press, 1958); Harris D. Riley, Jr., "Medicine in the Confederacy," *Military Medicine* 118 (1956):53–64, 144–53; Courtney R. Hall, "Caring for the Confederate Soldier," *Medical Life* 42 (1935):443–508; Hall, "The Lessons of the War Between the States," in *History of American Medicine*, ed. Martí-Ibáñez, 72–94; George H. Tichenor, Jr., "Medicine During Reconstruction Period, 1865–1901, in the South," *Western Medical Times* 41 (1922):339–43. The literature on the meaning of the war for black health is considerably sparser; see Gaines

M. Foster, "The Limitations of Federal Health Care for Freedmen, 1862–1869," *Journal of Southern History* 48 (1982):349–72; J. Thomas May, "The Louisiana Negro in Transition: An Appraisal of the Activities of the Freedmen's Bureau," *Bulletin of the Tulane University Medical Faculty* 26 (1967):29–36; Todd L. Savitt, "Politics in Medicine: The Georgia Freedmen's Bureau and the Organization of Health Care, 1865–1866," *Civil War History* 28 (1982):45–64; Marshall Scott Legan, "Disease and the Freedmen in Mississippi during Reconstruction," *Journal of the History of Medicine and Allied Sciences* 28 (1973):257–67.

41. Friedrich Prinzing, *Epidemics Resulting from Wars,* ed. Harald Westergaard (Oxford, England: Clarendon Press, 1916), 180. See also Erwin H. Ackerknecht, *Malaria in the Upper Mississippi Valley, 1760–1900* (Baltimore: Johns Hopkins Univ. Press, 1945), 56; Marshall A. Barber, *A Malariologist in Many Lands* (Lawrence: Univ. of Kansas Press, 1946), 6–7; Blanton, *Medicine in Virginia in the Nineteenth Century,* 258; Waring, *A History of Medicine in South Carolina, 1825–1900,* 178.

42. United States Board of Experts Authorized to Investigate the Yellow Fever Epidemic of 1878, *Proceedings of the Board of Experts Authorized by Congress to Investigate the Yellow Fever Epidemic of 1878. . . .* (New Orleans: L. Graham, 1878); George Augustin, *History of Yellow Fever* (New Orleans: privately printed, 1909), 767–1024 passim. Memphis bore the brunt of the epidemic; see J.M. Keating, *A History of the Yellow Fever. The Yellow Fever Epidemic of 1878 in Memphis, Tenn. . . .* (Memphis: The Howard Association, 1879); Thomas H. Baker, "Yellowjack: The Yellow Fever Epidemic of 1878 in Memphis, Tennessee," *Bulletin of the History of Medicine* 42 (1968):241–64.

43. Howard N. Rabinowitz, "From Exclusion to Segregation: Health and Welfare Services for Southern Blacks, 1865–1890," *Social Service Review* 48 (1974):327–54; Marion M. Torchia, "Tuberculosis among American Negroes: Medical Research on a Racial Disease, 1830–1950," *Journal of the History of Medicine and Allied Sciences* 32 (1977):252–79.

44. The social ills of tenancy are movingly depicted in two classic documentaries: James Agee and Walker Evans, *Let Us Now Praise Famous Men: Three Tenant Families* (Boston: Houghton Mifflin, 1931); and Erskine Caldwell and Margaret Bourne-White, *You Have Seen Their Faces* (New York: Viking, 1937).

45. George Brown Tindall, *The Emergence of the New South, 1913–1945* (Baton Rouge: Louisiana State Univ. Press, 1967), 227.

46. Lawrence H. Larsen, *The Rise of the Urban South* (Lexington: Univ. Press of Kentucky, 1985), ch. 6; David R. Goldfield, *Cotton Fields and Skyscrapers: Southern City and Region, 1607–1980* (Baton Rouge: Louisiana State Univ. Press, 1982), 91–97.

47. Representative studies of health reform in the late nineteenth-century South are Howard D. Kramer, "Agitation for Public Health Reform in the 1870's," *Journal of the History of Medicine and Allied Sciences*

3 (1948):473–88 and 4 (1949):75–89; Duffy, ed., *Rudolph Matas History of Medicine in Louisiana,* vol. II, ch. 17; Dennis East II, "Health and Wealth: Goals of the New Orleans Public Health Movement, 1879–1884," *Louisiana History* 9 (1968):245–75; John H. Ellis, "Businessmen and Public Health in the Urban South during the Nineteenth Century: New Orleans, Memphis, and Atlanta," *Bulletin of the History of Medicine* 44 (1970):197–212, 346–71; Gordon E. Gillson, *Louisiana State Board of Health: The Formative Years* (New Orleans: Louisiana State Board of Health, 1967); Holley, *A History of Medicine in Alabama,* ch. 12; Richard J. Hopkins, "Public Health in Atlanta: The Formative Years, 1865–1879," *Georgia Historical Quarterly* 53 (1969):287–304; James B. Speer, Jr., "Pestilence and Progress: Health Reform in Galveston and Houston During the Nineteenth Century," *Houston Review* 2 (1980):120–32; Margaret Warner, "Local Control versus National Interest: The Debate Over Southern Public Health, 1878–1884," *Journal of Southern History* 50 (1984):407–28.

48. Histories of the campaigns against malaria and yellow fever in the South remain to be written. For the crusades against pellagra and hookworm, see Elizabeth W. Etheridge, *The Butterfly Caste: A Social History of Pellagra in the South* (Westport, Conn.: Greenwood, 1972); Daphne A. Roe, *A Plague of Corn: The Social History of Pellagra* (Ithaca: Cornell Univ. Press, 1973); John Ettling, *The Germ of Laziness: Rockefeller Philanthropy and Public Health in the New South* (Cambridge, Mass.: Harvard Univ. Press, 1981).

49. The most thorough account of southern Progressivism is C. Vann Woodward, *Origins of the New South, 1877–1913* (Baton Rouge: Louisiana State Univ. Press, 1951); and Tindall, *The Emergence of the New South, 1913–1945;* an enlightening recent analysis is Dewey W. Grantham, *Southern Progressivism: The Reconciliation of Progress and Tradition* (Knoxville: Univ. of Tennessee Press, 1983). For medicine in the Progressive era, see James G. Burrow, *Organized Medicine in the Progressive Era: The Move toward Monopoly* (Baltimore: Johns Hopkins Univ. Press, 1977).

50. Tindall, *The Emergence of the New South, 1913–1945,* 276–81; John Samuel Ezell, *The South Since 1865,* 2d ed. (New York: Macmillan, 1975), 391–93; Burrow, *Organized Medicine in the Progressive Era,* ch. 6; Grantham, *Southern Progressivism,* 310–18; Gordon E. Gillson, *Public Health in the Progressive Era: A Louisiana Prospective* (Alamosa, Colo.: Adams State College, 1977); Shirley G. Schoonover, "Alabama Public Health Campaign, 1900–1919," *Alabama Review* 28 (1975):218–33; Stuart Galishoff, "Germs Know No Color Line: Black Health and Public Policy in Atlanta, 1900–1918," *Journal of the History of Medicine and Allied Sciences* 40 (1985):22–41; Mary Breckinridge, *Wide Neighborhoods: A Story of the Frontier Nursing Service* (New York: Harper & Bros, 1952); Carol

Crowe-Carraco, "Mary Breckinridge and the Frontier Nursing Service," *Register of the Kentucky Historical Society* 76 (1978):179–96.

51. Tindall, *The Emergence of the New South, 1913–1945*, 282; Ezell, *The South Since 1865*, 393.

52. For an enlightened discussion of the theme of benightedness and its meaning for the South, see George B. Tindall, "The Benighted South: Origins of a Modern Image," *Virginia Quarterly Review* 40 (1964):281–94.

53. Tindall, *The Emergence of the New South*, 209.

54. H.L. Mencken, *Prejudices: Second Series* (New York: Knopf, 1920), 136; see also Fred C. Hobson, Jr., *Serpent in Eden: H.L. Mencken and the South* (Chapel Hill: Univ. of North Carolina Press, 1974).

55. Frank Tannenbaum, *Darker Phases of the South* (New York: G.P. Putnam's Sons, 1924).

56. Etheridge, *The Butterfly Caste*, ch. 6.

57. Newby, *The South: A History*, 402–22.

58. The best survey of the New Deal in the South is Tindall, *The Emergence of the New South*; see chs. 11–19.

59. John Duffy, *The Healers: The Rise of the Medical Establishment* (New York: McGraw-Hill, 1976), 317.

60. Tindall, *The Emergence of the New South, 1913–1945*, ch. 14; Ezell, *The South Since 1865*, 428–36; Roy Lubove, "The New Deal and National Health," *Current History* 45 (1963):77–86, 117; Virgil C. Mitchell, "Louisiana Health and the Civil Works Administration," *Red River Valley Historical Review* 7 (1982):22–32; O.M. Derryberry, "Health Conservation Activities of TVA," *Public Health Reports* 68 (1953):327–33; D. Clayton Brown, "Health of Farm Children in the South, 1900–1950," *Agricultural History* 53 (1979):170–87; E.H. Beardsley, "Making Separate Equal: Black Physicians and the Problems of Medical Segregation in the Pre–World War II South," *Bulletin of the History of Medicine* 57 (1983):382–96. A tragic chapter of southern medicine during the era of the New Deal, and one that lasted until 1972, was the participation by a number of the region's public health officials and private physicians in the infamous Tuskegee Syphilis Experiment, in which 400 black men suffering from syphilis were deliberately denied treatment. See James H. Jones, *Bad Blood: The Tuskegee Syphilis Experiment* (New York: Free Press, 1981).

61. Tindall, *The Emergence of the New South, 1913–1945*, 687–731.

62. Newby, *The American South: A History*, 465–66.

63. For conflicting interpretations of contemporary southern health, see Thomas D. Clark, *The Emerging South*, 2d ed. (New York: Oxford Univ. Press, 1968), ch. 3; and the special issue on health, "Sick for Justice: Health Care and Unhealthy Conditions," *Southern Exposure* 6, no. 2 (1978). The most accurate picture is provided by the statistics of the U.S. Dept. of Health and Human Services; see, for example, Center for

Disease Control, *Morbidity and Mortality Weekly Report* (Washington, D.C.: Dept. of Health and Human Services/Public Health Service, 1951–).

64. Michael O'Brien, *The Idea of the American South, 1920–1941* (Baltimore: Johns Hopkins Univ. Press, 1979), xiv.

65. Dewey W. Grantham, *The Regional Imagination: The South and Recent American History* (Nashville: Vanderbilt Univ. Press, 1979), ix.

66. For an informative discussion of the debate over the enduring South, see Newby, *The South: A History,* ch. 17.

2

The Impact of Malaria
On the South

.

JOHN DUFFY

A disease which most Americans today equate with tropical lands, malaria was a major scourge in the United States from colonial times until well into the twentieth century. It was firmly established in England and on the Continent by the seventeenth century, and it soon came to North America. Diaries, journals, and letters of the colonists speak constantly of enduring the "seasonings" or "fevers." While these terms encompassed a wide range of disorders, malaria was probably the most common one. Generally known as "fever and ague," the disorder, which in colonial times was experienced from New England to Georgia, followed American frontiersmen all the way to California. The best and most fertile acres, those in the bottom lands of rivers, creeks, and streams, held the greatest appeal to settlers, but these were also the areas where the anopheles mosquitoes flourished.

The first settlers who crossed the Appalachians expressed their amazement at the beauty and healthiness of the Ohio Valley. Within a short time, however, they commented upon the appearance of "fevers and agues," and soon travelers were noting the sallow skin and anemic appearance of the residents. In the early nineteenth century, sections of Illinois, Indiana, and other western states as far north as Wisconsin were notorious for their omnipresent fevers. Fortunately, as the land was cleared and drained and the introduction of cattle provided the reduced mosquito population with preferred feeding grounds, the incidence of malaria declined. Moreover, the cold winters killed the in-

Spraying to kill anopheles mosquitoes (malaria carriers) just after
World War II. Courtesy Centers for Disease Control, Atlanta, Georgia.

fected mosquitoes each year, and by the end of the nineteenth century, with the exception of a few small areas, malaria had virtually disappeared from the North.

In the warm southern climate, however, mosquitoes could survive the year around. Once malaria gained a firm foothold, as it did by the end of the seventeenth century, it became an endemic plague, striking down newcomers of all ages and contributing notably to the high rate of infant mortality among the residents. Those who survived the initial attack remained subject to repeated bouts of fever and chills which reduced their vitality and laid them open to other disorders. The descriptions of thin, sallow-skinned settlers in the early Midwest applied equally to the residents of the South. But clearing southern land brought little relief, and the classic picture of the lazy southerner was undoubtedly conditioned in part by the omnipresence of malaria as late as World War II.

Malaria is a parasitic disorder which takes three major forms—two relatively mild ones, *Plasmodium vivax* and *Plasmodium malariae;* and a more severe type, *Plasmodium falciparum,* which is often fatal. The plasmodium is carried by the anopheles mosquito, an insect that breeds in still, fresh-water pools, swamps, river bottoms, and lakes. The main symptoms are acute chills followed by high fever with headache, nausea, and profuse sweating. Depending upon the type of malaria, the chills and fever recur with regular remissions of from 24 to 72 hours. It was these symptoms which gave rise to the general names of "fever and ague," remittent or intermittent fever. So familiar were the early settlers with the various forms of malaria that they differentiated between them on the basis of the recurrence of the fever: a daily bout of fever and chills was called quotidian; when it recurred every forty-eight hours, tertian; and every seventy-two hours, quartan. The deadly falciparum malaria, which quickly could prove fatal by literally blocking the blood vessels, was known variously as blackwater fever, congestive fever, hemorrhagic malaria, and pernicious malaria.

In the Deep South, the presence of mosquitoes on a year-round basis meant that malaria was constantly present. Once the parasite gains entrance to the bloodstream, it is difficult to eradicate. The only specific until well into the twentieth century was quinine, a derivative of the cinchona plant. Before the isolation of quinine in 1820, the pulverized bark of the plant was the standard remedy for "fever and ague." While the "bark," as it was called, could temporarily reduce symptoms, its quality varied widely, and it was impossible to standardize the dosage. Moreover—and this was true even after the introduction of quinine—the need to continue the medicine for long after the disappearance of the symptoms was not generally recognized. Consequently the malarial parasite remained in the patient's system, periodically flooding into the blood stream. This meant that whenever a certain percentage of any given population was infected, the disease could survive even in areas where winter was cold enough to kill all mosquitoes. Each spring the new crop of anopheles mosquitoes could become infected and thus maintain or spread the malarial parasite. For this reason, in the colonial period malaria was widespread in New England, and in the nineteenth century it ravaged as far north as Wisconsin and Minnesota. The southern climate, however, was far more conducive to the survival of malaria than that of the North.

The two milder forms of malaria, *P. vivax* and *P. malariae*, can survive in the body for many years, as long as thirty years in the case of *P. malariae*. But chronic exposure to these two forms enables the body to produce enough antibodies to lessen their effects. If untreated, assuming the patient survives the initial attack, the severe form, *P. falciparum*, ordinarily disappears in from six months to two years. In the South, where one or more forms of the disorder were endemic, most adult southerners, white and black, had acquired some measure of immunity. The blacks, however, had an advantage, in that 90 percent of those coming from West Africa, the chief source of slaves, had a natural immunity to vivax, and another 10 to 20 percent, those carrying the sickle cell trait, were highly resistant to falciparum. While observant southerners recognized the relative immunity of slaves quite early, they were puzzled by the periodic outbreaks of malaria among them. Since blacks who were immune to vivax were not necessarily resistant to other forms of malaria, the explanation is clear today. Moreover, the transfer of slaves to the South and West from the older plantation areas exposed them to unfamiliar strains of the disease.

Malaria, like nearly all endemic diseases, flares into epidemic proportions on a seasonal basis. Its incidence rises in the late spring and early summer, falls off slightly, and then rises again in late August and early September. Since temperature, humidity, and amount of rainfall affect the mosquito population, while social and economic conditions influence the health of the human population, the incidence of malaria even in an endemic area may vary considerably from year to year. Thus areas where the mild forms of the disorder are of minor consequence occasionally may experience a serious outbreak. When a series of local epidemics occurs over a wide region, the disease may be described as hyperendemic.

In discussing any medical problem of the past, historians are always faced with the question of an accurate diagnosis. Despite the apparent ability of actor-physicians on television programs to glance at a patient and instantly recognize some obscure complaint, diagnosis is far from easy even today. A little over one hundred years ago, physicians were still debating the existence of specific diseases, with some arguing that all clinical symptoms arose from one basic cause. To complicate matters, fever is characteristic of nearly all infectious diseases, and lacking an understanding of the germ theory, early physicians used a variety of descriptive terms to categorize fevers—slow fever, nervous fever, continued fever, pernicious fever, putrid fever, malignant fever, long fever, pestilential intermittent fever, remittent fever, and so forth. As late as 1900 a diagnosis of typho-malaria was still common. Typho-malaria illustrates yet another difficulty in diagnosis. A patient weakened by chronic malaria was quite likely to fall prey to typhoid fever, respiratory or enteric disorders, or a host of other infections; hence typho-malaria may have been an accurate diagnosis. On the other hand, it is conceivable that the patient had neither malaria nor typhoid.

Fortunately for historians, the distinctive periodic bouts of fever and chills (ague), the characteristic enlargement of the spleen in chronic malaria, the association of the disease with low swampy areas, and a long experience with malaria in Europe meant that the early settlers and their descendents could generally differentiate malaria from the other fevers. Typhoid, for example, was called long, continued, or slow fever. Typhus, because of its eruptions, was given various names, including putrid or eruptive fever. Nonetheless, one cannot assume that all epidemic outbreaks attributed to fever and ague, blackwater fever, hemorrhagic fever, or pernicious fever were in fact malaria.

Despite these caveats, we do know that the milder forms of malaria were established in areas of Western Europe relatively

early. In sixteenth-century England, for example, malaria was
known as the Kentish disorder or the lowlands disease, from its
association with the Dutch and Flemish. The exact date of its
arrival in North America is open to dispute, although medical
historians generally agree that the disease was not present prior
to the advent of Europeans. England experienced a series of
epidemics during the seventeenth century, and the disease was
undoubtedly carried by the settlers to the American colonies.
Wyndham B. Blanton, in his medical history of Virginia, argues
that in the seventeenth century malaria occurred there only
sporadically and was not a significant cause of the excessive
morbidity or mortality among the early arrivals. St. Julien
Ravenel Childs, in his monograph, *Malaria and Colonization in the
Carolina Low Country, 1526–1696*, maintains that malaria was
highly endemic in Tidewater Virginia.[1] Both men are probably
correct. The so-called "burning fevers" and "bloody fluxes"
which decimated the early Virginia settlements were far more
likely to have resulted from typhoid fever and intestinal infections rather than malaria. By the second half of the century,
malaria, as Childs maintains, was widely prevalent in the Virginia settlements, but only in its milder forms.

Whatever the case, by the latter third of the seventeenth century, "fever and ague" was widespread among settlers in the
southern colonies. In 1670 one of the first arrivals in South
Carolina wrote that it was present, "but we observe little mortality in the distemper. . . ."[2] The importation of slaves into South
Carolina in the 1680s may have introduced new strains of malaria,
in particular falciparum, the most deadly form, and thus led to
the intensification of the disease in the succeeding years. From
Virginia the Reverend John Clayton wrote in 1687 that intermitting fever was first among the diseases attacking English settlers.
Another colonist reported that his sister, having suffered from
two or three fits of fever and ague, was now well over the
"seasoning."[3] A student at William and Mary College argued in
1699 that Virginians, by remaining in the colony for their education, could avoid the double risk of the climate and diseases of
England and the necessity of readjusting to the "Fevers and
Agues" of Virginia on their return home.[4] The French who jour-
neyed down the Mississippi to the Gulf in the late seventeenth
century probably carried malaria with them. Father Jacques
Gravier wrote in 1701 that one of his companions was suffering

from tertian fever and reported from Louisiana several years later that "Brother fortin [sic] has been ill . . . with a quartan fever."[5]

The eighteenth century saw an increase in the prevalence of malaria in all the American colonies except for New England. But as a result of the South's warmer climate, the southern settlements bore the brunt of the onslaught. A businessman wrote in 1720 that South Carolina was such a sickly country that he was resolved to move North.[6] Between 1709 and 1717, three Anglican missionaries to the Carolinas reported that they and their families had suffered serious illness from "Fever and Ague." One declared cheerfully that he and his family had endured a "severe fitt" of "Fever and Ague" from August to December of the previous year, but that they were all now recovered. Ironically, he died of the same disorder the following fall. Between 1738 and 1742, no less than six other ministers in the Carolinas wrote that they had been incapacitated for months with malaria. Four of them urgently requested permission to return to England, one asserting that he had been afflicted with fever and ague every summer for seven years.[7] The South Carolina plantations were notorious for fever and ague, and many planters and their families retreated to Charleston during the late summer and fall. The city was relatively free of malaria, since it was surrounded by salt or brackish water unsuitable for breeding anopheles mosquitoes. A typical comment in the *South Carolina Gazette* in September 1732 stated: "The town at present is very healthy, except some few with an intermitting Fever."[8]

Since North Carolina was sparsely settled and lacked major towns, documentary evidence of malaria is limited, although it is clear that the milder forms of malaria were present. In 1735 William Byrd wrote to the governor of North Carolina, who was suffering from malaria, warning him to take repeated dosages of the "Bark" (cinchona) or else his "feaver" would "as surely return as speech to a silent woman."[9] An eighteenth-century tract advertising the advantages of North Carolina admitted that newcomers must endure agues, fluxes, and intermitting fevers from July through September but claimed that "these do not prove mortal."[10] They may not have been fatal, but the diaries and letters of North Carolinians during the period clearly show that fever and ague were endemic.

Malaria may have been relatively mild in North Carolina, but in Tidewater Virginia, as in South Carolina, it was a major com-

plaint of settlers. A Scottish settler complained in 1723 of suffering from "fever and Ague" wch is a very violent distemper here."
He added rather bitterly that the place was "only good for doctors
and ministers. . . ."[11] Thomas Salmon, describing Virginia in
1738, asserted that "Fevers and Agues, the Gripes, and Fluxes are
the most common Distempers," a statement fully borne out by
contemporary diaries, journals, and correspondence. Philip V.
Fithian recorded in his journal on 12 August 1774, "The conversa-
tion at Table was on the Disorders which seem growing to
be epidemical, *Fevers, Agues, Fluxes*—A gloomy train."[12] A
newly-arrived settler in Virginia wrote in 1785 that the colony was
"Esteem'd the most sickly Province this Except Georgia & South
Carolina. Fevers and Agues, Plurises [sic], Bilious Fevers rage
Terribly . . . it appears to me like a general plague." Seven of his
roommates, he continued, "were raging out of their senses" with
"Agues and Fevers."[13]

The Gulf Coast region was even more conducive to malaria,
since the warmer climate increased both the number and activity
of mosquitoes and lengthened the malarial season from May to
November, incapacitating or debilitating the inhabitants for
much of the year. A British physician detailed to study the health
of British troops in Mobile in 1769 reported that "billious, remit-
ting and intermitting fevers" flared up in June and continued for
several months. In September, he wrote, no less than two-thirds
of the officers and men stationed in the town were down with
fevers.[14]

The movements of troops and civilians during the Revolutionary War intensified the impact of all infectious diseases, including malaria. The retreat of this disorder from New England
by the time of the Revolution meant that New England troops
were particularly susceptible to it when fighting in the South. As
early as 1776, the Continental Congress ordered that three
hundred pounds of Peruvian (cinchona) Bark be sent to the
Southern Department.[15] A report from the Continental General
Hospital in South Carolina in 1780 showed that almost half of the
patients were suffering from intermittent or "continued" fevers.[16] The so-called "continued" fevers were probably typhoid,
although the exact diagnosis is uncertain. Malaria and typhoid
were frequently confused, and it was this confusion which contributed to the common nineteenth-century diagnosis of
typho-malaria. Both French and American troops besieging

Yorktown took heavy casualties from malaria in 1781. One-third of the patients in an American field hospital outside of Yorktown in October of that year had intermittent fever. In September 1782, almost half of General Nathanael Greene's men in camp near Charleston were sick with malaria. Aside from the large number of troops incapable of duty, the Southern Army suffered one hundred deaths from the disease during this same fall.[17]

Clearly malaria was a greater problem in the southern colonies than in the North, but did it affect settlement and growth in the South? For colonists from Great Britain and northwestern Europe, New England and the Middle Colonies were obviously more appealing. These colonies were more accessible, and the climate more closely resembled that of northwestern Europe. The settlers could raise familiar crops, and even the diseases they encountered, although somewhat harder on newcomers, were familiar to them. The southern colonies represented an altogether different way of life. Here colonists had to adjust to raising tobacco, corn, rice, indigo, and other new products; reconcile themselves to what they felt was excessive heat and humidity; and face new diseases such as yellow fever and more deadly forms of the familiar fevers, agues, and fluxes. All of these factors tended to inhibit the growth of the southern colonies. While malaria was widespread in all of the colonies except for those in New England, it was both more fatal and more debilitating in the southern ones. The disease was not a decisive factor in settlement, but during the colonial period the South's reputation for fevers and agues undoubtedly discouraged many prospective immigrants, and the longer malarial season tended to reduce the energy quotient of those who settled there.

The early nineteenth century brought no relief from malaria in the southern states. Writing of the Mississippi Valley in 1832, Timothy Flint stated that although intermitting fevers were seldom severe, they were always debilitating. Graphically describing the symptoms and course of the fever and ague, which he called "the general scourge of the valley," he stated: ". . . these agues, when often repeated, and long continued, gradually sap the constitution, and break down the powers of life. The person becomes enfeebled and dropsical. Marasmus, or what is called 'Cachexy,' ensues. A common result is, that enlargement of the spleen, vulgarly called 'an ague cake.' " This form of the disease, he added, "is most perceptible in the southern parts of the valley."[18] Daniel Drake, in his treatise on the principal diseases of the Mississippi Valley, devoted 163 pages to what he called "autumnal fever," a term, he said, which embraced the many names given to the different forms of fever and ague. After giving several reasons for devoting so much space to one disease, he concluded: "It is, moreover, the *great* cause of mortality, or infirmity of constitution, especially in the southern portions of the Valley. . . ."[19]

The records of U.S. Army posts in the southern states fully bear out the comments of Flint and Drake. In the 1820s and 1830s, Baton Rouge, Louisiana, and Fort Gibson, Arkansas, were considered the most sickly army posts in the country. Among the 210 deaths of soldiers at Fort Gibson in these decades, 49 were attributed to remittent and intermittent fever. In speaking of the First Regiment of Infantry, Samuel Forry wrote in 1842: "Baton Rouge, or more properly speaking, the swamps of the Mississippi, proved literally the grave of the regiment." According to one of the post surgeons at Baton Rouge, the diseases were "mostly bilious intermittents and remittents, tending to a typhoid character."[20] Other southern military posts shared top ranking for morbidity and mortality. Surgeon (later Surgeon General) Thomas Lawson referred to Fort Scott in Georgia and Baton Rouge as the "two most deadly" stations.[21]

In her history of the Second Seminole War, U.S. Army medical historian Mary C. Gillett states that the inordinately high incidence of fevers and diarrheal disorders prevented the army from campaigning against the Seminoles in Florida during the summer months. In the course of this war, army surgeons in Florida began to realize that relatively large doses of quinine were effective against the paroxysms of malaria, and their requests for additional supplies caused Surgeon General Lawson, an officer noted for economizing, to fly into one of his characteristic rages. On occasion, severe outbreaks of malaria caused Florida army posts to be temporarily abandoned, and in 1841 the Florida climate was considered so conducive to fever and ague and other disorders that an entire regiment was sent North to recover its health.[22]

According to J.I. Waring, medical historian of South Carolina, the rising incidence of malaria in country districts after 1790 led all planters who could afford it to move to Charleston and other areas known for their freedom from fever and ague. A history of Williamsburg County, South Carolina, in the mid-nineteenth

century declared that "the great continuous curse of this period
was malaria." "Malarial fever, as it developed in the fifties, on the
Santee," the author continued, "surpasses human capacity for
description. When the germ overpowered a human system, it
was relentless. It took away life slowly and certainly." The
"sickly" or malarial season generally began early in May, and
May 10 was considered the last safe day to remain in the country.
Even in Charleston, which was relatively free of the disorder,
between 1828 and 1845 malarial fevers ranked fifth among the
causes of death.[23] Most of these victims, however, may have
contracted the disease while residing or visiting in the back
country. As with most endemic disorders, malaria on occasions
struck in a particularly virulent form. Marlboro County in the
northcentral section of South Carolina experienced a particularly
severe form of malaria during summer and fall 1825. A local
resident recalled that scarcely a family escaped the disease, and
the county's two physicians were almost overwhelmed by demands for their services until the first killing frost put an end to
the epidemic.[24]

Malaria moved westward with the American frontier, along its
entire length, but in the northern states malaria declined once the
land was cleared and drained and cattle were introduced. In the
South this development occurred to some extent, but the survival
of mosquitoes throughout the winter months insured the constant presence of malaria. Moreover, settlement increased the
population density, creating another situation favorable for endemic disease. Howard Holley, in his medical history of
Alabama, asserts that with the settlement of the land around
1820, the severity of malaria steadily increased. Two of the state's
early capitals had to be abandoned because of fevers, and congestive malarial fever on occasions literally devastated sections of the
state. In early Conecuh County, a vicious outbreak of malaria
created panic, and a series of epidemics in Catawba ascribed to
fever and ague during 1821–22 killed twelve percent of the population. In 1867 an Alabama physician wrote: "Malarious affec-
tions constitute, undoubtedly and preeminently, the most
familiarly-known . . . , of the endemic diseases. . . . Intermittents and remittents of every known type and intensity, and with
almost every imaginable mask and complication, may be found
somewhere within the county (or state), in almost every sickly
season."[25]

While chronic malaria debilitated its victims and frequently rendered them easy prey to other disorders, a severe form of the disease known as congestive malaria was largely responsible for deaths directly attributed to malaria. Dr. P.H. Lewis of Alabama wrote in 1847 that to ascertain the most malignant malady responsible for the majority of deaths during the summer and fall it was "only necessary to be brought to the bed-side of one laboring under congestive fever, and the search is at an end."[26]

Dr. Charles C. Bass of Louisiana, one of the first scientists to obtain limited growth of the malarial parasite in pure culture, wrote that at the time of the Civil War, malaria was possibly the largest single cause of death in the South. The southern states most affected by the disease were Arkansas, Georgia, Mississippi, Louisiana, and South Carolina.[27] No part of Louisiana escaped malaria, but the bottom lands in the vicinity of the Mississippi and the state's other rivers were the most notorious for their fevers and agues. The diary of Kate Stone, a planter's daughter living on the floodplain of the Mississippi River in northeast Louisiana reveals the omnipresence of malaria. As Louisiana was settled in the antebellum years, a great many slaves were brought in or imported from the eastern states, many of whom were susceptible to the new strains of malaria they encountered. Kate Stone wrote on 24 August 1861 that so many of them had died that the "place must indeed seem like a graveyard to the poor Negroes." The following day she described a neighboring family as not having "an ounce of red blood between them—the whitest, weakest looking set of people." Shortly afterward she mentioned that she had slight chills and fever and that there was "danger of congestion or swamp fever at this season." Throughout the entire fall she made constant references to the presence of chills and fever in her own and neighboring families. Toward the end of November she wrote sadly that her brother had died of "swamp fever," a term usually applied to congestive malaria.[28]

By the time of the Civil War, malaria had definitely receded from New England and was declining in most of the settled northern states. There are indications that this situation held true for certain areas in the South as well. The association between wet swampy land and malaria was long established, and in the nineteenth century many individuals recommended draining land as a preventive measure. A special committee of the

Richmond Academy of Medicine appointed to study "the best method of counteracting the Influences of Malarial Poison in Eastern Virginia" claimed that prior to 1861 malaria had almost disappeared owing to the drainage and cultivation of low-lying land.[29] Since malaria remained endemic in virtually all sections of Virginia, the statement is probably an exaggeration, but undoubtedly a marked decline in malaria had occurred. The outbreak of the Civil War ended this promising state of affairs. The large-scale mobilization and movement of soldiers and civilians made malaria hyperendemic in the South and spread the disease widely in all of the northern states.

Throughout the war years, malaria was the major cause of morbidity among both northern and southern troops. In the period from 1 May 1861 to 30 June 1866 approximately one-fourth of all reported cases of disease among the Union forces involved malaria, and many soldiers, fearful of hospitals and dubious of army surgeons, dosed themselves with quinine and patent medicines containing quinine rather than make sick call. The records of the Union forces show a total of 1,213,814 cases and 12,199 deaths from malaria.[30] In the Deep South, malaria took an exceedingly heavy toll on Federal troops. The mean strength of officers and men in the Department of the Gulf, which included Mobile Bay; Ship Island, Mississippi; and a part of Louisiana, was 47,035 during the year ending 30 June 1864. The sick returns for that year showed a total of 47,999 cases of remittent and intermittent fever, an average of slightly better than one case per man.[31]

During 1862, the 30th Massachusetts Volunteers were first stationed in Louisiana, across the Mississippi River from Vicksburg, and then moved to Baton Rouge. Despite leaving 150 of its sick behind before moving up towards Vicksburg, over half of the regiment's 800 remaining men were on the sick list while in front of Vicksburg. In August the regiment was ordered to Baton Rouge, where the "sick list . . . was never below 400, almost entirely from malarial diseases, chiefly remittent fevers." In September and October, the regiment was encamped at Carrollton, Louisiana, at that time a suburb of New Orleans. The surgeon's report stated: "Nearly all those who had remittent fever from the exposure at Vicksburg had repeated attacks at Carrollton, and of the few who had escaped up-river, not one, officer or private, escaped illness from the effect of malaria at the latter locality."[32]

Malaria was even more prevalent among Confederate troops,

but, possibly because they had some measure of immunity, it proved less fatal. The Army of the Valley of Virginia, with a mean strength of 15,582 men, suffered 3,885 cases of malaria in the first ten months of 1862.[33] The 878 officers and men in a Confederate battery stationed below Savannah reported 3,313 cases of malarial fevers between October 1862 and December 1863.[34] Approximately 27 percent of all admissions to a Charleston, South Carolina, hospital during the Civil War were diagnosed under the various names given to malaria.[35] Inasmuch as malaria plagued troops on both sides, it is doubtful that it had any major impact upon the outcome of the war. Although the disease was more likely to take a serious form with northern troops, they were better fed, clothed, and housed, which helped them to resist disease, and their superior numbers more than compensated for any losses incurred from malaria.

Disease has always been a concomitant of warfare, and the Civil War was no exception. Among the infectious disorders spread far and wide through the movement of soldiers and civilians, malaria ranked high and no area escaped it. Even New England, which had been virtually free of it for half a century or more, witnessed a large-scale recurrence. According to Erwin Ackerknecht, the disease was hyperepidemic in New England from 1870 to 1890. In other areas, too, where malaria had been declining, epidemics flared up with the return of troops from the South. The net effect was a major wave of the disease that did not begin to subside until the end of the century.[36]

The effect on the South was even worse. In the antebellum years, clearing and draining land for cultivation had reduced the impact of malaria in many sections. The war, however, by disrupting all normal life and impoverishing the South, paved the way for an increase in endemic and epidemic disorders of all types and of malaria in particular. The rising incidence of hemorrhagic malarial fever was discussed by the North Carolina State Medical Society in 1874. One discussant declared that before the war, due to the large amount of cultivated land, "the malignant forms of malarial disease, as a general rule, were not known except in very low badly-drained swamp lands." Within the past eight years, he continued, "owing to much land lying waste, defective drainage and the general unsanitary condition of the country . . . the malarial poison has acted with intense virulence."[37]

This same point was made by a committee of the Richmond (Virginia) Academy of Medicine in 1869. Its report asserted that due to the cultivation of land malaria had almost disappeared by 1861, but that since the devastation caused by the war, the disease was once again rampant. In 1871, a Virginia physician from Princess Ann County reported that he had seen 514 cases of malaria within the past four years. [38] Medical journals and board of health reports from every southern state tell the same story of recurrent severe outbreaks of malaria. The war stimulated the northern economy and resulted in a high standard of living for its people, one of the most effective forms of disease control. The South, on the other hand, saw its economy ravaged, a good share of its work force killed or disabled, its transportation system worn out or destroyed, and its traditional social structure drastically altered. Small wonder that malaria and other disorders intensified their attacks and that for another seventy or eighty years the South found itself enmeshed in a bitter cycle of poverty and disease.

The impoverishment of the South intensified all prevalent disorders, and as the incidence of typhoid, diphtheria, smallpox, and other more dramatic diseases rose, malaria, despite its intensification, was relegated to the position of a familiar endemic complaint, troublesome but acceptable. Virtually no part of the South was exempt from it. A study by Walter Reed in 1895 showed that, in two army posts on the Virginia side of the Potomac River near Washington, intermittent and remittent fevers were present constantly from 1871 to 1895. Interestingly, in view of the imminent discovery of the role of mosquitoes, Reed argued in his article that since the water supply at the two posts had been improved, the source of the disease did not lie in the water itself. [39] In Charleston, South Carolina, which had always been relatively free of malaria, the occurrence of the disorder in the postwar years led to a proposal to plant a grove of eucalyptus trees across the neck of the peninsula to filter out the offending germ. On two occasions in the 1880s, statewide malarial outbreaks in South Carolina reached serious proportions. [40]

In the larger southern cities, malaria began to decline by the 1890s. The famous New Orleans surgeon, Rudolph Matas, in a paper on continued fevers in Louisiana, declared that "the true malarial type of fever—the strictly intermittent—is gradually disappearing from the city limits, and is now almost restricted in its prevalence to the swampy portion of our suburbs."[41] This same year, however, the Louisiana State Board of Health, which functioned primarily as a city health department, reported 340 deaths in New Orleans from malaria. Of this total, 58 were listed as typho-malaria, a common diagnosis throughout much of the nineteenth century. One can only assume that these 58 deaths were misdiagnosed or, more likely, that the victims were suffering from both diseases. In its *Biennial Report* for 1894–95, the Board of Health listed the number of cases of diphtheria, scarlet fever, smallpox, and leprosy, but not of malaria.[42] Although the two-hundred-page report discussed sanitary conditions, food and water supplies, and infectious diseases of men and animals, the only mention of malaria came in the annual mortality reports. What this probably indicates is that most malarial sufferers, in New Orleans as elsewhere throughout the South, treated themselves with one of the many antifever tonics, most of which contained quinine. And physicians, who were likely to see only the more severe cases, did not consider them worth reporting unless the patient died.

Even as late as 1940, two factors make it difficult to ascertain the precise role of malaria in the South. The first was the failure of southern states, with one or two exceptions, to gather vital statistics. Concern for public health traditionally has been an urban phenomenon, and the South was largely rural. The second factor was that rural and small-town physicians were apathetic or resistant in reporting cases. In 1922, Dr. Oscar Dowling of the State Board of Health complained about this to the Louisiana State Medical Society. Physicians justify their negligence, he declared, on the grounds that "the population is scattered in the country, that diseases seldom become epidemic and, most forcibly, that nothing is ever done about it anyway so what's the use." To illustrate his point, he cited an epidemic of 44 cases of typhoid fever in a small community of between 300 and 400 residents. None of the attending physicians bothered to report the cases, and the health board only learned of the outbreak when it was reported by a layman.[43]

As the South's standard of living began to rise slowly at the end of the nineteenth century, the incidence of malaria began a gradual decline. Even more promising, the discovery of the mosquito vector at the turn of the century opened the way to eliminating malaria. Unfortunately many southern leaders were reluctant to accept the mosquito hypothesis and even more were unwilling to spend the necessary funds for antimosquito campaigns. The basic problem, however, was the endemic poverty of the South in the years before World War II. Neither state nor municipal resources were available for expensive drainage and sanitary projects, and the federal government, which spent millions of dollars for mosquito control in Panama, gave little assistance.[44] The prime factor in eliminating malaria, as well as other disorders, is a high standard of living; until the majority of southerners were adequately housed, clothed, and fed, only limited gains could be made.

The author recalls that on his first trip into the Deep South in 1937, he was struck by the miserable shacks in which many rural workers and tenant farmers lived. These cabins not only lacked screens at doors and windows, but most did not even have window panes; their inhabitants were dependent on crude wooden shutters for warmth in cold weather. Two years earlier, Dr. Mark F. Boyd of the Rockefeller Foundation had written that he saw little hope for eliminating malaria from the South until "there are radical improvements in the housing facilities at the disposal of the rural inhabitants, both white and black. . . ." The quality of rural homes was so bad, he added, as to make screening and mosquito-proofing impossible.[45]

Despite the obvious success of antimosquito campaigns in Panama and other sections of the United States, little effort was made in this direction in the South. In 1905, responding to what was to be the last great yellow fever outbreak in the United States, New Orleans began a major effort to eliminate the *Aedes aegypti* mosquito. In the process it temporarily eliminated the anopheles.[46] Aside from this and several less strenuous drives by other port cities threatened by yellow fever, little was accomplished before 1912–13, although a few scattered attempts to eliminate the malarial mosquito were made before this date. In 1909, for example, the town council of West Bennettsville, South Carolina, concerned over the town's high malaria rate, began a systematic drainage campaign to combat mosquitoes.[47] About the same time, Dr. J.M. Barnett, physician to a small mill village in Dougherty County, Georgia, decided to take action against the omnipresent malaria and blackwater fever. Under his direction, the county began a systematic program of screening, oiling, and drainage combined with quinine treatment for the sick, in the process demonstrating that these fevers could be controlled.[48] The Louisiana State Board of Health, in its 1909 report made only one reference to malaria other than ascribing a total of 201 deaths to it. In a lecture given to public school teachers, one of the board's medical inspectors mentioned that eliminating mosquitoes could prevent malaria, adding that some midwestern states had eradicated the disorder by this method. Significantly, in giving the mortality statistics from the state's parishes (counties), a cryptic warning preceded them: "These reports are to be accepted at their face value," and a chart showing the morbidity figures for the parishes was preceded by the phrase, "as presented to this office."[49]

By 1912 the growing awareness of the role of mosquitoes in malaria led to a number of antimalarial campaigns in the United States. In the South some gestures were made, but the old combination of apathy and poverty prevented any real headway. The second decade of the century was one in which health trains were widely used to spread the gospel of public health; many state health boards adopted this tactic. A train consisting of several railway cars carrying health personnel and equipped to perform laboratory work and provide illustrated lectures would tour the state. The health inspectors would investigate the town or village water and food supplies and general sanitary conditions and lecture on health subjects. In describing the work of the Louisiana health train in 1913, Dr. Oscar Dowling mentioned that the board had supplied pamphlets on exterminating mosquitoes and that one parish, as a result of the train's visit, had established a commission to eliminate mosquitoes. He added, however, that the idea of eradicating mosquitoes had "not yet taken so great a hold," since many "people are skeptical as to results of measures recommended."[50]

Nevertheless, the success of occasional local campaigns (particularly those which proved economically and politically successful), a slow rise in living standards, and years of public health agitation gradually reduced the amount of malaria in the South during the first thirty years of the twentieth century. The decline of malaria was most striking after World War I. Two students of malaria estimated that the number of cases in Mississippi dropped from 118,370 in 1920 to 57,709 in 1937.[51] By the mid-1920s, New Orleans physicians were convinced that the disease was about to be conquered. Fearful of yellow fever, the city had continued to fight mosquitoes and thus kept both the *Aedes aegypti* and the anopheles under reasonable control. Dr. C.C. Bass, a world authority on malaria, in 1926 quoted the state health officer of Mississippi to the effect that malaria had declined by 52 percent in that state during the previous ten years. Attributing the decrease to clearing and draining the land, an understanding of the role of mosquitoes, and the more common use of quinine, Dr. Bass asserted that malaria was leaving the United States and would shortly be a negligible disorder except in a few undeveloped areas.[52]

The optimism seemed fully justified on the basis of returns from southern state health boards. In Louisiana, for example, the death rate from malaria declined from 33.9 per 100,000 in 1920 to 11.0 in 1926, and similar figures obtained for other states.[53] Even bearing in mind that these statistics were largely estimates, a real decrease in the incidence of malaria did occur, although much of it came in the larger cities and towns which were most likely to inaugurate antimosquito campaigns. In rural areas the improvement was only slight. In a Baton Rouge industrial plant which drew most of its workers from rural areas, the malaria rate in 1923 was 110.4 per 1,000 employees. After a program of diagnosis and treatment was instituted, the rate fell to 82.8 in 1928.[54] Beginning the following year, however, the malaria rate rose sharply among these employees, reflecting a general rise in the disease throughout the entire South. In Louisiana the total number of deaths attributed to malaria increased from 180 in 1930 to 427 in 1933, remained between 360 and 370 for the next two years, and fell to 258 in 1936. It was 1940 before the annual number of malaria deaths dropped below 100.[55]

The rise in malaria coincided with the onset of the Great Depression, and, although other factors undoubtedly played a role, it is probably more than a coincidence that the malarial wave did not subside until preparations for World War II stimulated the southern economy. The increase in malaria in the 1930s came about despite the beginning of relatively large-scale mosquito abatement programs under the sponsorship of the federal government. With the help of the Works Progress Administration, Public Works Administration, and other relief agencies, state and local governments, urged on by their boards of health, began drainage and oiling programs. On the other hand, the Tennessee Valley Authority (TVA) and other government and private agencies began damming streams for flood control, hydroelectric power, and navigational and recreational purposes, thereby creating large bodies of still water, ideal for breeding anopheles mosquitoes. The threat these waters posed in terms of malaria was well recognized by the 1930s. In 1932, for example, the South Carolina State Board of Health required a permit before damming or impounding waters and established regulations to limit the breeding of mosquito larvae in them.[56] The TVA devoted considerable time and effort to finding the best methods of mosquito control. One technique used with artificial lakes was periodically to lower the water level back of the dams. Mosquitoes lay their eggs in shallow water and reducing the water level left the eggs and larvae stranded on the shore. Equally important, TVA embarked on an educational program to create an awareness of the malarial problem.

Despite all these efforts, progress was slow, particularly in rural areas. Endemic malaria was all too familiar a disorder, one which rarely killed and could easily be mitigated by such standard proprietary drugs as "666," a tonic manufactured in Jacksonville, Florida, or forty or fifty other over-the-counter medicines containing quinine. Many rural and small-town physicians tended to be as casual towards malaria as laymen, seeing little reason for reporting cases. For this reason the perennial problem of determining the extent of malaria still remained as late as 1940. Epidemiologists C.L. Browne and Waldo L. Treuting of Louisiana reported in that year, "we have no really accurate statistics concerning malaria." The morbidity rates, they added, are "obviously very incomplete." While the reporting of deaths was more accurate "except from certain areas," the low case fatality rate means that "the number of deaths reported is not a good index of prevalence of the disease nor of its economic effect." The Louisiana State Board of Health had programs for malaria control, the two men concluded, but these were dependent upon local interest and financial support, which in many areas of the state was simply not forthcoming. Too many large plantation owners who controlled local governments were simply unwilling to assume the financial cost of controlling malaria.[57]

The advent of World War II, which brought thousands of Americans into southern army camps, had a twofold effect on malaria. First, the armed forces could not needlessly expose large groups of men to a dangerous, debilitating, and controllable disease. The army medical units promptly began moving against the disorder, and federal authorities encouraged local health departments to join in the drive. These programs were consolidated in 1942, with the establishment of the Office of Malaria Control in War Areas under the United States Public Health Service. The most effective antimosquito programs up to this date had been those which combined large-scale drainage work, the application of light oils and paris green to standing water, and the screening of homes and buildings. Fortunately, about this time a new and extremely effective insecticide, DDT (chlorophenothane), came into use. To supplement the standard antimosquito methods, emulsions of DDT were sprayed in homes, buildings, and other areas offering haven to mosquitoes. Within the next ten years, an estimated one hundred million dollars were spent on antimalarial work. As a result, malaria in the United States was reduced to negligible proportions.[58]

World War II and the Korean and Vietnam Wars reintroduced the more deadly strains of malaria, most notably *P. falciparum*, into the United States, but the higher standard of living throughout the South precluded any of them from gaining a foothold. Postwar prosperity gradually eliminated the tenant farmer shacks and substituted mosquito-proof screened homes; yielded a better-educated, healthier, and more disease-resistant population; and improved drainage and sanitation programs and health departments. In 1950, only two thousand cases of malaria were reported in the United States, a figure that was reasonably accurate since by this date even most rural counties had effective health departments.[59] Since then the majority of malaria cases reported in the United States has resulted from individuals contracting the disease abroad.

Of the three chronic disorders associated with the South—hookworm, pellagra, and malaria—malaria was undoubtedly the most serious. It affected all age and economic groups, could be fatal and was always debilitating, and was more widespread and survived longer than the other two. As a chronically debilitating disease, it shared with the other two the responsibility for the term "lazy southerner." In part because malaria was familiar and in part because quinine in one form or another could quickly relieve its symptoms, the South was slow to move against it. Its elimination was due as much to changes in the southern economy as it was to the active public health measures taken against it. The boll-weevil revolution, which moved cotton-growing to the Southwest, and the mechanization of farming caused a major shift in the southern population. The large black populations of the rich malaria-ridden bottom lands were forced to seek employment elsewhere, while at the same time diversified farming helped raise the entire southern standard of living. It is possible that either social and economic changes or public health measures alone could have solved the problem of malaria, but the process would have been much slower. Fortunately for the South, the two conjoined to eliminate malaria by the mid-twentieth century.

The forces that shaped southern distinctiveness were many, but undoubtedly malaria was a contributing factor. The lack of accurate statistics and the difficulties in identifying early diseases preclude precise comparisons between the North and the South. But all evidence—diaries, letters, newspapers, medical journals—shows that malaria was more widespread and fatal in the South. The disease was brought to the American colonies by the early settlers and became endemic in all of them during the colonial period. The warmer climate of the South, however, which in many sections enabled mosquitoes to survive throughout the winter, made malaria both more extensive and intensive. The influx of slaves from West Africa, some of whom carried falciparum malaria, added new and more virulent strains to those already in the South. Beginning in the latter half of the eighteenth century, as the disorder slowly withdrew from the North it appeared to strengthen its attack on the South, thus contributing to the South's reputation as a fever-ridden area. This view of the South was further enhanced in the Revolutionary and Civil Wars, when northern troops fighting in the South proved highly vulnerable to the omnipresent malaria.

In the antebellum period, southern nationalists argued that southern diseases were distinct from northern ones and that blacks differed anatomically and physiologically from whites. Consequently, they said, southern medical practice must vary considerably from that of the North. The recurrent threat of yellow fever and the omnipresence of malaria, which attacked nearly all newcomers to the South even well into the twentieth century, lent credence to the argument for distinctive southern diseases. Whatever the truth in the southern nationalist argument—and there was some truth in it—it helped to create a sense of southern uniqueness.

Early in the nineteenth century, made defensive by growing antislavery sentiment in the Western world, the South became hypersensitive to criticism. Undoubtedly the failure of southern states to adopt antimosquito tactics against malaria in the early twentieth century was in part the result of a lower living standard, but it also arose from a refusal by many southerners to admit that malaria was a problem. This same sensitivity to northern criticism made southern representatives deny the existence of pellagra among its poor, long after its presence had been demonstrated; and led Senator James Eastland and other Mississippi representatives to deny, in the face of overwhelming evidence, that poverty existed in their state during the 1960s.

The impact of malaria in itself directly influenced the economy and lifestyle of the South and helped to create an unfavorable image of that sector within the United States. Many southerners, already hypersensitive as a result of slavery and the race question, refused to acknowledge the problem of malaria until well into the twentieth century. This failure strengthened the picture of a backward South, further sensitized its people to outside criticisms, and drew southerners even closer together.

NOTES

1. Wyndham B. Blanton, *Medicine in Virginia in the Seventeenth Century* (Richmond, Va.: William Byrd Press, 1930), 54–55; St. Julien Ravenel Childs, *Malaria and Colonization in the Carolina Low Country, 1526–1696* (Baltimore: Johns Hopkins Univ. Press, 1940), 30.

2. Joseph I. Waring, *A History of Medicine in South Carolina, 1670–1825* (Columbia, S.C.: South Carolina Medical Association, 1964), 10.

3. John Duffy, *Epidemics in Colonial America* (Baton Rouge: Louisiana State Univ. Press, 1953), 207.

4. "Speeches of Students of the College of William and Mary Delivered May 1, 1699," *William and Mary College Quarterly*, ser. 2, vol. 10 (1930):326.

5. R.G. Thwaites, *The Jesuit Relations and Allied Documents* (Cleveland: Burrows Bros., 1896–1901), vol. 65, p. 103; vol. 66, p. 124.

6. Thomas Amory to Edward Chester, Jr., 15 Apr. 1720, in Business Letterbook of Thomas Amory, June 1717 to Oct. 1720, Thomas Amory

Letterbooks, Library of Congress Manuscript Division, Washington, D.C.

7. Duffy, *Epidemics in Colonial America*, 210–11.

8. *South Carolina Gazette*, 23 Sept. 1732.

9. "Letter of William Byrd, 2d, of Westover, Va.," *Virginia Magazine of History and Biography* 9 (1902):232.

10. "Information concerning the Province of North Carolina," *North Carolina Historical Review* 3 (1926):608.

11. Erskine Hume, "A Colonial Scottish Jacobite Family," *Virginia Magazine of History and Biography* 38 (1930):110.

12. Hunter D. Farish, ed., *Journal & Letters of Philip Vickers Fithian, 1773–1774, A Plantation Tutor of the Old Dominion* (Williamsburg: Colonial Williamsburg, Inc., 1943), 208.

13. "Virginia in 1785," *Virginia Magazine of History and Biography* 23 (1915):411.

14. Laura D.S. Harrell, "Colonial Medical Practice in British West Florida, 1763–1781," *Bulletin of the History of Medicine* 41 (1967):545.

15. Wyndham B. Blanton, *Medicine in Virginia in the Eighteenth Century* (Richmond, Va.: Garrett & Massie, 1931), 259.

16. Waring, *A History of Medicine in South Carolina, 1670–1825*, 98.

17. Mary C. Gillett, *The Army Medical Department, 1775–1818* (Washington, D.C.: Center of Military History, United States Army, 1981), 121–22, 124.

18. Timothy Flint, *The History and Geography of the Mississippi Valley* . . . , 2 vols. (Cincinnati: E.H. Flint and L.R. Lincoln, 1832), 1:38–39.

19. Daniel Drake, *Malaria in the Interior Valley of North America*, ed. Norman D. Levine (Urbana, Ill.: Univ. of Illinois Press, 1964), 866.

20. Samuel Forry, *The Climate of the United States and Its Endemic Influences. Based Chiefly on the Records of the Medical Department and Adjutant General's Office, United States Army* (New York: J. & H.G. Langley, 1842), 184–87, 200–202.

21. P.M. Ashburn, *A History of the Medical Department of the United States Army* (Boston: Houghton Mifflin, 1929), 46–47.

22. Mary C. Gillett, "The Army Medical Department, 1818–1865," ch. 3 (in press).

23. Waring, *A History of Medicine in South Carolina, 1670–1825*, 35–37, 63.

24. Suzanne C. Linder, *Medicine in Marlboro County, 1736–1980* (Baltimore: Gateway Press, 1980), 15.

25. Howard R. Holley, *The History of Medicine in Alabama* (Birmingham: Univ. of Alabama School of Medicine, 1982), 6, 274.

26. P.H. Lewis, "Medical History of Alabama," *New Orleans Medical and Surgical Journal* 4 (1847–48):12.

27. Charles C. Bass, "The Passing of Malaria," *New Orleans Medical and Surgical Journal* 79 (1926–27):714.

28. John Q. Anderson, ed., *Brokenburn, The Journal of Kate Stone, 1861–1868* (Baton Rouge: Louisiana State Univ. Press, 1955), 39, 46–49, 57, 63–64, 68.

29. Wyndham B. Blanton, *Medicine in Virginia in the Nineteenth Century* (Richmond, Va.: Garrett & Massie, 1933), 258–59.

30. *The Medical and Surgical History of the War of Rebellion*, vol. 1, pt. 3 (Washington, D.C.: Government Printing Office, 1888), 77–80.

31. Ibid., vol. 1, pt. 1 (Washington, D.C.: Government Printing Office, 1870), 397. These figures were obtained by subtracting the cases of typhoid, typhus, and typho-malaria from the total number of fever cases.

32. Ibid., vol. 1, pt. 3, 153–54.

33. Blanton, *Medicine in Virginia in the Nineteenth Century*, 292.

34. Mark F. Boyd, "An Historical Sketch of the Prevalence of Malaria in North America," *American Journal of Tropical Medicine* 21 (1941):235.

35. Joseph I. Waring, *A History of Medicine in South Carolina, 1825–1900* (Columbia, S.C.: South Carolina Medical Association, 1967), 136–37.

36. Erwin H. Ackerknecht, *Malaria in the Upper Mississippi Valley, 1760–1900* (Baltimore: Johns Hopkins Univ. Press, 1945), 56.

37. *Medical and Surgical History of the War of Rebellion*, vol. 1, pt. 3, 127n.

38. Blanton, *Medicine in Virginia in the Nineteenth Century*, 258–59.

39. Hugh R. Gilmore, Jr., "Malaria at Washington Barracks and Fort Meyer, Survey by Walter Reed," *Bulletin of the History of Medicine* 29 (1955):346–51.

40. Waring, *History of Medicine in South Carolina, 1825–1900*, 178.

41. Rudolph Matas, "Remarks on the Continued Fevers of Louisiana," *New Orleans Medical and Surgical Journal* 23 (1895–96):41.

42. *Biennial Report of the Board of Health to the General Assembly of the State of Louisiana, 1894–1895* (Baton Rouge: Printed by the *Morning Advocate*, 1896), 102.

43. Oscar Dowling, "Some Phases of Rural Health," *New Orleans Medical and Surgical Journal* 75 (1922–23):424–25.

44. Gordon Harrison, *Mosquitoes, Malaria and Man: A History of the Hostilities since 1880* (New York: E.P. Dutton, 1978), 168.

45. Earl B. McKinley, *A Geography of Disease* (Washington, D.C.: George Washington Univ. Press, 1935), 378.

46. John Duffy, *The Rudolph Matas History of Medicine in Louisiana*, 2 vols. (Baton Rouge: Louisiana State Univ. Press, 1958–1962), 1:433–36.

47. Linder, *Medicine in Marlboro County*, 77.

48. "Notes & Queries," *Journal of the History of Medicine and Allied Sciences* 1 (1946):175–76.

49. *Biennial Report of the Louisiana State Board of Health to the General Assembly of the State of Louisiana, 1908–1909* (New Orleans: Brandao Printing Company, n.d.), 76ff., 190.

50. Ibid., 1912–1913, pp. 117, 127.

51. Ackerknecht, *Malaria in the Mississippi Valley*, 57.

52. C.C. Bass, "The Influence of Malaria on the Progress of Civilization," *Southern Medical Journal* 19 (1926):855–56; Bass, "The Passing of Malaria," *New Orleans Medical and Surgical Journal* 79 (1926–27):714–15.

53. *Biennial Report of the Louisiana State Board of Health to the General Assembly of the State of Louisiana, 1926–1927* (n.p., n.d.), 185.

54. James M. Adams, "The Standard Treatment of Malaria," *New Orleans Medical and Surgical Journal* 84 (1931–32):382–83.

55. *Biennial Report of the Louisiana State Board of Health to the General Assembly of the State of Louisiana, 1940–1941* (n.p., n.d.), 208.

56. Linder, *Medicine in Marlboro County*, 77.

57. *Biennial Report of the Louisiana State Board of Health to the General Assembly of the State of Louisiana, 1940–1941* (n.p., n.d.), 152.

58. Wesley W. Spink, *Infectious Diseases, Prevention and Treatment in the Nineteenth and Twentieth Centuries* (Minneapolis: Univ. of Minnesota Press, 1978), 374.

59. Franklin A. Neva, "Malaria, Recent Progress and Problems," *New England Journal of Medicine* 277 (1967):1242.

3

Yellow Fever:
Scourge of the South

.

JO ANN CARRIGAN

Even without yellow fever, the South would have had its heat and humidity, plantations and slavery, Civil War and defeat. The American South as a geographical and social arena had already begun to develop the features that would shape its distinctive history before the disease first appeared as an occasional visitor around the turn of the eighteenth century. And the South has continued as a distinctive region and as a state of mind since the last yellow fever epidemic in 1905. Yet the "scourge of the South," as yellow fever was often called by nineteenth-century southerners and northerners alike, did have a special history in the region. For almost a century the disease served as one more peculiar, exotic element among the many peculiarities which, at one time or another, have characterized the South.

Although it should not be surprising that medical historians might view disease as a central theme in history (if not quite *"the* central theme"), a more restrained approach would argue only that yellow fever—or disease in general—was a significant but perhaps not a primary component in southern distinctiveness. More basic conditions such as the semitropical climate, the region's historical involvement with plantation agriculture and slave labor, and a biracial population of African as well as European origins eventually gave rise to other sectional differences, including disease patterns. Both climate and slavery played a crucial role in yellow fever's peculiar history, as in that of the South itself.[1]

Front-page cartoon from New Orleans newspaper during 1905 epidemic of yellow fever. Jack Frost blows away the yellow fever mosquito, Mme. Stegomyia, for the last time. From the New Orleans *Daily Picayune*, 13 October 1905.

The climate that made possible the cultivation of tobacco, rice, cotton, and sugar also provided a suitable environment for the *Aedes aegypti* mosquito, the transmitter of the yellow fever virus. Transplanted to the New World from Africa through the slave trade, the virus and its mosquito vector eventually found an ecological niche in the new tropical setting and became a permanent year-round source of infection in some of the port cities of Mexico, Central America, and the West Indies, and in some of the coastal towns and interior forests of South America. The coming of frost, which terminated mosquito activity, always brought an end to yellow fever epidemics in North America, but southern winters were sufficiently mild that some mosquitoes could hibernate and eggs could survive until the return of warm weather. While the *Aedes aegypti* established permanent residence in the American South, yellow fever never became an endemic infection—that is, present at all times. Only in tropical regions where mosquitoes remained active throughout the year, and only in communities where the size, density, and growth of the human population allowed the host-vector cycle of transmission to proceed without interruption, could the virus be propagated continuously and the disease maintained on a permanent basis. Yellow fever was reintroduced to the South again and again, however, during warm weather, by infected persons or infected mosquitoes arriving on ships from tropical America, often from Havana and occasionally from Veracruz, Honduras, Santo Domingo, Martinique or other yellow fever foci in Central America and the Caribbean. Once in port, the disease could be spread by the native southern *Aedes aegypti*.[2]

One of the great medical puzzles of the eighteenth and nineteenth centuries, yellow fever provoked much controversy among physicians and laymen in the attempt to explain its origin and transmission. Was it contagious or not? Was it an imported malady which quarantine measures might prevent? Or was it an indigenous product of local causes, such as heat and moisture acting upon accumulations of filth and producing "noxious effluvia"? Was it spread through the atmosphere, by infected materials, or by sick persons? Even after the development of germ theory in the 1870s the disease continued to defy explanation, prediction, and control. Not until the early twentieth century was the role of the mosquito scientifically demonstrated, thereby providing the means for preventing or limiting the spread of yellow fever.[3]

Prior to that discovery, the erratic and unpredictable spread of the pestilence, its awful symptoms, the lack of effective therapy, and the high mortality during epidemics inspired considerable private terror and public panic. Symptoms of the disease include chills, fever, vomiting, and muscular pain; and in severe cases, jaundice or yellowness of the skin and hemorrhaging from various parts of the body. Partially digested blood from hemorrhaging within the stomach produces the dreaded "black vomit," resembling coffee grounds in appearance. In the terminal stage, violent delirium, convulsions, or coma will occur, with death resulting from damage to the liver, kidneys, heart, and blood vessels.[4] Little wonder that many who could afford it fled their communities when yellow fever appeared, or that the coastal cities of the South had a large absentee population seeking the amenities and comforts of northern summer resorts each year during the so-called "sickly season."[5]

Yellow fever had not always been mainly a southern scourge. In fact, its early ravages in North America were concentrated in northern seaports, the colonial population centers engaging in regular commerce with the West Indies. The earliest clearly identified yellow fever epidemics had occurred in the mid–seventeenth century in Barbados, Guadeloupe, Havana, and Yucatan. By the 1690s the disease began to appear in the Atlantic ports of North America, and intermittently throughout the eighteenth century, outbreaks occurred in Boston, New York, and Philadelphia, as well as Charleston, Norfolk, and Baltimore. The French or Spanish colonial settlements of Biloxi, Mobile, and Pensacola on the Gulf coast, and New Orleans on the Mississippi also experienced yellow fever attacks at various times during the eighteenth century. In the North, the most destructive epidemic ever to occur was the Philadelphia visitation of 1793.[6]

Largely confined to port cities with relatively dense populations, eighteenth-century epidemics were highly variable in extent and intensity, and the specific nature of the fever remained in question. The disease would appear several summers in succession, disappear for decades, then strike again.[7] It was a mystery. But it was not a southern mystery—until the nineteenth century, when the disease unaccountably seemed to retreat below the Mason-Dixon line, or thereabouts, and after the 1820s to focus its attacks mainly upon the towns of the South Atlantic and the Gulf coasts and along the southern rivers, especially the lower Mississippi. Ironically, the North ceased to be troubled with yellow fever about the same time that slavery was completely eliminated there; by the 1820s, in this American Union, both slavery and yellow fever were peculiar to the South. Except for a few outbreaks in Norfolk and Baltimore, thereafter Charleston was the northernmost point on the Atlantic coast to suffer epidemics on a fairly regular basis.[8]

Meanwhile, New Orleans, as a major port and center for the Latin American trade, had become the principal point of entry for the infection and the yellow fever capital of the South. As the pestilence was reintroduced every summer from the late 1790s until the Civil War, many New Orleans residents developed an attitude of fatalistic acceptance, even indifference, along with their acquired immunity to "Yellow Jack," the "Saffron Scourge," the "Strangers' Disease," their familiar names for the malady. In the antebellum Crescent City, the illness soon achieved the status of a common, ordinary, expected summer phenomenon. Each year saw a few cases, and several times in each decade the infection reached epidemic proportions, spreading outward from New Orleans along the lines of trade and travel to the various towns on the coast and the inland waterways, extending over a wider southern territory with each successive epidemic.[9]

Three features of the "southern pestilence" are noteworthy (and in some ironic sense, almost "un-southern"). First, in a South defined as mainly rural, yellow fever was almost exclusively a disease of towns and cities.[10] Second, in those ports where yellow fever occurred frequently, recently arrived foreign immigrants and "strangers" from the North provided most of the victims, whereas native southerners and longterm residents seemed to enjoy some measure of immunity.[11] And third, the black population, more than native whites, always exhibited a striking resistance to the malady, even in areas where yellow fever was only an occasional visitor.[12] One medical authority in the 1850s described this particular phenomenon as the "inferior susceptibility" of blacks.[13]

Although this urban "strangers' disease" received more widespread attention than any other nineteenth-century southern health problem, yellow fever usually had little or no direct effect on the health of rural southerners, black or white—the vast majority. Other ailments, so commonplace they seemed as inevitable as the changing seasons, attracted slight public notice yet caused far more sickness and death year after year among rural and urban southerners of both races than the occasional dramatic epidemic occurrences of the mysterious, highly-feared yellow fever.

Transmitted by a household mosquito which rarely travels far from home on its own power, the yellow fever virus does not spread easily within a scattered rural population. Infected persons or mosquitoes traveling on ships, riverboats, or trains may introduce the virus into an area, but a certain "critical" population size and density, both of mosquitoes and susceptible humans, is required for an epidemic to develop. The growth of antebellum coastal cities and river towns supplied more potential fever victims, and the use of steam navigation in river commerce and later the development of railroads facilitated the spread of the infection.

In another ironic coincidence (which did not escape the notice of abolitionists), the peculiar scourge of the South reached a peak of virulent activity during the 1850s, even as the sectional controversy and debate over slavery intensified. Four major epidemics struck New Orleans within the decade—1853, 1854, 1855, and 1858—destroying almost 20,000 lives in that city alone and spreading throughout the South more than ever before. In 1853, yellow fever attacked every town on the Mississippi from New Orleans to the mouth of the Arkansas River, almost every village in Mississippi and Louisiana south of Vicksburg, and many large plantations along the Mississippi River south of Natchez, where densely populated quarters were the equivalent of villages. The disease also struck Galveston, Biloxi, Mobile, Pensacola, Tampa, Key West, Savannah, and Norfolk, and spread to interior communities where it had never been seen before.[14]

Both the opponents and defenders of slavery found ways to use the Great Southern Plague of 1853 in their respective arguments. Some abolitionists suggested that yellow fever was not only the result of slavery, having been introduced by the African slave trade, but that the disease served as a penalty or punishment, afflicting those areas where the institution prevailed. Responding to this "theory" when it appeared in the New York

Tribune in 1853, the New Orleans *Weekly Delta* denied the African origin of the disease and contended that the relative immunity of blacks from the ravages of the fever provided a strong argument in favor of slavery. Only those blacks who had spent some time in the North and then returned to the South had been susceptible to the disease, the editor explained, and among those few blacks who died, almost all had been free. Therefore, "slavery is the condition best suited to . . . [the Negro] as it exempts him from a destructive disease, to which he would render himself liable by the exercise of his freedom." Considering the extremely high death rate among the white laboring class in New Orleans, the editorial concluded that yellow fever mortality would have been catastrophic beyond imagining had white labor instead of black slaves been employed on southern plantations.[15]

The same newspaper had previously published a letter arguing that slavery was "a blessing in our Southern States to both races" and not a curse, as the abolitionists believed. According to the writer, yellow fever was actually generated by the practice of "rank poison abolitionism"—that is, when white laborers violated nature's laws "in making negroes of themselves by doing the work in hot noonday summer sun that negroes ought to do."[16] Almost identical views were expressed in a New Orleans medical journal that year by Dr. Samuel Cartwright, whose enduring reputation rests largely on his discovery of *Drapetomania* ("the disease causing slaves to run away"), his formulation of the medico-Biblical proslavery argument, and his advocacy of a distinctive medical practice for the South. Cartwright was certain that yellow fever resulted from the violation of nature's laws, mainly by the recently arrived Europeans and northerners, who fell victim to the disease when they engaged in "laborious employments" appropriate only to the black constitution. Explaining further, he wrote:

> Nature scorns to see the aristocracy of the white skin . . . reduced to drudgery work under a Southern sun, and has issued her fiat, that here at least, whether of Celtic or Teutonic origin, they shall not be hewers of wood or drawers of water, or wallow in the sloughs of intemperance, under pain of three fourths of their number being cut off. Until this immutable law, which has made the white race rulers . . . be properly respected, the deaths arising from its violation will continue to swell the bills of mortality . . . .[17]

The New Orleans *Daily Picayune* observed in September 1853 that the pestilence had provided the occasion for the *London News* to offer a critique of slavery along with a report that New Orleanians had been terrified by the possibility of a slave uprising during the outbreak of fever. Denying that such a thought had occurred to anyone in the city, the southern editor was sorely distressed by "our amiable transatlantic cousins" and their "moralizing upon the subject of slavery . . . [while] contemplating the beauties of a servile insurrection."[18]

The suggestion by the London journalist that southerners might worry about urban slave rebellions was not altogether without foundation. In fact, an alleged slave plot had been revealed in New Orleans in June 1853, producing a brief but intense scare in and near the city. The New Orleans *Picayune* minimized the alleged conspiracy as the fantasy of one white fanatic and several slaves; about the same time the newspaper was also discounting the rumors of a serious yellow fever outbreak in the city. However little substance behind the plot, the officials took it seriously enough to place armed patrols on the streets, to call out some units of the local militia, and to make several arrests. On at least two other occasions in Louisiana history, in 1804 and 1837, slave conspiracies or rumors of planned insurrections were reported during yellow fever outbreaks.[19] From the epidemics of the 1790s onward, whites had noticed and commented upon yellow fever's differential impact on the races, even as blacks must also have observed their apparent resistance to the disease. Blacks were sometimes employed as nurses and gravediggers during epidemics because of their presumed immunity.[20] Certainly if the master class ever felt anxious about the possibility of urban slave revolt, a severe yellow fever epidemic would have been an appropriate time to worry about white vulnerability in the midst of health crisis and social emergency.

Southern physicians in the 1840s and 1850s, responding to the sectional controversy, focused attention on the South's peculiar diseases, including yellow fever, and initiated a drive for southern medical independence. They established medical schools and associations in the region where few had existed before, and some began publishing journals and medical texts, hoping to encourage research by other southern practitioners. Various medical periodicals urged students intending to practice medicine in the South to study medicine in the South, where they might receive instruction and acquire experience—not available elsewhere—in the peculiarities of southern diseases, as influenced by climate and manifested in various ways in black and white populations.[21]

As the widespread epidemics of the 1850s clearly demonstrated, blacks were not immune to yellow fever, but they usually presented mild symptoms, and relatively few died of the disease. With freedom and increased mobility in the post–Civil War era, many plantation blacks relocating in southern towns experienced yellow fever attacks in time of epidemics, but always with a remarkably low case-fatality rate compared to whites in the same communities. This pattern would continue through the last epidemic in 1905.[22]

Differences in degrees of vulnerability to the fever also appeared among white residents of the Gulf and South Atlantic ports, which one northern medical writer called "our southern yellow fever cities." Wherever yellow fever was a frequent occurrence, the native-born and the longterm resident, although not invariably immune, did appear less liable to attack during epidemics than newcomers from the North or from Europe, the "strangers" who always figured prominently in the mortality lists. Climate played an important role in nineteenth-century medical theory, and physicians generally believed that the native-born enjoyed immunity because they were accustomed since birth to the subtropical heat and humidity, while the "unacclimated stranger" was highly vulnerable because he had not yet adapted to the climate and therefore had no resistance to the diseases associated with that climate. Gradual habituation to the local atmospheric influences supposedly modified an individual's physical system and gave protection against fevers common to the locality. Five or six years of continuous residence in the area, living through one or more epidemics, with or without having experienced a clearly identified case of yellow fever, were considered sufficient for purposes of acclimation and immunity.[23]

Only those persons who had actually experienced a case of fever, however, and lived through it could be absolutely certain that they were among the privileged immune class. These survivors, confident of their immunity, tended to scoff at those who expressed fear; they asserted that the "acclimating fever" was not a serious hazard when treated in time, and furthermore it

supplied "a safeguard against all other ills indigenous to a southern latitude."[24] Outsiders moving to the yellow fever zone with
the intention of residing there had to face this "ordeal by
disease"—a dangerous process of naturalization (or as some
called it, "creolization") by which a safe and secure southern
residency was achieved.[25] One physician writing in the 1830s
admitted that the process of acclimation was "sometimes severe, [but] it is the only ordeal we have to pass through—no such
immunity is enjoyed in the northern portion of the United
States—no period of acclimation can protect the pulmonary organs of the natives or emigrants . . . [against consumption]," one
of the principal causes of mortality in northern cities.[26]

The acclimated survivors as well as the natives of southern
ports (who had acquired their yellow fever immunity from mild,
undiagnosed cases in childhood) explained the high mortality of
the "strangers' disease" as the fault of the lower orders—the
filthy, intemperate, ignorant foreigners and northerners in the
ranks of the laboring poor. Local physicians and journalists con-
curred in this judgment, claiming excellent urban health except
during epidemics, which posed no threat except to strangers in
the lower classes, who brought on their own ills and gave southern cities an undeserved reputation as centers of pestilence. Yellow fever reinforced southern nativism and xenophobia and intensified class consciousness in the antebellum urban South.
Labeling the fever the "strangers' disease" diminished its importance, made it appear a disease of the poor, the foreign, the
expendable. The associated belief in native immunity supported
an elitist, exclusionist, upper-class, laissez-faire bias, and a cal-
lousness and indifference which undermined most efforts at public health improvements until the late nineteenth century.[27]

During the Civil War, northern newspapers expressed concern
for Union troops exposed to southern diseases, especially in the
summer months. When northern forces occupied New Orleans
in May 1862, some rebels hoped that the saffron scourge would
appear that summer and destroy the unacclimated invaders. But
the disruption of trade by the blockade, General Ben Butler's
firmly enforced system of quarantine and sanitation, and a large
measure of luck preserved the Yankee troops in New Orleans
from an all-out confrontation with Yellow Jack.[28]

After the war the disease struck the southern coast less frequently, and only twice, in 1867 and 1878, was an epidemic even

New Orleans newspaper advertisement suggesting people leave the city during the yellow fever epidemic for a North Carolina resort community where there are no quarantine restrictions. From the New Orleans *Daily Picayune*, 6 August 1905.

comparable to the antebellum experience. The 1878 visitation surpassed the record of the 1850s in terms of territory affected, and indeed was the most extensive yellow fever epidemic ever to occur in the United States. Spreading throughout the South and up the Mississippi Valley as far north as Missouri and Illinois, transported by railroad as well as river steamer, this epidemic stimulated an awareness of regional, even national, interdependence in matters of health—especially in the interior states of the valley. Reaction to the epidemic also led to the establishment of a National Board of Health, a short-lived experiment, and opened a lengthy debate over the proper limits of federal action in quarantine and health policy. Business leaders in southern cities became increasingly concerned with the economic impact of disease and began to organize and work for sanitary reform. [29]

Epidemics, yellow fever or otherwise, if extensive in scope and costly in terms of lives and commerce, always aroused public concern and usually resulted in local or state legislation creating advisory health committees or boards to administer quarantine regulations or sanitary measures. Without understanding the processes by which various diseases spread from person to person and place to place, antebellum health officials were operating in the dark, and their work was sporadic and limited in effectiveness. Even so, as the preeminent southern pestilence, yellow fever continued to be the main force driving southern efforts at health reform throughout the nineteenth century and into the early years of the twentieth. Other social and scientific developments converged with epidemics in the post–Civil War years and brought about a national public health movement with greater promise. From the 1870s on, states and municipalities throughout the country began to establish permanent health agencies with more extensive powers and responsibilities. [30] In the forefront of the health crusade, the American Public Health Association, organized in 1872, held its annual meeting for the first time in a southern city, Richmond, late in 1878, soon after the great pestilence of the Deep South and the Mississippi Valley had subsided. The main topic for discussion by the convention delegates would be "the scourge of the South" (as yellow fever was still called) and its impact upon the nation as a whole. [31]

The epidemic of 1878 occasioned much suffering and distress among fever victims and their families, as well as many others left without employment or resources when most normal economic

activities were disrupted or suspended during the crisis. Northern generosity had been exhibited before during yellow fever
epidemics in the South, but this time contributions of food,
medicines, and money literally poured in from the North to
southern relief associations—it was said, from every quarter and
every class. Some northern brethren even came in person to
assist in the care of the sick and the poor. Many southerners
expressed deep appreciation for this benevolence in time of their
great need and despair, and several did so in poetic form. One
allegorical monstrosity, which won a prize offered by the New
Orleans *Times* for the best poem expressing southern gratitude,
lurched on for more than three hundred lines of unrhymed iam-
bic pentameter, describing how Hope had been driven out by
Despair and Terror, until brave Rescue from the North arrived
and saved the day.[32]

A similar creation by a Mississippi judge entitled "The Welded
Link" offered up almost six hundred lines describing the northern response to the awful southern pestilence and the resulting
emotional impact in the South. In the preface to his book of verse,
the judge declared that "kindness, charity, and love did what
arms never could have done. It conquered the Southern people
and the Southern heart." In his overwrought rhymes he expressed a sentiment that seems to have been widely shared.[33]
The New Orleans *Daily Picayune* said it more simply: "In the
name of that philanthropy which has overswept all geographical
and party lines, we declare that the war is over, now at last and
forever."[34]

Aside from completing the task of Reconstruction through
emotional reunion, as some would have it, the experience of 1878
had other lasting effects. The epidemic intensified fear of the
disease in hundreds of towns, fear that persisted for years and
motivated the shotgun quarantines in the 1890s. As yellow fever
became less frequent and less familiar, it seemed to inspire more
panic than ever. Almost two decades passed with very few cases
occurring, even in New Orleans. Then when the disease appeared on the Gulf coast in Mississippi and spread to New Orleans in 1897, panic erupted throughout the region. Although the
outbreak was a relatively mild one and the fever less virulent than
in previous years, local and state quarantines throughout the
South, enforced by "cordons of shotguns," disrupted rail and
steam transportation and in some areas halted commerce al-

together. According to the New Orleans *Picayune*, "The entire country south of the Ohio River and the Kansas State line is dominated by madmen."[35]

In its final decade as a threat to the South, yellow fever (and even the rumor of fever) engendered much conflict within and between southern states. Panic-stricken citizens continued to interfere with commerce, sometimes refusing to allow trains even to pass through their communities. They engaged in vigilante or mob action with occasional violence, hoping to protect themselves against this seemingly unpredictable, hence especially terrifying, disease. Northern newspapers denounced this behavior as stupid, irrational, primitive, and definitely unscientific. On the road to modernization, the South was obviously way behind.

Southern state health officials met in 1898, drafted a set of uniform quarantine regulations, and agreed to provide early notification of infectious diseases, hoping to reduce the influence of suspicion and rumor and to keep the trains and steamboats running in interstate commerce. Despite the efforts of state and federal health authorities, problems of distrust, suppression of information, and local quarantine barriers continued to plague southern trade and travel through the last epidemic in 1905.[36]

A massive amount of evidence from newspapers, medical literature, official documents, and private papers clearly reveals the sectional character and southern identification of yellow fever from the 1820s through the final episode in 1905. Both southerners and northerners recognized it as a disease of the South, most prevalent in several coastal and river cities, but potentially active in towns throughout the region (except in the highlands). Medical authorities in the mid–nineteenth century usually declared the thirty-fifth parallel as the approximate northern limit of epidemic yellow fever.[37] By the 1890s federal regulations for inspection and certification of interstate passengers and freight leaving infected areas required different treatment for trains destined for "POINTS SOUTH" (defined as "infectible territory") and those heading for "POINTS NORTH" (or "noninfectible territory"). The southern boundary of Maryland was considered the dividing line between infectible and noninfectible territory. Detention of passengers and fumigation of freight were not required for through trains destined for the North, beyond the yellow fever zone. While a case of disease might be transported into a noninfectible area, health authorities felt confident that it would spread no further. This judgment was grounded on years of observation and experience, although the effective basis for the distinction between infectible and noninfectible territory—that is, the presence or absence of the *Aedes aegypti* mosquito—was not understood until the early twentieth century.[38]

If newspaper reports and editorials can be accepted as indicators of sectional image projection and reception, disease in general and yellow fever in particular began to appear as a factor in southern distinctiveness fairly early in the nineteenth century. Editors often published extracts from journals in other sections of the country, then commented on the content. As early as 1817, a New Orleans editor was complaining about the exaggerations of a Boston paper on the subject of disease in the southern states, and he offered his on-the-spot observations to the northern friends to counter their "horrid picture."[39]

DeBow's Review noted in 1848 the vast amount of ignorance exhibited in the North regarding southern health. "Their insurance companies exact a higher premium if the party, being a southerner, remain at *home during summer*; but . . . permit him to *spend his winter in New-England*, where, perhaps, his chances of life would be diminished one half." In 1867, when postwar bitterness raged on both sides of the Mason-Dixon line, northern newspapers accused the New Orleans journals of being in league with local authorities to suppress the facts about the ravages of yellow fever. The New Orleans *Bee* indignantly denounced this charge as an "abominable lie," but found it not at all surprising "that this is believed in the north for they are ready to believe anything unfavorable about us."[40]

Some forty years later, during the epidemic of 1905, the New Orleans *Picayune* wondered why people thought yellow fever would ruin New Orleans, when no-one expected a smallpox epidemic or any other disease to cause permanent destruction to the commerce of New York or Chicago. The people of the Crescent City were "no more affected by the light outbreak of yellow fever than the inhabitants of Northern cities by their periodic invasions of typhoid and diphtheria." While the outbreak might temporarily affect certain business interests, the New Orleans editor was certain that the South would not be held back in "its great material progress."[41]

For more than a hundred years the negative economic effects of yellow fever epidemics had been visited upon the South, including the disruption of trade and its diversion to other areas; delay of commerce associated with the harvest; and the consumption of energy and resources in the care of the sick, burial of the dead, provision for orphans, and relief of the families of the sick and the unemployed. The threat of yellow fever had discouraged foreign immigration as well as internal migration to southern cities, and it had also resulted in a substantial absentee population each year during the "sickly season" of summer and early fall. Or so it was believed by many southern observers and analysts, who repeatedly cited yellow fever as "the South's greatest drawback," or at the very least, one of the main obstacles to population growth, capital investment, commercial expansion, and economic prosperity. The final victory over Yellow Jack in 1905 was expected to usher in a great new age of southern prosperity.[42]

The "Sickly South" (or the "Pestilential South") was an important facet of the image of "otherness" projected by the region in the nineteenth and early twentieth century, perhaps as potent in its impact on northern consciousness as the image of the "Violent South," the "Backward South," or the "Lazy South."[43] Yellow fever was exotic, bizarre, and dreadful in its symptoms; and baffling in its invisible movement from place to place and its apparently random attacks, all potentially fatal. The disease struck morbid fascination if not terror into the hearts of those at a distance as well as those nearby. Northern newspapers sometimes gave more attention to the scourge of the South than the journals in the region affected.

As a deviation from the normal expected patterns of illness, epidemic disease has always attracted much more public attention than ordinary endemic maladies which result in far greater mortality over a period of years. Hence, southern yellow fever epidemics focused the attention of the nation on the region and supplied material for front-page drama in the northern press. While focusing attention on the South, epidemics provided the occasion for the expression of sectional antagonism, mutual criticism, charges and countercharges with regard to disease and other matters, as well as occasional cooperation and benevolence.

Yellow fever epidemics also served as a lens through which other negative aspects of the southern image were projected and reinforced in the rest of the country—racism, xenophobia, violence, shotgun vigilantism, poverty, economic stagnation, ignorance, irrationality, resistance to modern science, and the usual defensiveness and hypersensitivity. In addition to the real injuries inflicted on the South, yellow fever also revealed and magnified the region's worst blemishes for all the world to see.

NOTES

1. There is an enormous body of literature that attempts to define, assess, magnify or discount, and determine the persistence or alteration of the elements of southern distinctiveness. One work which I found especially useful and thought-provoking in writing this paper was Carl N. Degler's *Place over Time: The Continuity of Southern Distinctiveness* (Baton Rouge: Louisiana State Univ. Press, 1977). Also of value was a collection of essays, *Myth and Southern History*, ed. Patrick Gerster and Nicholas Cords, 2 vols. (Chicago: Rand-McNally College Publishing, 1974). Ever since U.B. Phillips began the search for "the central theme" of southern history in the 1920s, others have continued to explore that wilderness, finding many diverse themes and increasing ambiguity and complexity. For a recent insightful treatment of the interaction of environment, population, and culture in the making of southern history, with considerable emphasis on the impact of disease, see Albert E. Cowdrey, *This Land, This South: An Environmental History* (Louisville: Univ. Press of Kentucky, 1983).

2. Richard M. Taylor, "Epidemiology," in *Yellow Fever*, ed. George K. Strode (New York: McGraw-Hill, 1951), 445–51; Sir Macfarlane Burnet and David O. White, *Natural History of Infectious Disease*, 4th ed. (Cambridge, England: Cambridge Univ. Press, 1972), 242–45; Henry Rose Carter, *Yellow Fever: An Epidemiological and Historical Study of Its Place of Origin* (Baltimore: Williams and Wilkins, 1931); George Augustin, *History of Yellow Fever* (New Orleans: Searcy and Pfaff, 1909), 760–80.

3. Réné La Roche, *Yellow Fever, Considered in its Historical, Pathological, Etiological and Therapeutical Relations*, 2 vols. (Philadelphia: Blanchard and Lea, 1855); Charles-Edward A. Winslow, *The Conquest of Epidemic Disease: A Chapter in the History of Ideas* (Princeton: Princeton Univ. Press, 1943), 193–235, 352–56. See also Jo Ann Carrigan, "The Saffron Scourge: A History of Yellow Fever in Louisiana, 1796–1905" (Ph.D. diss., Louisiana State Univ. 1961), 280–363.

4. J. Austin Kerr, "The Clinical Aspects and Diagnosis of Yellow Fever," in *Yellow Fever*, ed. Strode, 389–422; *Merck Manual of Diagnosis and Therapy*, ed. Robert Berkow, 13th ed. (Rahway, N.J.: Merck and Company, 1977), 57–58.

5. Newspaper commentary every summer and early fall exhibited concern about the absentee population and questioned why anyone should go off to northern resorts when "our own beautiful coast" had so

much to offer. See for example, New Orleans *Daily Picayune,* 21 Aug.
1838; New Orleans *Daily Crescent,* 22 June 1853; *DeBow's Review* 2 (July
1846):73; *Southern Medical Reports* 2 (1850):142–43; *New Orleans Medical
and Surgical Journal* 7 (Mar. 1851):591. See also New Orleans *Times-
Democrat,* 17 and 20 Aug. 1905, for samples of advertisements by hotels
and resort areas of the North and Upper South, and notices of special
fares on the Illinois Central and other rail and steamer lines. Virtually
every source examined reported the emptying out of towns by a substantial portion of the population as yellow fever approached, at various
times during the nineteenth century.

6. John Duffy, *Epidemics in Colonial America* (Baton Rouge: Louisiana
State Univ. Press, 1953), 138–63; Wilson G. Smillie, *Public Health, Its
Promise for the Future: A Chronicle of the Development of Public Health in
the United States, 1607–1914* (New York: Macmillan, 1955), 33–38; Augustin, *History of Yellow Fever,* 769–73; J.M. Toner, "The Distribution
and Natural History of Yellow Fever as it has Occurred at Different Times
in the United States," American Public Health Association, *Public Health
Papers and Reports* 1 (1873):359–84.

7. John B. Blake, "Yellow Fever in Eighteenth Century America,"
Bulletin of the New York Academy of Medicine 44 (June 1968):673–86;
David Geggus, "Yellow Fever in the 1790s: The British Army in Occupied Saint Domingue," *Medical History* 23 (1979):38–44, 58. The
chronological pattern of eighteenth-century epidemics in the Atlantic
and Gulf ports of North America reflected the periods of greatest prevalence in the Caribbean, when yellow fever was fueled by rapid population growth or by European troops deployed in the contest for empire.
These periods included the late 1690s and early 1700s; the 1730s and
1740s; the 1760s; and the 1790s, when an extensive and virulent series of
epidemics was sparked by the troops and refugees of war and revolution.

8. John Duffy, "Yellow Fever in the Continental United States During
the Nineteenth Century," *Bulletin of the New York Academy of Medicine*
44 (June 1968):692–97; Josiah C. Nott, "Yellow Fever Contrasted with
Bilious Fever," *New Orleans Medical and Surgical Journal* 4 (Mar.
1848):590–91; John Duffy, *A History of Public Health in New York City,
1625–1866* (New York: Russell Sage, 1968), 118–21, 450–51. Why yellow
fever no longer invaded the North Atlantic ports after the 1820s is not
altogether clear. Although cases of the disease continued to appear on
ships arriving in northern ports throughout the nineteenth century, the
infection almost never spread beyond the quarantine stations or marine
hospitals. Whether the quarantine systems had become more effective,
or whether conditions favoring the mosquito's importation and warm-
weather proliferation had somehow altered, the fact remains that the
center of yellow fever activity in North America shifted southward in the

early nineteenth century, and its incursions became much more frequent. See Augustin, *History of Yellow Fever*, 769–80, for list of epidemic years and places affected. See also James D. Goodyear, "The Sugar Connection: A New Perspective on the History of Yellow Fever," *Bulletin of the History of Medicine* 52 (Spring 1978):5–21, for a fascinating hypothesis relating sugar and molasses production and shipping to yellow fever epidemiology.

9. Elisha Bartlett, *The History, Diagnosis, and Treatment of the Fevers of the United States*, 3d ed. (Philadelphia: Blanchard and Lea, 1852); Erasmus Darwin Fenner, *History of the Epidemic Yellow Fever, at New Orleans, Louisiana, in 1853* (New York: Hall, Clayton and Co., 1854); Carrigan, "The Saffron Scourge," 471–77.

10. Daniel Drake, *A Systematic Treatise, Historical, Etiological, and Practical on the Principal Diseases of the Interior Valley of North America as they appear in the Caucasian, African, Indian, and Esquimaux Varieties of its Population*, 2 vols. (1850, 1854; reprint, New York: Burt Franklin, 1971), 2:188–89; La Roche, *Yellow Fever* 1:593; Taylor, "Epidemiology," 447–53.

11. John Ellis, "The New Orleans Yellow Fever Epidemic in 1878: A Note on the Affective History of Societies and Communities," *Clio Medica* 12 (June–Sept. 1977):189–90; Jo Ann Carrigan, "Privilege, Prejudice, and the Strangers' Disease in Nineteenth-Century New Orleans," *Journal of Southern History* 36 (Nov. 1970):568–75.

12. Kenneth F. Kiple and Virginia H. Kiple, "Black Yellow Fever Immunities, Innate and Acquired, as Revealed in the American South," *Social Science History* 1 (Summer 1977):419–36; Fenner, *History of the Epidemic Yellow Fever*, 56–57; Carrigan, "Privilege, Prejudice, and the Strangers' Disease," 576–78.

13. La Roche, *Yellow Fever* 2:64.

14. Erasmus Darwin Fenner, "Report on the Epidemics of Louisiana, Mississippi, Arkansas, and Texas in the year 1853," *Transactions of the American Medical Association* 7 (1854):421–553; Toner, "The Distribution and Natural History of Yellow Fever," 366–84; Augustin, *History of Yellow Fever*, 844–902; *DeBow's Review* 15 (Dec. 1853):631–33. Large sugar plantations along the lower Mississippi and in the bayou country had a population of sufficient size and density to fuel an outbreak of yellow fever, easily introduced from New Orleans through trade along the waterways. In 1853 many plantation slaves experienced yellow fever for the first time, and some died. Physicians commented on this feature of the 1850s outbreaks, but continued to find black case-fatality rates much lower than those of white populations. In the late nineteenth century, sugar plantations with a work force of hundreds, including many Italians, had serious problems with yellow fever. See *Annual Report of the Supervising Surgeon-General of the Marine Hospital Service of the United States for . . . 1897* (Washington, D.C.: Government Printing

74   JO ANN CARRIGAN

Office, 1899), 638; New Orleans *Daily Picayune*, 20–24 Oct. 1897; 14 and 15
Oct. 1905; Jean Anne Scarpaci, "Immigrants in the New South: Italians in
Louisiana's Sugar Parishes, 1880–1910," in *American Workingclass Cul-
ture: Explorations in American Labor and Social History*, ed. Milton Cantor
(Westport, Conn.: Greenwood Press, 1979), 377–95.

15. New Orleans *Weekly Delta*, 2 Oct. 1853.

16. Ibid., 14 Aug. 1853.

17. *New Orleans Medical and Surgical Journal* 10 (Nov. 1853):312. For a
discussion of "drapetomania" and other facets of the medical proslavery
argument, see Samuel A. Cartwright, "Report on the Diseases and
Physical Peculiarities of the Negro Race," *New Orleans Medical and
Surgical Journal* 7 (1851):692–713. See also James O. Breeden, "States-
Rights Medicine in the Old South," *Bulletin of the New York Academy of
Medicine* 52 (Mar.-Apr. 1976):354–60.

18. New Orleans *Daily Picayune*, 29 Sept. 1853.

19. New Orleans *Daily Picayune*, 14, 15, 16, 19, and 23 June 1853. A
small article on the "Attempted Negro Revolt in New Orleans" made the
front page of the *New York Times*, 17 June 1853. See also John Duffy,
Sword of Pestilence: The New Orleans Yellow Fever Epidemic of 1853 (Baton
Rouge: Louisiana State Univ. Press, 1966), 15; and Herbert Aptheker,
American Negro Slave Revolts (1943; new ed., New York: International
Publishers, 1969), 343–44. For references to the other two incidents, see
William C.C. Claiborne to Thomas Jefferson, 18 Sept. 1804, in *The Terri-
tory of Orleans, 1803–1812*, vol. 9 of *The Territorial Papers of the United
States*, ed. Clarence E. Carter (Washington, D.C.: Government Printing
Office, 1940), 298; R.F. McGuire Diary, Sept.-Oct. 1837, Louisiana State
Univ. Archives, Baton Rouge.

20. Todd L. Savitt, *Medicine and Slavery: The Diseases and Health Care
of Blacks in Antebellum Virginia* (Urbana: Univ. of Illinois Press, 1978),
242–43; Carrigan, "Privilege, Prejudice, and the Strangers' Disease,"
576–78.

21. Breeden, "States-Rights Medicine in the Old South," 348–72;
James D. Guillory, "Southern Nationalism and the Louisiana Medical
Profession, 1840–1860" (M.A. thesis, Louisiana State Univ., 1965); *New
Orleans Medical and Surgical Journal* 9 (July 1852):120; 9 (Sept. 1852):282; 9
(May 1853):763; 10 (Sept. 1853);278.

22. La Roche, *Yellow Fever* 2:60–65; Kiple and Kiple, "Black Yellow
Fever Immunities, Innate and Acquired," 425–29; Carrigan, "The Saffron Scourge," 394–96.

23. La Roche, *Yellow Fever* 2:18–38, 564; J.C. Nott, "Sketch of the
Epidemic of Yellow Fever of 1847, in Mobile," *Charleston Medical Journal
and Review* 3 (Jan. 1848):4, rptd. in *Yellow Fever Studies*, ed. Barbara
Guttman Rosenkrantz et al. (New York: Arno Press, 1977).

24. [William L. Robinson], *The Diary of a Samaritan* (New York: Harper

and Brothers, 1860), 88; see also New Orleans *Weekly Delta*, 24 July, 7 Aug. 1853; and Isaac H. Charles to John Edward Siddall, Sept.-Nov. 1847, Isaac H. Charles Letters, Louisiana State Univ. Archives, Baton Rouge.

25. According to Dr. Bennett Dowler of New Orleans, "Long urban residence (with or without having had yellow fever) is, in a sanitary sense, an equivalent to nativity, among the people of the city. It is a kind of naturalization, or rather creolization. . . ." *New Orleans Medical and Surgical Journal* 7 (July 1850):67. La Roche, *Yellow Fever* 2:25, 38, also used the term "creolization" for the acquisition of immunity through habituation to the climate, with or without an obvious case of the disease. (Both native and longterm residents, after living through several major epidemics, probably had experienced one of those "inapparent infections," now known to be extremely common, which caused little more than headache and slight fever but conferred lasting immunity nonetheless.) La Roche and others also believed that immunity was lost through living outside the South for any extended period (2:27, 61, 765). Such a view was theoretically consistent with "acclimation," but what the theoreticians used for evidence is not apparent.

26. Edward Hall Barton, *Introductory Lectures on Acclimation, Delivered at the Opening of the Third Session of the Medical College of Louisiana* (New Orleans: Commercial Bulletin, 1837), 13. Although southerners generally considered it a northern disease, consumption (tuberculosis) also claimed many victims in the South. It was the greatest single cause of death in Charleston during an eighteen-year period, 1828–1845, exceeding both yellow fever and Asiatic cholera. See J.C. Nott, "An Examination into the Health and Longevity of the Southern Sea Ports of the United States, with reference to the subject of Life Insurance," *Southern Journal of Medicine and Pharmacy* 2 (Mar. 1847):124–27, 133. In New Orleans in 1849, consumption was the third leading cause of mortality, outranked only by Asiatic cholera and yellow fever; New Orleans also had a higher consumption death rate that year (relative to population) than Boston, Philadelphia, or New York. The New Orleans Board of Health, however, in its report for 1849 declared the Crescent City especially "favored" in suffering less from lung disease "than any large city in this hemisphere." This statistical feat was achieved by calculating the tuberculosis deaths as a percentage of total mortality and finding that consumption caused a smaller proportion of the total mortality in New Orleans than in the major northern cities. When standardized as number of deaths per thousand population, the figures tell a very different story. See James Stark, "Vital Statistics of New Orleans," *Edinburgh Medical and Surgical Journal* (Jan. 1851):142; E.H. Barton, "Annual Report of the New Orleans Board of Health [1849]," *Southern Medical Reports* 1 (1849):85–86; J.C. Simonds, "Report on the Hygienic Characteristics of

New Orleans," *Transactions of the American Medical Association* 3
(1850):276–77, 287–90; Stanford E. Chaille, "Vital Statistics of New Orleans," *New Orleans Journal of Medicine* 23 (Jan. 1870):3–4.

27. *DeBow's Review* 4 (Nov. 1847):401; *New Orleans Medical and Surgi-
cal Journal* 5 (July 1848):52–53; 11 (Jan. 1855):503–4; Nott, "Sketch of the
Epidemic of Yellow Fever of 1847, in Mobile," 4; Carrigan, "Privilege,
Prejudice, and the Strangers' Disease," 571–74, 578; Ellis, "The New
Orleans Yellow Fever Epidemic in 1878," 189–91.

28. *New York Times,* 18 and 24 May, 16 July, 11 Aug., 19 Nov. 1862; Jo
Ann Carrigan, "Yankees versus Yellow Jack in New Orleans, 1862–
1866," *Civil War History* 9 (Sept. 1963):248–60.

29. Dennis East II, "Health and Wealth: Goals of the New Orleans
Public Health Movement, 1879–1884," *Louisiana History* 9 (Fall
1968):245–75; John Ellis, "Businessmen and Public Health in the Urban
South During the Nineteenth Century: New Orleans, Memphis, and
Atlanta," *Bulletin of the History of Medicine* 44 (May–June 1970):197–212;
(July–Aug. 1970):346–71.

30. John M. Toner, "Boards of Health in the United States," American
Public Health Association, *Public Health Papers and Reports* 1 (1873):499–
521; Elisha Harris, "General Health Laws and Local Ordinances, Considered with Reference to State and Local Sanitary Organization," ibid.,
472–82; see also Duffy, "Yellow Fever in the Continental United States
During the Nineteenth Century," 699–701; Margaret Warner, "Local
Control versus National Interest: The Debate over Southern Public
Health, 1878–1884," *Journal of Southern History* 50 (Aug. 1984):407–28.
Louisiana had established the first state board of health in the country in
1855, as a direct response to the Great Epidemics of 1853–54. Southern
state and local governments, reacting to the persistent threat of yellow
fever and the pressure of commercial interests, established health boards
in the late nineteenth century and experimented with quarantine and
sanitary regulations, supporting health reform in principle at least, if not
always with adequate funding. According to a survey of the work of state
health boards, undertaken in 1914 under the sponsorship of the American Medical Association, Florida and Louisiana were the only two southern states in the top 50 percent of states ranked by per capita expenditures for public health purposes. Not one southern state appeared
among the ten top-ranking states in an overall assessment of health
work; and only Virginia, Louisiana, Mississippi, and Florida ranked
within the top half of the states. See Charles V. Chapin, *A Report on State
Public Health Work based on a Survey of State Boards of Health* (Chicago:
American Medical Association, 1916; reprint, New York: Arno Press,
1977), 190–95 and Table 1. Only after yellow fever was brought under
control in the early twentieth century did southern health officials begin
to realize the magnitude of the region's poor health status and how much
work remained to be done.

31. American Public Health Association, *Public Health Papers and Reports* 4 (1877–78):170.

32. Henry Guy Carleton, "Andromeda Unchained" (clipping, New Orleans, 1878), Howard-Tilton Memorial Library, Tulane Univ., New Orleans.

33. Judge J.F. Simmons, *The Welded Link, and Other Poems* (Philadelphia: J.B. Lippincott, 1881), 14.

34. New Orleans *Daily Picayune*, 22 Sept. 1878.

35. Ibid., 29 Sept. 1897.

36. *Atlanta Convention of the South Atlantic and Gulf States. Uniform Regulations for the Management of Yellow Fever Epidemics . . . .* (New Orleans: L. Graham and Son, 1899); *Annual Report of the Supervising Surgeon-General of the Marine Hospital Service . . . 1897*, 580–676; *New York Times*, 15 Sept., 26 Oct. 1897; 22 July–27 Oct. 1905; *Report of the Public Health and Marine-Hospital Service* (1906), 59th Cong., 2d sess., H. Doc. 199; Jo Ann Carrigan, "The Yellow Fever Panic of 1897 in Louisiana," *Louisiana Studies* 6 (Spring 1967):7–25.

37. Bartlett, *History, Diagnosis, and Treatment of the Fevers of the United States*, 495–96; Drake, *Principal Diseases of the Interior Valley* 2:188; La Roche, *Yellow Fever* 1:118–19, 592. Because of its high elevation, Atlanta was considered virtually uninfectible territory.

38. *Yellow Fever: Its Nature, Diagnosis, Treatment, and Prophylaxis, and Quarantine Regulations Relating Thereto, by Officers of the U.S. Marine Hospital Service* (Washington, D.C.: Government Printing Office, 1898), 77–78, 85, 94–103, reprinted in *Yellow Fever Studies*.

39. *Louisiana Gazette* (New Orleans), 23 Oct. 1817. Such exchanges occurred not only between southern and northern papers, but similar charges and countercharges were hurled back and forth between the journals of competing southern towns and cities. See the *Louisiana Courier* (New Orleans), 15 Nov. 1819, refuting the charges of the *Baltimore Morning Chronicle*; New Orleans *Daily Picayune*, 21 Aug. 1853, contending with the *Charleston Mercury*. See also David R. Goldfield, "The Business of Health Planning: Disease Prevention in the Old South," *Journal of Southern History* 42 (Nov. 1976):563–68.

40. *DeBow's Review* 6 (Sept. 1848):226; New Orleans *Bee*, 4 Sept. 1867.

41. New Orleans *Daily Picayune*, 26 Sept. and 1 Oct. 1905.

42. *New Orleans Medical and Surgical Journal* 2 (Sept. 1845):129; 5 (Sept. 1848):261; 6 (Mar. 1850):666; 7 (Mar. 1851):591; 9 (Nov. 1852):415–16; *DeBow's Review* 2 (Dec. 1846):422; *Southern Medical Reports* 2 (1850):142–43; *Proceedings of the Board of Experts Authorized by Congress to Investigate the Yellow Fever Epidemic of 1878* (New Orleans: L. Graham, 1878), 31–35; Ellis, "Businessmen and Public Health in the Urban South During the Nineteenth Century," 204–5, 210–12; New Orleans *Times-Democrat*, 28 July 1882; New Orleans *Daily Picayune*, 26 Sept. and 1, 7, 19 Oct. 1905. No effort has been made to calculate or estimate the economic consequences

of yellow fever on southern urban development. Many other negative
forces were also at work, and it is doubtful that yellow fever was the
"greatest drawback." On the other hand, it would be hard to argue that it
was no drawback at all or that the longterm costs, direct and indirect,
were negligible.

43. See George B. Tindall, "Mythology: A New Frontier in Southern
History," in *The Idea of the South: Pursuit of a Central Theme*, ed. Frank E.
Vandiver (Chicago: Univ. of Chicago Press, 1964), rptd. in Gerster and
Cords, *Myth and Southern History*, 1–15, for an exploration of various
myths, stereotypes, and images of the South. Although the "Sickly
South" was not among the images Tindall developed, his essay provided
insight and the inspiration for the label.

4

The South's Native Foreigners: Hookworm as a Factor in Southern Distinctiveness

·

ALAN I MARCUS

Much has been written about the impact of disease on society. But the process by which a population is identified as having a particular malady has been explored less fully. This is especially true for longstanding endemic disorders, a class of illness usually more difficult to identify because the population's familiarity with a certain disease often masks its consequences. Though the impact of endemic disease on society is usually great, it is rarely dramatic; it does not appear disruptive because society continues to operate "normally," the way it has always functioned. As a result of the population's long acquaintance with a disease's symptoms, the disorder itself remains undetected.

The state of medical knowledge as well as the training of physicians surely plays a large part in the identification process, but sometimes other factors also contribute. Society's ideas about particular endemic diseases are among those usually not considered. Yet such notions may prove crucial, because changes in society's conception can convert long-standing previously unremarkable situations into problems; old conditions often become visible because people interpret them in a different way. Such appears to have been the case in the American South. At the end of the nineteenth century, a new notion of American nationality crystalized, one in which the South was defined as fundamentally distinct from and inferior to the rest of the American nation. This definition of the South as deficient set off a widespread discussion of the causes of southern differentness. It was within

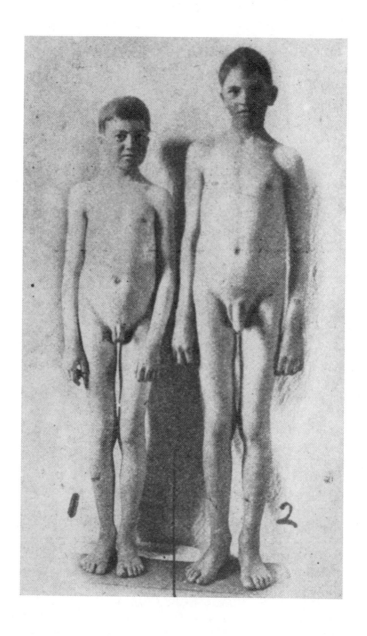

Comparison of two adolescent brothers, one infected with hookworm, the other not. From *Journal of the American Medical Association* 41 (1903), 10.

the context of these investigations of southern distinctiveness that hookworm was detected as endemic in the southern United States.

Victims of hookworm disease show a characteristic set of symptoms. They display a pronounced anemia, often accompanied by diarrhea, a slight fever, and sometimes a seemingly insatiable appetite for clay or dirt. Sufferers usually exhibit lethargy, sallow skin, and a lack of physical development and mental acuity. The disease is particularly prevalent among children, in whom it may cause grotesque anatomical deformities, but it also strikes adults. Though generally not fatal, a severe infestation of hookworm can plague its host for up to a decade and render her or him incapable of performing even the most rudimentary physical tasks.[1]

That the hookworm-producing nematode found a haven in the southern United States is not surprising. It thrives in wet, warm climates and in rural sandy regions such as the southern lowlands. Nor is it surprising that an estimated two million southerners bore the affliction. The key to understanding its extensive distribution in the South lies in the disease's mode of transmission. The agent is discharged in and spread by human feces. When hookworm-contaminated fecal material comes in contact with an individual, the parasite burrows through the victim's skin, enters the bloodstream, and finally takes up residence in the lower intestine, where it robs the body of vital nutrients.[2] The absence of sanitary facilities, even the simple box privy, placed most rural southerners in proximity to the noxious matter, while the tendency of many southern children to go without shoes gave the worm easy access to the skin.

Ample evidence exists to suggest that hookworm possessed a long history in the South. While it was not until 1893 that the first case of the disease was diagnosed and identified as such in America and nearly ten years later before it gained notoriety as "the vampire of the South," travelers had reported on the physical manifestations of hookworm much earlier. Indeed, after 1808, physicians and others journeying to the rural South had often described some inhabitants as exhibiting what we would call the classic hookworm portrait. Dwarfishness, misshapen heads, a blank stare, laziness, and dirt eating all stood out as unsavory curiosities worthy of mention when encountered on these sojourns.[3]

It is the casual yet frequent reporting of the symptoms of hookworm that fascinates. Although apparently endemic to the South, the disease—not its symptoms—went undetected in that region until the twentieth century. Certainly, well before that time many American medical practitioners, as well as those of foreign origin practicing in the United States, knew of hookworm as a distinct parasitic disease. European investigators had identified the hookworm-producing entity in 1843, established the disease in the 1850s as a particular disorder caused by a specific agent, and by 1870 included that knowledge in medical school courses. Presumably, then, the perennial stream of Americans crossing the ocean for medical or postgraduate training, some of whom were from the South, learned of the hookworm.[4]

But American medical students did not have to travel to Europe to learn about hookworm. The subject appeared regularly in popular American medical textbooks of the 1870s. For example, Austin Flint, in his classic *Clinical Medicine* (1879), identified hookworm as a specific disease and took care to describe the parasite's anatomical features as well as its hosts' symptoms, mentioning geophagia prominently. He also speculated that the worm "infests . . . the African race" and, as a consequence, probably "is common in certain of the Southern States of the Union, namely, Alabama, Georgia, Florida, and South Carolina." Nor did discussions of hookworm disappear from textbooks in subsequent years. Johns Hopkins' William Osler, one of America's leading physicians in the 1890s, included in his *Principles and Practice of Medicine* (1892) a consideration of the disease's symptoms and took great pains to identify its agent's physical characteristics. While he maintained that the nematode had been "described many years ago by physicians in the Southern States," Osler underscored that "no recent observations upon the disease have been made in this country."[5]

If by the 1870s many physicians who practiced in America had been taught about hookworm and if the disease was widespread in the South, the question remains as to why it went undiagnosed. That question also plagued early-twentieth-century medical professionals. In the first years of the new century, investigators offered several propositions in an effort to account for their colleagues' ignorance of the longstanding presence of hookworm in the southern United States. Despite the creativity of some of these suggestions, none serves as an adequate expla-

nation for the lack of recognition of the disease. One often repeated statement, that the anemia was associated with hookworm led to its confusion with malaria, while no doubt true in a
few instances, ignores the fact that other symptoms of the two
diseases are so markedly different that cases of repeated misdiagnosis are difficult to justify. Indeed, Osler thought errors of
that type impossible and regarded such utterings as slander
against his southern medical brethren.[6]

Others explained the hookworm problem in a different way.
They contended that the disease flourished in sparsely populated
environments, whose residents had little use for doctors, and
that as a consequence well-trained and experienced physicians
rarely had the opportunity to view or treat cases of hookworm. In
short, urban doctors, particularly those affiliated with medical
schools, hospitals, colleges, and the like, did not come into contact with rural dwellers and therefore could not identify what
they did not see.[7] While an interesting proposal, it fails to bear up
under close scrutiny. It was incorrect to deem the country people
isolated and beyond the physician's pale. Many rural inhabitants
moved to cities—the abandoned farm problem attracted significant interest in the late nineteenth century—while others
regularly visited urban markets. In both cases, they carried the
visible symptoms of their malady with them—the very same
symptoms that appalled many travelers—and so subjected themselves to the doctor's gaze. In addition, the sons and daughters of
farmers flocked to urban medical schools, universities, and especially the new tuition-free agricultural colleges. There they established intimate relations with their professors, often medical doctors. In fact, southern college students constituted one of the first
populations examined for hookworm after 1900 and demonstrated a high incidence of the disease.[8] Certainly the opportunity
for physicians to check them had existed earlier.

Others argued that the diagnosis of hookworm outside the
human body necessitated the use of a microscope. They maintained that hookworm ova, the material transported in human
feces, required magnification before it could be identified or even
seen.[9] Though an accurate proposition, it does not account for the
failure to detect the disease. By 1860, there was a flourishing
American microscope manufacturing industry, while by the late
1870s, microscopes had become a valuable diagnostic tool, especially among doctors exposed to the European medical regime. It

remained neither difficult nor expensive, moreover, to secure an instrument adequate to the task at hand. For example, Orange Judd, through his paper the *American Agriculturist*, made, in the late 1870s, French achromatic microscopes available to subscribers for three dollars. [10] Nor was it always essential to use microscopes to uncover the disease. Autopsies, a practice not unknown in southern medical schools and hospitals, stood as a case in point. During necropsies, attending physicians would find not the ova, but the worm. And the worm needed no magnification for observation because it measured nearly one-half inch in length, a size easily visible to the naked eye. Indeed, hookworm was first detected, identified, and described in the 1840s by a keen-eyed Italian physician during an autopsy. [11]

A final explanation offered for the hookworm anomaly is disciplinary in nature and concerns the science of parasitology. Surprisingly, this suggestion came not from a physician, but from an historian over a half-century after the fact. He noted that parasitology in the United States originated as a veterinary or zoological, not medical, specialty and indicated that this disciplinary demarcation placed knowledge of the nematode outside the province of medical practitioners. To be sure, parasitology did indeed seem a most fit subject for veterinarians and zoologists. But the idea of disciplinary restrictions is misleading. It certainly should not be construed to indicate that all American-schooled physicians lacked access to the information necessary to identify hookworm in humans. Quite the opposite was the case, for neither veterinary medicine nor zoology was a firmly established discipline in late-nineteenth-century America; most veterinarians and more than a handful of zoologists received their training as medical practitioners. Although they paid more attention to animals than to people during their careers, many also ministered to at least a few human patients, particularly in rural areas. In these lightly populated districts where hookworm abounded, the acquaintance and involvement of physicians with the parasitology of animals, rather than hindering their efforts, should instead have increased the likelihood of unearthing the worm. [12]

The question remains, then, why was hookworm in the South not detected earlier? It appears that physicians possessed both the ability and the opportunity to unmask the scourge. They lacked only motive. The disease's character, in part hidden, did little to goad doctors into searching for it. Hookworm is a chronic, not an acute, illness, and it was endemic, not epidemic, in the South. It manifested neither the ferocity of yellow fever or cholera nor the apparent capacity to disrupt the normal functioning of society. The worm rests silently in the body, slowly but continually sapping its victim's strength. It was not until the very end of the nineteenth century that the medical profession acquired a motive, and that motive did not come from new medical advances or discoveries. Instead, it emerged as a consequence of a new perception of the nation and its people, a perception that had nothing directly to do with medical knowledge.

Crystallizing around 1900, this broad-based consensus included most of America's rising political and social leaders. Indeed, it might be argued that this new vision—especially the assumption that it was shared by many of their silent countrymen—permitted these politicians, literateurs, muckraking journalists, professionals, businessmen, and the like to achieve prominence. Though a list of participants could not approach completeness, men and women as dissimilar as Theodore Roosevelt, William McKinley, Herbert Croly, analysts of the 1890 and 1900 federal censuses, Richard Ely, Walter Rauschenbush, Simon Patten, Albert Shaw, Theodore Dreiser, Jane Addams, Samuel Hopkins Adams, Harvey Wiley, George Perkins, Irving Fisher, and Madison Grant apparently embraced a similar vision of the United States. They concluded that America comprised, or ought to comprise, a distinct national entity. Aside from disputing who should govern, their primary area of disagreement was the cause of the nation's distinctiveness—what made it a complete unit, different from other nations. They differed as to whether that distinctiveness stemmed or would stem from what they recognized as its Teutonic or Anglo-Saxon racial stock or from the ability of its people generally to form themselves into a differentiated, hierarchically arranged socioeconomic and political system. In either case, the notion of nationality led them to designate any group inconsistent with the national standard as foreign, deviant, or in some other way outside the norm. Put more simply, these people defined the national standard as the correct racial group or the capacity for finding the appropriate niche within American society.[13]

Historians of American thought and culture have been sensitive to this movement. The emergence of a national vision at the end of the nineteenth century has become a standard historical interpretation. Two scholars have carried the analysis further. They have explicitly considered American nationality by investigating the nation's perception of groups defined as outside the new American nationality. Henry D. Shapiro, in his *Appalachia on our Minds: The Southern Mountains and Mountaineers in the American Consciousness, 1870*–1920, has discussed the transformation of the idea of Appalachia and Appalachians during the last decade of the nineteenth century. Shapiro found that Americans ceased to view Appalachians as curiosities and began to define the group's persistence and actions as a problem within American civilization. John Higham has approached conceptions of immigrants in much the same manner. In his *Strangers in the Land: Patterns of American Nativism, 1860–1925*, he has pinpointed "the Nationalist Nineties" as the time in which new notions of immigrants crystallized; they had become a particular type of problem within the context of American nationality.

Both Higham and Shapiro have discussed the literature of advocacy and patterns of action that stemmed from the new definitions. Their insights can be generalized. Designation of groups as contrary to the national standard produced two basic sets of proposals, both of which sought to create or preserve American nationality. The first consisted of physical exclusion from the country, segregation from society, or the withdrawal of society's blessings. Before 1910 this approach found expression in only a few instances, although it affected large numbers of people. The Supreme Court's ruling in *Plessy v. Ferguson*, enforcement of Jim Crow laws, attempts to deport socialists as foreign-inspired anarchists, and efforts to halt the influx of southern European immigrants are examples of this thrust. More common was the second type of proposition, namely that deviants/foreigners be reformed, and, despite their God-given attributes or potentials—often considered quite meager—integrated into the American socioeconomic and political machine. This sentiment translated into diverse forms of public action. The settlement house movement, efforts to revitalize rural America through the Country Life Movement, campaigns to establish mandatory public school attendance, establishment of Americanization programs for immigrants, and development of vocational training[14] are only a handful of the more conspicuous examples of efforts during the late nineteenth and early twentieth centuries to keep or make America a peculiar national entity.

Nowhere did the idea of American nationality cause as much consternation and soul-searching as in the South. Indeed, the notion of American nationality marked the South as fundamentally distinctive, or more properly deviant or foreign, and set off a quest for the cause of the distinctiveness. To be sure, earlier critics had spoken of southern differences. But they had characterized those differences as ephemeral—for example, in the early nineteenth century, in terms of climate or "the peculiar institution." Both hurdles then had seemed readily surmountable; after all, people could be acclimated to southern meterological conditions, while slavery seemed an aberration that could and ought to be abolished. For several decades after the Civil War, critics persisted in viewing southern differences as temporary. To some, the differences were the result of the ravages of war, the legacy of slavery, or the dislocation caused by freeing the slaves. A short period of adjustment was necessary for the South to rebound. It was in this milieu that the southern local colorists of the 1870s and 1880s flourished. Seeking to entertain rather than explain, they wrote about the South's quaintness and accentuated its seeming ephemeral curiosities. Advocates of the "New South creed" held a similar perspective. To be sure, these men and women deemed southern economic practices outmoded. But the South seemed different in form, not substance; proponents of the creed, such as Henry Grady, felt confident that archaic ways easily could be shucked. They looked forward to a day in which "the words 'the South' will have only a geographic significance."[15]

The optimistic view of southern differences crumbled during the 1890s. At the end of the century, southern distinctiveness seemed fixed, something fundamentally a part of the South that kept the South apart from the rest of America. One manifestation of this sentiment was the decline of southern local color writing; the condition of the South was no laughing matter. Another was the rejection of the "New South creed." For example, North Carolina's Walter Hines Page and Virginia's Lewis H. Blair maintained that the promise of a speedy regeneration of the South had been a pipe dream; several decades of concerted action had proven that southern differences were intractable. Kentucky's Nathaniel Shaler, then at Harvard, offered a similarly gloomy assessment. He claimed that the South was "dwelling in the mediaevil [sic] age" and that progress awaited "the death of the generation" that had lived through the Civil War. W.P. Trent raised the same point, but with explicit respect to American nationality. To Trent, the persistence of the prewar generation constituted a problem because these people "inculcate social and political principles alien to American ideas."[16]

In probing for the origins of southern distinctiveness, Trent, Shaler, and like-minded men and women performed a crucial function. The process of explanation—articulating the reasons that the South was fundamentally unlike the rest of America— often dictated or circumscribed potential remedies. For instance, those who attributed southern distinctiveness to a lack of education attempted to begin to remove that deficiency by cooperating through the Conferences for Education in the South.[17] But not all critics indicted the entire South or even its leadership. Some focused instead on specific groups within the region, labeled them deviant, and argued that their deviance destroyed southern vigor. Blacks certainly were treated in this manner. So too were poor whites, the "crackers" and "dirt eaters." Investigators in the late nineteenth century had described poor white males as possessing "inimitable drawling speech," a "sallow complexion, lanky frame, lazy habits, and immorality." Females seemed no better; portrayed as "ugly, feeble, dumb," these women commanded "no romantic charm" and appeared "even too dull witted for factory work." Poor whites seemed to engage in a series of nasty habits, not only refusing to wear shoes or use privies, but also devouring clay. Even more astonishingly, some of their number were so degraded as to publicize their practice, establishing dirt-eating clubs and sending the material through the United States' mail. The terrible trait of clay-eating was not confined to adults, moreover, but also was indulged in by poor white children. One unnamed black commentator summed up the situation succinctly. "De little children begin 'fore dey kin walk," he reported, "and dey eat it till dey die; dey chaw it lake 'backer. It makes all dar stumacs big like as you seed 'em and spiles dar 'gestion. It'm mighty onhealfy."[18] It was the identification of these people as a distinctive and aberrant group within the context of American nationality and southern deviance that possibly provided physicians with the impetus to look for the cause of the group's distinctiveness, an event that led to the discovery of hookworm as indigenous to the southern United States.

Put another way, the idea of American nationality and southern distinctiveness converted the white crackers from an appalling curiosity of local color writers and other observers—or, to followers of Hinton Rowan Helper, victims of slavery—into a social problem. As a problem, they became an important subject for investigation because their existence demanded explanation and their situation amelioration if the South was to shed its foreignness and assume its rightful place within the nation. The group's Anglo-Saxon heritage only compounded the difficulty; it made it hard to ascribe their repulsiveness to defective or inferior racial stock. Nonetheless, many critics adopted a hereditarian approach. One author explained not only how crackers became degenerates, but also why they had drawn little notice prior to the late nineteenth century. Identifying them as "descendants of the lowest grade of humanity on the British Island," with "only enough Anglo-Saxon spirit to make a poor chattel," he suggested that southern poor whites had come to America as indentured servants in the first half of the seventeenth century. Disinclined to labor, they quickly were replaced by black slaves and, freed of bondage, took to the hills of Appalachia. There they remained isolated, inbred, and inbreeding until after the Civil War. Then for reasons unknown, poor whites left the mountains, moved to the southern lowlands, and were discovered by their shocked countrymen to be in ghastly condition.[19]

While some observers managed to develop a hereditarian solution to the problem of the South's native foreigners, others explored different possibilities. Several men trained in medicine were among those who sought an alternative. They would establish that southern dirt eaters suffered from hookworm and offer suggestions for curing the region.

Ironically, however, poor whites were not associated with the first cases of hookworm identified in America. Although physicians reported nine instances of the disease between 1893 and 1901, seven of them coming from south of the Mason-Dixon line, each instance received a similar interpretation. All were considered with reference to American nationality but not southern distinctiveness. Attending physicians regarded each occurrence as isolated and not originating in the United States. Instead, they attributed the disease's appearance in America to the nation's contact with foreigners, as a result either of lower-class southern European immigration or of more intimate connections with tropical countries in wake of the Spanish-American War.[20] During this period, then, hookworm was not a disease of Americans, but rather a disease of foreigners in America.

F.G. Möhlau, a Buffalo physician, underscored this point. He insisted in 1896 that the ailment would continue to crop up periodically in America, but would affect only recent arrivals, their friends, families, and coworkers. Relying on his Buffalo experience, Möhlau explained that immigrants carried the disease to the United States. Aware that Italian laborers "employed in brickyards, miners and potmakers" had been "the principal sufferers of hookworm in Europe," he thought it "natural" that when these men "took to the notion of traveling . . . they imported the disease to America." This had been the case in the past and would be in the future, he contended, because "if laborers are afflicted with the disease while in Europe, how can it disappear while coming over the ocean?"[21]

Medical professionals explained hookworm in the United States in terms of its foreign derivation, no doubt, because they knew the parasite was native to Europe and the tropics. But even as they offered their pronouncements, at least one doctor suggested that it was "probable that the disease exists in some of the Southern States." William Pepper, a Philadelphia physician, published his speculations in 1894. They drew little attention, however. Not until 1902 did the subject appear in print again, and at that time it created a stir. Like Pepper, Charles Wardell Stiles, a helminthologist then employed in the Bureau of Animal Industry, thought it possible for the South to harbor the worm. And in the process of examining several specimens of the nematode taken from patients in America, he determined that these worms differed structurally from those found in Europe. He reported his findings, hypothesizing that "although it is rarely recognized," hookworm probably "is endemic in the southern United States."[22]

Stiles selected a most propitious forum in which to announce his conclusions. Unlike Pepper, who buried his opinion in a textbook, Stiles presented his material to the Pan-American Sanitary Conference. Meeting in Washington, D.C., in 1902, the gathering was insured of at least some newspaper coverage. But while such coverage presented the possibility of public dissemination of Stiles's views, it did not account for the sensation that his revelations produced. Perhaps the notion of southern distinctiveness—the problem of the foreignness of the South and its poor whites—within the framework of American nationality contributed to the intense reaction. Stiles's technical paper was converted into a major public event; newspapers across America picked up on and reported the speech, often offering support or rejoinders. Although Stiles frequently was the object of ridicule, his suspicions rapidly became known.[23]

Based on such limited evidence, Stiles's supposition required extensive verification, and between 1902 and 1904 medical research provided the necessary corroboration. No less than eight investigators surveyed all or part of the southern lowlands as they sought to confirm that hookworm victimized rural southerners. In every instance, the results were the same; each researcher uncovered numerous cases of the disease and provided concrete evidence that hookworm was indeed a condition from which many in the South suffered.[24] They not only published their studies, but also brought the matter repeatedly before local and state medical societies, while urging their colleagues to do the same. Their efforts met with such success that by 1905 the contention that hookworm was widespread in the South went virtually unchallenged in the medical profession.[25]

While physicians demonstrated that the South's peculiar people, its native foreigners, bore the disease, they achieved no similar consensus as to whether it stood as the cause of the group's deviance or as a consequence of that deviance.[26] Ultimately, however, it did not matter. Simply identifying poor whites as sick transformed the problem of distinctiveness into a medical one. Redefining deviance in terms of medicine was crucial, for it demanded that health be restored and maintained. This redefinition also held important practical and policy implications. Those believing that the depravity of crackers resulted in hookworm sought to cure the disease and to prevent its recurrence by removing deviance; they favored what was in effect a cultural attack, including the reformation of not only the uncivilized habits of the rural South, but also of its institutions. Those arguing that disease caused the deviance offered a similar plan. They sought to heal sufferers and to wipe out the disease by a process necessitating the institution of new behaviors on the part of rural southerners so as to prevent their reinfestation.

In the five years after 1905, medical theorists suggested several forms of public action to resolve the hookworm problem. Each plan stressed the importance of integrating the South within the American socioeconomic and political system. William Weston brought his proposal before the South Carolina Medical Association. Arguing in 1808 that "certain portions of the South are notoriously unprogressive," Weston, a doctor in Columbia, South Carolina, attributed the region's economic ills to the lack of white labor and the substantial number of diseased poor whites. Securing the venture capital necessary to industrialize posed no difficulties, he maintained, but the prevalence of hookworm hampered attempts to create a reliable labor force. Two methods of forming a stable work force presented themselves, but he found only one feasible. While some wanted to bring Europeans to labor in southern mills, Weston reasoned that the answer ought to lie with the poor whites. After all, he concluded, our native foreigners "speak our language [and] are familiar with our laws and customs."

To make crackers into an adequate labor force demanded the eradication of hookworm, and Weston urged "physician-citizens" to lead the fight. His proposal remained somewhat vague, but did entail the formation of a state-financed and sponsored commission of physicians. Presumably, its members would scour the state, treat disease victims, and preach the sanitary privy and the wearing of shoes to both poor whites and their medical practitioners. [27]

While Weston sketched his program in only its grossest detail, others were more specific. For example, Stiles too considered the question of southern aberrance. He complained that although "we have numerous schools and colleges for the education of the negro" and while "the Indian is the ward of the government," little activity had been "directed especially to the elevation of any considerable number of the 'crackers.' " He proposed to correct the omission through the creation of a regionwide hookworm eradication campaign. He pleaded for "the introduction of Public Health Week into all" southern schools and programs to teach mothers the "great sanitary principles." Stiles hoped to "bring about a sanitary reform on the farms, by persuasion if possible," but he recognized that voluntary compliance might fail. As a consequence, he urged the passage of national legislation that would "send to the chain gang any person who deliberately pollutes" either public or private land.[28]

Others chose not to involve the government because coercion might increase resistance. For instance, the *Medical Record*'s Thomas L. Stedman maintained that any effort to compel "the children of the southern small farmers" to use sanitary privies and to wear shoes would surely fail. Instead, he called on the South's better classes to employ community pressure and concerted action. He especially appealed to "the charitably disposed and the patriotic people of the South" to establish "leagues for combating the hookworm" modeled "after the plan of the antituberculosis leagues." Action of this type was imperative, he maintained, because "the regeneration . . . of the South depended absolutely upon the extermination" of the disease "that is literally sucking its lifeblood."[29]

H. Edwin Lewis, editor of *American Medicine*, next took up the cause. He too focused on education by an elite group but wanted to rely on medical practitioners to furnish both the impetus and the knowledge. In his analysis, he dealt with hookworm in explicitly national terms. Indeed, the disease was "a matter of national concern" because it stood as "a removable cause of part of our own racial deterioration." Although acknowledging that southerners "are now suffering from their notorious neglect of cleanliness," Lewis knew that a physician-directed educational campaign would eliminate "the lack of intelligence" which prevents crackers from "learning how to be as clean as [members of] civilized communities should be." But while calling for doctors to mobilize their professional societies to end "the defective development which has apparently removed [poor whites] from national control," he was not above feeding southern egos. He reminded his readers that the South formerly had been an integral part of the nation, but now "the presidents and leaders who once came from south of Mason's and Dixon's line, . . . nearly all come from the north." Eradicating hookworm would redress the regional imbalance.[30]

These proposals marked the climax of public medical discussions about the disease, prior to the formation of the Rockefeller Sanitary Commission for the Eradication of Hookworm. Launched in 1909, the commission worked to set up state and county boards of health and, through these institutions, both to treat hookworm victims and to prevent the scourge's recurrence. A campaign was launched, dedicated to the proposition that use of sanitary privies, wearing shoes, and health education would emancipate the South from the curse of hookworm.[31] In a fundamental way, the commission's creation marked the culmination of previous ideas. Like those plans offered earlier but not enacted, it considered hookworm a national problem and focused exclusively on the South's medical sickness. It reflected the post-1905 accord among doctors, defining southern deviance as a simple medical issue without regard to cause or effect—a tacit acknowledgment that made southern aberrance appear amenable to a concrete and harmonious yet swift program of public action. But that concept was possible only in a context that already defined the South as distinctive and at least some of its population as defective. Indeed, labeling the South as foreign to and out of concert with the American nation, in an era of American nationality, led to efforts to explain and correct the deviance. It was that rubric that enabled medical professionals to identify hookworm as endemic to the South. And those notions led to the employment of hookworm as a vehicle to make the South American.

NOTES

Abbreviations:

JAMA Journal of the American Medical Association
AJMS American Journal of the Medical Sciences
GPO Government Printing Office

1. Paul Chester Beaver, Rodney Clinton Jung, and Eddie Wayne Cupp, *Clinical Parasitology*, 9th ed. (Philadelphia: Lea and Febiger, 1984), 269–87.
2. Charles Wardell Stiles, "Report Upon the Prevalence and Geographic Distribution of Hookworm Disease (Uncinariasis or Anchylostomiasis), in the United States," *Hygienic Laboratory Bulletin* 10, (Washington, D.C.: GPO, 1903). Also see the following articles by Claude A. Smith: "Uncinariasis in the South," *JAMA* 40 (1903):709–13; "Some Remarks Upon Hook-Worm Disease," *Mobile Medical and Surgical Journal* 5 (1904):47–59; "Uncinariasis in the South, With Special Reference to Mode of Infection," *JAMA* 43 (1904):592–96; "Further Remarks on the

Mode of Infection in Uncinariasis," *JAMA* 45 (1905):1142–45; "[Proceedings of the American Society of Tropical Medicine]," *JAMA* 45 (1905):1899; and "The Causative Factor in the Production of the Dermatitis of Ground Itch (Uncinariasis)," *JAMA* 47 (1906):1693–95.

3. See, for example, Joseph Pitt, "Observations on the Country and Diseases Near Roanoke River, in the State of North Carolina," *Medical Repository* 2d Hexade, 5 (1808):340–41; J.R. Cotting, "Analysis of a Species of Clay Found in Richmond County, Which is Eagerly Sought After, and Eaten, By Many People, Particularly Children," *Southern Medical and Surgical Journal*, N.S., 1 (1845):430–31; Robert Edmonds Little, "Remarks on the Climate, Diseases, &c., of Middle Florida— Particularly of Gasden County," *AJMS*, N.S., 10 (1845):70; James B. Duncan, "Report on the Topography, Climate, and Disease of the Parish of St. Mary, La.," *Southern Medical Repository* 1 (1850):194–95; Thomas Pollard, "More Than 150 Gravel Taken From the Bowels of a Dirt-Eating Child," *Stethoscope* 2 (1852):185; and E. Lewis Sturtevant, "Earth As Food," *Scientific Farmer* 4 (1879):126. "Vampire of the South" was a label commonly given hookworm by muckrakers towards the end of the first decade of the 20th century.

4. John Ettling, *The Germ of Laziness: Rockefeller Philanthropy and Public Health in the New South*, (Cambridge, Mass., Harvard Univ. Press, 1981), 24; and Thomas N. Bonner, *American Doctors and German Universities: A Chapter in International Intellectual Relations, 1870–1914* (Lincoln: Univ. of Nebraska Press, 1963).

5. Austin Flint, *Clinical Medicine: A Systematic Treatise on the Diagnosis and Treatment of Disease. Designed For the Use of Students and Practitioners of Medicine* (Philadelphia: Henry C. Lea, 1879), 363–64; and William Osler, *The Principles and Practice of Medicine* (New York: D. Appleton and Co., 1892), 1031–32.

6. For the suggestion that hookworm was often confused with malaria by physicians, see "Discussion on Uncinariasis," *JAMA* 40 (1903):311. Osler's response was found in the following retrospective works: Mark Sullivan, "An Emancipation," *Our Times: Pre-War America*, (New York: Scribners, 1930), 306; Charles Wardell Stiles, "Early History, in Part Esoteric, of the Hookworm (Uncinariasis) Campaign in Our Southern United States," *Journal of Parasitology* 25 (1939):288–89; and Frances Maule Björkman, "The Cure For Two Million Sick," *World's Work* 18 (1906):11608.

7. "Discussion on Uncinariasis," 311.

8. For the examination of college students, see Allen J. Smith, "Uncinariasis in Texas," *AJMS* 126 (1903):769–98; and J.L. Nicholson and Watson S. Rankin, "Uncinariasis As Seen in North Carolina: Its Frequency, Etiology, Pathological Significance, Symptoms and Treatment," *Medical News* 85 (1904):981. The path along which a railroad traveled produced many natural points for urban-rural interactions.

96 ALAN I MARCUS

H.F. Harris focused on cities along the Georgia, Southern, and Florida Railway and found a large percentage of the inhabitants of these villages suffering from hookworm. See H.F. Harris, "Uncinariasis (Ankylostomiasis): Its Frequency and Importance in the Southern States," *Transactions of the Medical Association of Georgia* (1903), 368–69.

9. Charles Wardell Stiles, "The Significance of the Recent American Cases of Hookworm Disease (Uncinariasis, or Anchylostomiasis) in Man," *Annual Report of the Bureau of Animal Industry for 1901*, (Washington, D.C.: GPO, 1902), 183.

10. For Judd's offer, which was repeated regularly, see, e.g., *American Agriculturist* 37 (1878):125. James Cassedy suggests that microscopes began to play a role in American medicine much earlier. He also describes the thriving business of U.S. microscope manufacture. See his "The Microscope in American Medical Science, 1840–1860," *Isis* 67 (1976):76–97.

11. Ettling, *Germ of Laziness*, 24.

12. The argument about disciplinary boundaries appears implicitly in Ettling, *Germ of Laziness*, 25–32. For the medical training of veterinarians and zoologists in the United States, as well as their efforts with human patients, see, for example, Bert W. Bierer, *A Short History of Veterinary Medicine in America* (East Lansing: Michigan State Univ. Press, 1955); P.B. Kirkeminde, *History of Veterinary Medicine in Tennessee* (Nashville: Modern Typographers, 1976); and J.F. Smithcors, *The American Veterinary Profession, Its Background and Its Development* (Ames: Iowa State Univ. Press, 1963). Also, parasitology was making inroads in medical college curricula during the last decades of the 19th century. That was especially true of prestigious and heavily enrolled schools, such as Johns Hopkins, Georgetown, and the Army Medical College. Courses in medical zoology—parasitology—were required of students expecting to spend time overseas or in the tropics. See Stiles, "Early History," 288–89.

13. Of use are Sidney Fine, *Laissez Faire and the General-Welfare State* (Ann Arbor: Univ. of Michigan Press, 1956); Roy Lubove, *The Progressives and the Slums* (Pittsburgh: Univ. of Pennsylvania Press, 1962); Stephen Wood, *Constitutional Politics in the Progressive Era* (Chicago: Univ. of Chicago Press, 1969); Alan I Marcus, "Disease Prevention in America: From a Local to a National Outlook, 1880–1910," *Bulletin of the History of Medicine* 53 (1979):184–203; Samuel P. Hays, *The Response to Industrialism, 1885–1914* (Chicago: Univ. of Chicago Press, 1957); and Robert H. Wiebe, *The Search for Order, 1877–1920* (New York: Hill and Wang, 1967). The notion of America as a distinct national entity had other consequences. It made it possible to envision a new role for the federal government, an event explored by Fine, Wood, and Marcus in the works cited above.

14. Henry D. Shapiro, *Appalachia on Our Minds: The Southern Mountains and Mountaineers in the American Consciousness, 1870–1920* (Chapel Hill: Univ. of North Carolina Press, 1978), esp. 59–132; and John Higham, *Strangers in the Land: Patterns of American Nativism, 1860–1925* (New Brunswick, N.J.: Rutgers Univ. Press, 1955), 69–130. For examples of these thrusts, from an extensive literature, see, Ray Stannard Baker, *Following the Color Line* (New York: Doubleday, Page and Co., 1908); C. Vann Woodward, *The Strange Career of Jim Crow*, 3d ed. (New York: Oxford Univ. Press, 1974), 67–109; August Meier and Elliott M. Rudwick, *From Plantation to Ghetto: An Interpretive History of American Negroes* (New York: Hill and Wang, 1966), 156–88; Barbara Miller Solomon, *Ancestors and Immigrants: A Changing New England Tradition* (1956; rpt. ed., Chicago: Univ. of Chicago Press, 1972); Allen F. Davis, *Spearheads for Reform: The Social Settlements and the Progressive Movement* (New York: Oxford Univ. Press, 1967); William L. Bowers, *The Country Life Movement in America, 1900–1920* (Port Washington, N.Y.: Kennikat, 1974); Olivier Zunz, *The Changing Face of Inequality: Urbanization, Industrial Development, and Immigrants in Detroit, 1880–1920* (Chicago: Univ. of Chicago Press, 1982), 309–18; Marvin Lazerson, *Origins of the Urban School: Public Education in Massachusetts, 1870–1915* (Cambridge, Mass.: Harvard Univ. Press, 1971); and Edward A. Krug, *The Shaping of the American High School, 1880–1920* (Madison: Univ. of Wisconsin Press, 1969).

15. See, e.g., Paul M. Gaston, *The New South Creed: A Study in Southern Mythmaking* (Baton Rouge: Louisiana State Univ. Press, 1970); and J.V. Ridgely, *Nineteenth-Century Southern Literature* (Lexington: Univ. of Kentucky Press, 1980), 89–112. The quotation is from Gaston, 191.

16. Ridgely, *Nineteenth-Century Southern Literature*, 110; Shields McIlwaine, *The Southern Poor White: From Lubberland to Tobacco Road*, (Norman: Univ. of Oklahoma Press, 1939), 242; Gaston, *New South Creed*, 198–207; Walter Hines Page, *The Rebuilding of Old Commonwealths* (New York: Macmillan, 1902); Nathaniel S. Shaler, "The Peculiarities of the South," *North American Review* 151 (1890):477–88; and W.P. Trent, "Dominant Forces in Southern Life," *Atlantic Monthly* 79 (1897):47–51. Also useful is Paul H. Buck, *The Road to Reunion, 1865–1900* (New York: Vintage, 1937), esp. 310 ff.

17. Charles William Dabney, *Universal Education In the South*, 2 vols. (Chapel Hill: Univ. of North Carolina Press, 1936), 2:3–53.

18. *New York Times*, 10 May 1896, p. 10; and 31 May 1898, p. 7. "Dirt-Eaters," *American Medicine* 3 (1902):94. While poor whites long had resided in the rural South, they engendered a new type of concern in the late 19th century. Now the new concern required observers to explain why they had not noticed earlier that crackers constituted a discrete group. Often these commentators responded by claiming that the exis-

tence of "poor white trash" was in fact a new event; crackers were new to the rural South. For contemporary reflections on poor whites in the early and mid-19th century, see both Paul H. Buck, "The Poor Whites of the Ante-Bellum South," *American Historical Review* 31 (1926):41–54; and A.N.J. Den Hollander, "The Tradition of Poor Whites," in *Culture in the South*, ed. W.T. Couch (Chapel Hill: Univ. of North Carolina Press, 1935), 403–431.

19. *New York Times*, 10 May 1896, p. 10. For the local color literature on poor whites after the Civil War, see McIlwaine, *Southern Poor White*, 75–162.

20. W.L. Blickhahn, "A Case of Ankylostomiasis," *Medical News* 63 (1893):662–63; F.G. Möhlau, "Anchylostomum Duodenale, With Report of Cases," *Buffalo Medical Journal* 36 (1896–97):573–79; C.H. Tebault, Jr., "Anchylostomiasis," *New Orleans Journal of Medicine and Surgery* 52 (1899–1900):145–48; William B. Grey, "Anchlostomium Duodenale in Virginia," *Virginia Medical Semi-Monthly* 6 (1901):269–70; M. Charlotte Schaefer, "Anchylostoma Duodenale in Texas," *Medical News* 79 (1901):655–58; R. Lee Hall, "Anklyostomiasis—Report of a Case," *JAMA* 37 (1901):1464–65; Thomas A. Claytor, "A Preliminary Report Upon a Case of Uncinariasis (Ankylostomiasis)," *Philadelphia Medical Journal* 7 (1901):1251; J.H. Dyer, "Anchylostomiasis," *Interstate Medical Journal* (1901):94–96; and Herman B. Allyn and M. Behrend, "Ankylostomiasis In the United States: Report of a Case," *American Medicine* 2 (1901):63–66.

21. Möhlau, "Anchylostomum Duodenale," 574.

22. William Pepper, "Diseases of the Intestines," in *A Text-Book of the Theory and Practice of Medicine by American Teachers*, ed. William Pepper, 2 vols., (Philadelphia, 1893–1894), 2:833; Charles Wardell Stiles, "A New Species of Hookworm (Uncinaria Americana) Parasitic in Man," *American Medicine* 3 (1902):777–78.

23. For an excellent account of the commotion that Stiles's report raised, see Sullivan, "An Emancipation," 290–99.

24. H.F. Harris, "Ankylostomiasis, The Most Common of the Serious Diseases of the Southern Part of the United States," *American Medicine* 4 (1902):776; Claude A. Smith, "Uncinariasis in the South"; E.D. Bondurant, "The Hook Worm Disease in Alabama," *New York Medical Journal and Philadelphia Medical Journal* 78 (1903):8–11; Nicholson and Rankin, "Uncinariasis," 978–87; Louis M. Warfield, "Grave Anemia Due to Hook-Worm Infection," *Medical Record* 66 (1904):9–12; and Stiles, *Hygienic Lab Bulletin #10*.

25. See, for instance, Ralph N. Greene, "Hookworm Disease," *Memphis Medical Monthly* 24 (1904);521–24; W.P. Ivey, "Uncinariasis in the Mountains of North Carolina," *New Albany Medical Herald* (1904):204–207; Horace B. Blan, *Nashville Journal of Medicine and Surgery* 97 (1905):106–108; George Homan, "Remarks on Hookworm Disease (Un-

cinariasis), With Report of a Case," *Journal of the Missouri State Medical Association* 2 (1906):764–70; and W.P. Dunbar, "Uncinariasis—Report of a Case in Hunt County," *Texas State Journal of Medicine* (1906):71.

26. See, for example, Joseph A. Capps, "Uncinariasis or Ankylostomiasis," *JAMA* 40 (1903):31, Allen J. Smith, "Uncinariasis in Texas," 795–96; Isaac Ivan Lemann, "Importance of Uncinariasis to the Southern Practitioner," *Mississippi Medical Record* 7 (1903):214; and *New York Times,* 25 June 1905, p. 7.

27. William Weston, "Uncinariasis," *Journal of the South Carolina Medical Association* 4 (1908):124–27. A commission to combat hookworm had been established earlier in Puerto Rico. See George H. Simmons, "Tropical Anemia (Ankylostomiasis) in Puerto Rico," *JAMA* 43 (1904):334; Jane Howell Harris, "Uncinariasis," *Journal of the Medical Society of New Jersey* 2 (1905):302–306; and L.L. Seaman, "Uncinaria Duodenalis (Hookworm Disease), Its Presence in Puerto Rico and Treatment Suggested," *Southern California Practitioner* 20 (1905):161–66.

28. Charles Wardell Stiles, "Soil Pollution and Hookworm Disease in the South: Their Result and Their Prevention," *Mobile Medical and Surgical Journal* 12 (1908):193–203.

29. Thomas L. Stedman, "An Enemy to the South," *Medical Record* 76 (1909):608–609.

30. H. Edwin Lewis, "The Prevalence of Uncinariasis in America," *American Medicine* 15 (1909):497–98.

31. For the activities of the commission, see James H. Cassedy, "The 'Germ of Laziness' in the South, 1900–1915: Charles Wardell Stiles and the Progressive Paradox," *Bulletin of the History of Medicine* 45 (1971):159–69; Mary Boccaccio, "Ground Itch and Dew Poison: The Rockefeller Sanitary Commission, 1909–1914," *Journal of the History of Medicine and Allied Sciences* 27 (1972):30–53; and Ettling, *Germ of Laziness,* esp. 87–177. Also see Sullivan, "An Emancipation," 309ff.

5

Pellagra:
An Unappreciated Reminder
of Southern Distinctiveness

.

ELIZABETH W. ETHERIDGE

Pellagra came as an intruder to the American South in the early years of the twentieth century. This disease, loathsome to look upon and awful in its consequences, was distinctive in itself, marking its victims with a peeling rash across the face and on the extremities, sapping their energy, and often as not stealing away their sanity. Certainly the disease seemed to bear no definite relation to the region which stretched from Virginia to Texas, an area many of its prouder occupants believed had emerged from the devastation of the Civil War to preserve intact the very best of American culture. Rather, pellagra was something foreign and terrible. When it was recognized, first among the insane at a hospital in Alabama, and later among the region's tenant farmers and mill workers, many of the South's physicians rallied to look for the cause and a cure, calling on the medical profession across the nation and abroad to help track down the invader. A national conference to study the problem, held in 1909 in Columbia, South Carolina, attracted nearly four hundred people.[1] The mystery of pellagra had to be solved. Few suspected that the clue to the puzzle lay in the very aspects of southern life in which so many took pride—the fields of snowy cotton and the spreading textile mills. Later, when the invader was closely identified as a by-product of the southern economy and lifestyle, the pain of that discovery was as awful as the earlier panic.

Pellagra, although new to the South, was well known in Europe. A physician at the Spanish court, Don Gaspar Casal, first described it in 1735. Among the peasants of Asturias he noted a "disgusting" skin disease he called *mal de la rosa*. Red, crusty, peeling skin marked its victims on the face, arms, legs, and back, and especially around the neck, a mark thereafter known as "Casal's necklace." In addition, they suffered from extreme weakness, sensations of burning, and melancholia. The first published account, written by Casal's associate at the Spanish court, the French physician François Thiéry, appeared in a French journal in 1755. Casal's paper was published posthumously in 1762. Within a decade, the disease appeared in Italy, where Francesco Frapolli described it carefully and gave it the name pellagra, or "rough skin." The disease resisted all remedies, and no-one knew the cause.

As pellagra spread into central and northern Italy, the Austrian Tyrol, southeastern Hungary, Rumania, and lower Egypt, European physicians sought as frantically for the cause and a cure as their American counterparts would a century later. They noted that pellagrins always had maize as the main component of their diet. As early as 1810, pellagra and corn were firmly linked. The Zeists, as these proponents of the maize theory were called, at first believed that something crucial was missing in a diet composed largely of corn, but within a short time they abandoned this theory in favor of the idea that spoiled corn, not sound corn, was responsible. Cesare Lombroso of Turin spent a quarter century studying the various moulds and bacteria that grew on damp corn, trying without success to isolate the cause of the disease.[2] After infectious diseases like anthrax and tuberculosis were specifically linked to a bacillus in the late nineteenth century, European physicians actively sought a pellagra "germ," and when it was determined that mosquitoes carried both malaria and yellow fever, they looked for an insect carrier. The debate raged in the European medical community, but the argument always came back to two central facts: pellagrins always ate corn, and they were nearly always poor. An English expert on tropical medicine, Dr. F.M. Sandwith, was not surprised when pellagra appeared in the American South. The conditions with which it had long been associated in Europe existed there also.[3]

In America, as the disease became widely recognized, pellagraphobia swept across the land. The search for a cure was frantic. Unlike hookworm, another disease which seemed peculiar to the South but whose origin and treatment were well known, the

Dr. Joseph Goldberger, pioneer pellagra researcher. Courtesy History of Nutrition Collection, Vanderbilt University Medical Center Library.

cause and treatment of pellagra were a mystery. While much attention was directed toward corn, pellagra was variously blamed on other items of food, including cottonseed oil and cane sugar. Like their European counterparts, American researchers looked for a pellagra germ, perhaps one that was insect-borne. The *simulium* fly was blamed. So were mosquitoes. Even birds were suspect.[4] The life-giving sun was cited as the cause, since a victim's skin often turned red as if sunburned. The symmetrical lesions became pellagra's signature, and exposure to sunlight almost always made a pellagrin feel worse. Their misery was compounded when they were sometimes shunned as lepers. More than two hundred remedies, some of them purportedly inspired by the deity, appeared in the literature.[5]

Individual panic over this disease, which struck the poor particularly hard, quickly snowballed into regional fear that yet another affliction, like the ten plagues of Egypt, had been sent to the besieged South. A map showing the distribution of pellagra looked like one of the Confederacy with Kentucky and a corner of Missouri tacked on.[6] Southerners soon became sensitive to the implied criticism which the spread of pellagra brought to the region, and they took what comfort they could in the appearance of cases now and then in northern communities.[7]

The pellagra epidemic was another example of the difficulties southerners were having trying to fit in with their image of the region as a land of wealth, power, and prosperity. Henry W. Grady, editor of the Atlanta *Constitution*, gave this image a name in 1886 in an address to northern industrialists. A "New South" of union and freedom, he said, had replaced the Old South of slavery and secession.[8] For southern boosters, the phrase soon became a symbol. They believed that the new industries that came to the South in the late nineteenth century and a new emphasis on diversified agriculture would surely transform the region. Indeed, some promoters of the South insisted that the transformation had already taken place. Grady, a year after he coined the "New South" phrase, claimed that "southern prosperity has been established by divine law."[9]

A quarter of a century later, as victims of pellagra dealt with their own private misery and hoped for a cure, they did not concern themselves with the socially volatile issue of the South's image and their place in it. Other southerners, however, more affluent and articulate than pellagrins, were more concerned with what the onset of pellagra revealed about the South than with the suffering it caused. How could the South claim to be prosperous and successful, and as a result, respected and admired,[10] when such an awful malady was so widespread? Textile mills, the very symbol of the New South, were no longer harbingers of the new prosperity. Instead they were centers of a repulsive disease that set the South apart, as different from and inferior to the rest of the nation. In time, the most vocal defenders of the New South would deny that pellagra existed. Meanwhile, other southerners who loved the region no less but who took a more realistic attitude toward its problems and shortcomings, turned to northern philanthropy and southern humanitarianism to lift up the South.[11] Walter Hines Page, a southern expatriate who had made his mark in the editorial world of New York and Boston, forsook the optimistic view of the New South which had been his in the 1880s. On a tour of the region in 1899, he saw a land that appeared "listless, discouraged, poverty-stricken, and backward looking."[12] He hoped that millionaires of the North and middle-class southern humanitarians would be able to do for the South, and especially for what he called the "forgotten man," what industry had failed to do—make the region a better place to live. Page became a crusader for education and the eradication of hookworm and an advocate of the public health movement. It was public spiritedness like his that supplied the needed support for the campaign against pellagra.

The campaign itself was waged in large part by the United States Public Health Service, which entered the fight against the disease in a small way soon after it was diagnosed in the South. In 1909, Dr. Clarendon H. Lavinder, a member of the PHS staff, was dispatched to the South Carolina State Hospital for the Insane, where there were at first dozens and then hundreds of cases. Pellagra, like tuberculosis, was thought to be a communicable disease, but at the Columbia institution neither type of patient was separated from the general population. Instead, officials of that hospital addressed themselves to what appeared to be a more pressing problem, the separation of the colored insane from the whites, putting them in separate buildings for the first time. On the incidence of pellagra at the institution, they noted that the mortality rate was "very high" and that those patients who did not die were left "damaged in mind and body . . . ataxic in gait, emaciated in body, demented and mute."[13]

Dr. Lavinder, in the two small rooms at his disposal in the hospital, used the time-honored experimental techniques of the Italian investigators. He tried to induce the disease in rabbits, rats, chickens, and guinea pigs by injecting them with the blood, spinal fluid, and spleen pulp of pellagrins, but he got only negative results. He injected pellagrins with salts of mercury and arsenic, two popular treatments, and with serum from the blood of recovered pellagrins, all without success. He noted the widespread prevalence of the disease in the surrounding community, but with the exception of Dr. James Woods Babcock, the superintendent of the hospital, few local physicians seemed interested. The superintendent himself was criticized for directing the attention of the public to the extent of pellagra in the institution which he headed and in the state as a whole. "I cannot believe that such criticism is seriously made," Dr. Babcock noted. With evidence of the serious impact which pellagra had on society, he thought he should be criticized if he failed to deal with it.[14]

By 1912, however, as the number of pellagrins ballooned, the medical profession and the public became increasingly aware of the dangers it posed. Dr. Babcock called it "the greatest public health problem now before this State, as well as other Southern States." South Carolina had 30,000 cases that year, with a mortality rate of 40 percent. The North Carolina Medical Society and the State Board of Health passed a resolution at their meeting in 1912 recognizing pellagra as an interstate and not an intrastate problem. They sent an appeal to Congress, one which they believed was responsible for the subsequent appropriation making possible the inauguration of a program of field epidemiology and the establishment of a Pellagra Hospital in Spartanburg, South Carolina, where biochemical studies could be conducted. The Public Health Service put forty-one men in the field to study pellagra from every conceivable angle. The state health officers of the southern states were also converted to the cause. Dr. James A. Hayne of South Carolina described pellagra as "the greatest riddle of the medical profession . . . a sphinx of which we have asked a reply and gotten none, for nearly two hundred years." The problem was far too big for the states to solve alone, he maintained; it was a national issue.[15]

In February 1914 the Public Health Service assigned Dr. Joseph Goldberger to direct the pellagra study in the South. The son of Jewish immigrants from Hungary, Goldberger grew up on New

York's East Side. He trained first as a civil engineer and then turned to the study of medicine. After graduating from Bellevue Hospital College, he entered private practice but abandoned this after two years for a career in the Public Health Service. It was a career of marked success. He wrote a paper on yellow fever which so impressed his superiors in Washington that he was invited to join the small staff of the Hygienic Laboratory there, the research arm of the Public Health Service. He made important contributions to understanding the etiology of typhus, Rocky Mountain spotted fever, measles, and typhoid. He was at work on a diphtheria epidemic when Surgeon General Rupert Blue put him in charge of the pellagra investigations. Thereafter his name and the campaign against pellagra were irrevocably linked.

Goldberger left at once for the South, traveling from state to state, visiting pellagrins in hospitals for the insane, checking hundreds of sick children in orphanages, touring the cotton mill towns with their boxlike houses. He saw beyond the patients to the way in which they lived. Perhaps because he was an outsider, what he saw intrigued him. He looked especially hard at the food the people ate, and what impressed him was its monotony. He must also have remembered the history of pellagra and the association of the disease with corn. What he saw the poor people of the South eating was a diet of fat back, cornbread, and syrup. Within three weeks he decided that pellagra and what came to be called the "Three-M diet"—meat, meal, and molasses—were linked. If the southern people could be persuaded to change their dietary habits, he believed pellagra would disappear. He wrote a preliminary paper in which he discarded all other theories about the etiology of pellagra. He would pursue the role of diet and disease.[16]

The meat, meal, and molasses diet which looked so strange to Goldberger was a legacy of the South's frontier past. To southerners, who substituted the readily raised pig for the once plentiful game, meat meant salt pork. Pigs fattened on corn, the same grain which supplied the second staple of the frontier diet, cornbread. Molasses was any kind of syrup made from easily grown cane. The preparation of these foods was as simple as the foods themselves. A study of the diet of blacks in Alabama in the 1890s described it this way: "Corn meal is mixed with water and baked on a flat surface on a hoe or griddle. The salt pork is sliced thin and fried until very brown and much of the grease tried out.

Molasses from cane or sorghum is added to the fat, making what is known as 'sap,' which is eaten with the corn bread. Hot water sweetened with molasses is used as a beverage." Modified at times with boiled collards, turnips, or an opossum, this was the food, three times a day all year.[17] The diet of white tenant farmers was not very different, and when many of these people moved to the mill villages, their diets did not change. As Rupert B. Vance observed, "When a people in the midst of a land capable of variety limit their diet to a few staples, they are in the grip of tradition."[18]

Goldberger made another trip through the South in April and May 1914 visiting many sites where pellagra was prevalent and making arrangements to test through experiment his theory that pellagra could be wiped out by a change in the diet of the southern poor. In a pocket-sized notebook he made penciled jottings of his observations. He visited the State Hospital for the Insane in Columbia where Dr. Lavinder worked, and again he found that corn was an important item in the diet. While Dr. Babcock headed that institution, corn had been excluded. In nearby Clinton, he visited an orphanage where he thought a "modified diet" might be tried. In Georgia he toured the Atlanta penitentiary and found it free from pellagra, but at the Georgia State Sanitarium at Milledgeville, he saw hundreds of cases. One of his associates, Dr. D.G. Willets, was already established there to do experimental work on diet with a selected group of patients. In Louisiana he visited the Charity Hospital in New Orleans and another sanitarium at Pineville. Remembering that pellagra was sometimes thought to be caused by eating spoiled corn, he noted that the corn used at Pineville was grown at the institution. There he also noted what he had observed in Milledgeville: "Nurses and attendants live in the rooms connected with the ward and received the same food as the patients. (N.B. They undoubtedly help themselves at the expense of the patients. Getting the best helpings &c. None of the personnel had been known to contract the disease.)"

Late one afternoon in early May, he arrived at the East Louisiana State Hospital in Jackson, having hurried there "by auto from Baton Rouge," using what was then a somewhat novel form of transportation. He found the staff well and many of the inmates sick. The staff told him that pellagra occurred mostly in the " 'untidy' and the 'dements.' " No staff member at the Mount

Vernon Insane Hospital in Mobile, Alabama, which Goldberger visited a few days later, had the disease, either. The diet of these people was a "little more varied" than that of the inmates.

In Jackson, Mississippi, on May 11 and 12, he visited two orphanages run by churches, where many of the children had pellagra. The superintendent of the Baptist Orphanage told him they had "cases of 'sunburn' that some people are calling pellagra." The superintendent at the Methodist Orphanage, where a third of the children were ill, was willing, Goldberger noted, "to turn the institution over to us," and he would speak to the superintendent of the Baptist home. In his notebook, Goldberger jotted down the menu at the Methodist Orphanage:

Breakfast:	Grits & gravy or Rice & gravy
	Biscuit & syrup (Louisiana syrup)
	Larger boys & girls get coffee with cream and sugar
	Children (2–5 yrs) have milk 3 times a day
	Eggs about once a week when cheap enough.
Dinner:	Vegetables (3 or 4 kinds at one time) such as cabbage, turnip greens, beets, onions, lima beans, pork & beans, lettuce, spinach, okra, &c.
	Once or twice a week a desert such as a pie or pudding, apple butter, pickles, canned goods.
	In summer, berries. *Occasionally* fresh fish served.
Supper:	Grits & gravy
	Biscuits & syrup
	Light bread
	Iced tea for larger boys & girls
Sunday Dinner!	Boiled ham
	Light bread
	Teacakes
	Pickles & salad
	Apples or prunes
	Iced tea.[19]

The exclamation point said it all. The diet at the Baptist Orphanage, which he also recorded, was no better. As Goldberger later told an associate, the diet at the orphanage was "more suited to cattle than humans."[20]

The two Mississippi orphanages were the sites of the first test to prove the efficacy of diet in curing pellagra. Within two weeks after Goldberger's visit to Jackson, a member of his team, Dr. C.H. Waring, was on the scene to supervise the new diet prescribed by Goldberger and paid for by the government. It included meat, milk, and dried legumes. A year later pellagra had disappeared from both institutions. Meanwhile, under the direction of Dr. Willets and Dr. W.F. Lorenz, a similar test of diet was under way at the Georgia State Sanitarium for a group of patients. The task was different there, however, because the patients with pellagra were apathetic. "They would sit at the table head lowered, back stooped, perhaps aimlessly stirring the food with one finger," Lorenz reported. "If the food were taken away no protest was made." It was not enough to provide a pellagra-preventive diet. It had to be eaten. Again, no staff member was ill. Here as elsewhere, they helped themselves first and what was left was offered the inmates. Goldberger concluded that because of the need to economize, that was very little.[21]

Economy was the watchword at these southern institutions. No sooner had the government-subsidized diet program ended at the two Mississippi orphanages than one of them reverted to the old diet, and within a few months nearly half the children had pellagra again. At a Georgia orphanage from which pellagra disappeared after officials voluntarily changed the diet, the doctor in charge could offer no assurance that the children would continue to be healthy, "especially if the table supply is cut down . . . . remember the difficulty under which a doctor labors, as an institution of this kind desires to be run on as economical basis as possible."[22]

Despite the refusal of many southern physicians to accept Goldberger's belief that something was lacking in the pellagrin's diet, this mild-mannered Public Health Service officer was optimistic that the southern people would change their eating habits if they just knew what to eat. His task was to prove absolutely that a proper diet could eliminate the disease. Just as he stopped pellagra at the orphanages with a good diet, so in a dramatic experiment, he induced it among prison volunteers with a poor one.[23] Still there were unbelievers. It was when Goldberger linked pellagra to the basic poverty of the South, however, that he ran into the most opposition. He believed that people would eat the right things if they had the money to do so. Many of them became pellagrins when the price of cotton dropped or when wages were lowered in the mills.

In a brilliant epidemiological study conducted in seven South Carolina mill villages from 1917 to 1921, Goldberger and his associates proved that pellagra was a by-product of a depressed economy. Probing the lives of the workers there, they proved that the lower the income of the mill worker, the greater the incidence of pellagra. If you had more money, you bought better food; it was as simple as that. Availability of food was also a factor. Villages in the Cotton Belt were ravaged by pellagra; villages in areas where cotton was less profitable had access to more meat, milk, and vegetables. [24]

The elimination of a disease tied to the economy posed unprecedented problems for southern physicians. Two years before the mill village study was made, Dr. James Hayne of South Carolina, who had become one of Goldberger's loudest critics, observed, "When you tell the health officer that the way to stop this thing is to make the whole people of the state change their mode of living, you put a proposition up to him that is almost impossible." [25] But that is just what Goldberger did. He became an advocate for abandoning the one-crop system. He wanted southerners to stop growing so much cotton and plant more vegetables and keep a cow instead.

So closely was pellagra tied to economics, to the price of cotton and to wages in the mill villages, that Goldberger became alarmed in autumn 1920, when the price of cotton dropped precipitously and the wages of mill workers were cut almost in half. For some months he remained silent, but in summer 1921 he decided he must do something. He sent a blunt letter to Public Health Service headquarters in Washington. "For all practical purposes we have in our own country this summer thousands of people who are starving and dying. We are feeding the Near East and Far East but we are neglecting our own people here at home." [26] A conference of health officials was called to map out a plan of action. The New York Times reported that a state of "semi-starvation" existed in the South and that indeed a "veritable famine" had developed in the rural districts of the region. President Warren G. Harding read the accounts and expressed alarm that "Famine and plague" existed in the land. He proclaimed that the nation must save its own. [27]

The response of the South to the president's solicitous concern was rage and fury. Southern businessmen denied that pellagra had increased in the South. Certainly, nothing like famine existed. They did not want help from the Red Cross. At least one southern planter, however, agreed with Goldberger and with the president. "It will not do for you to be offended at the messages that have come from the South," the Mississippi landowner wrote President Harding. "Foolish pride is at the bottom of them all. . . . That there is an epidemic that is sapping the manhood and womanhood of the South no sensible observing man can doubt. The average southerner will starve himself and allow his wife and children to starve rather than beg. . . . The southern gentleman thinks he is being personally insulted when anybody charges that a considerable portion of the people of his county are in a starving condition. He takes it as a reflection on his generosity." He said there were such "clear lines of distinction between the working man and the gentleman that the latter really knows almost nothing of the home life of the former and is little impressed by what he may hear as to the working man's condition or that of his wife and children."[28]

But most southerners could not admit the truth of Goldberger's claim, nor could they accept President Harding's offer of help. If pellagra and the economy were linked, then any increase in the disease meant a deterioration in the region's claim to prosperity. Those steeped in the dogma of the New South could not bring themselves to admit this. It was easier to deny pellagra existed than to confront the harsh realities of dealing with it.

The resurgence of pellagra coincided with an extensive campaign by southern Progressives to lure yet more industry to the South. To advertise the region's defects as Goldberger and President Harding had done threatened to undercut the effectiveness of this campaign. In 1921, for the first time, a southerner, John E. Edgerton of Tennessee, headed the National Association of Manufacturers. For several years southern mills had used more cotton than those in New England, and industrialists anticipated that the South would pass New England in total textile production in the 1920s. Industrial promoters in Gaston County, North Carolina, had a slogan: "Organize a mill a week." The lure for investors, as always, was the cheap labor of the South.[29] *The Manufacturers' Record* of Baltimore joined the chorus of those denying that pellagra posed a threat to the region's well-being. It published an article during the height of the fray entitled "Pel-

lagra in the South Not a Menace Nor Due to Under Nourishment." Its author was Dr. E.M. Perdue, a professor at the Eclectic
Medical University in Kansas City and president of the American
Association of Progressive Medicine, who believed that pellagra
was caused by drinking "soft" or "freestone" water.[30] The editor
of the *Record* was Richard Hathaway Edmonds, a contemporary
of Henry Grady who had held his post at the *Record* since 1882.
Four decades earlier he had proclaimed that the South was pre-
destined to greatness.[31] He had not changed his mind.

Politicians came to the South's defense, too. Congress was the
forum for a national debate on the issue. The South was prosperous, southern senators and congressmen argued. There was
plenty of food. Certainly, times were hard since the price of
cotton had dropped from forty-five to ten cents a pound, but the
South would pull through. Georgia's Congressman W.C. Wright
invoked the guidance of an "All-Wise Being" to save the South.
"Cotton," he said, "will once more be enthroned as King, and the
Fair Southland will come again into her own, blossom as the rose,
and her people will be contented and happy."[32]

Northerners were mystified at the southern response to President Harding's concern. A Saginaw, Michigan, paper commented, "Almost it would seem that they did not wish a fight to
be made upon pellagra, that they had adopted that disease as
something quite expected, something indigenous to the South
and not to be interfered with."[33] The Michigan paper missed the
point. It was not that pellagra was desirable, but rather that its
existence said too much about the southern way of life.

Pellagra was but one sin of the South discussed nationally in
the 1920s, a bad decade for the region. Led by H.L. Mencken, who
made South-baiting a national pastime, northern critics concerned themselves with one abomination after another: hookworm, pellagra, child labor, peonage, lynching, the Scopes trial,
the fundamentalist crusade against Al Smith. George Tindall has
called these diatribes a part of the old abolitionist image of bru-
tality in the South, which now once again emerged into the
mainstream of American thought. The "benighted South" became an object of concern to every publicist in the country.[34]
Accounts of widespread pellagra fit the image that other sections
of the country had of the South, as a land of piney woods and po'
white trash. Not surprisingly, southerners reacted defensively to
so much criticism. Donald Davidson, the Vanderbilt University

Agrarian, writing in the 1930s, called these accounts a "legend of barbarism." He said they depicted the South as "a region full of little else but lynching, shootings, chaingangs, poor whites, Ku Kluxers, hookworm, pellagra, and a few decayed patricians whose chief intent is to deprive the uncontaminated spiritual-singing Negro of his life and liberty."[35] The hue and cry over pellagra in 1921 was a forerunner of what the decade of the twenties would hold for the South. The tactic generally adopted by southerners was to deny everything, call the charges "bosh and poppycock," and insist that the South was being maligned as part of a propaganda campaign for some other section.[36]

The ready denials of the existence of pellagra were part of what Paul Gaston describes as a "flight of fantasy" about the New South. The solid accomplishments which New South spokesmen promised in the late nineteenth century had not been achieved. Instead, southerners created a "mythic view of their own times that was as removed from objective reality as the myth of the Old South."[37] Blinded to the faults of the region by the dazzling vision of abundance held up to them for a third of a century, southerners refused to see that pellagra existed.

It is not always easy to see want and misery in your own backyard. By the 1920s southerners had lost interest in the mill village, once the shining symbol of the new prosperity. The mill population was cut off from the rest of the southern community. Mill village residents did not mix with people beyond village borders. At the lower end of the social and economic scale, millhands were a breed apart. Tenant farmers were equally invisible. They were left out of local activities of the community and were strangers in the neighborhood. They had few friends and were viewed as outsiders.[38] Articulate defenders of the South in 1921, those who said that pellagra did not exist probably thought that they spoke the truth, for they rarely if ever encountered the lower classes.

In 1921 Goldberger gave up his fieldwork and his advocacy of reform to return to the laboratory. From there he watched the marked increase of pellagra throughout the decade. It was a time of agricultural depression, and as Goldberger knew that it would, pellagra followed. In the laboratory he tried to determine exactly what was missing from the diet of pellagrins. In the South he had noticed that dogs fed a diet of cornbread died of black tongue, a disease that looked like pellagra. At the Hygienic Laboratory in

Washington he and his staff induced black tongue in dogs and then attempted to cure them by the addition of a single item in their diet. Meanwhile, at the Georgia State Sanitarium, experiments with humans were under way. Dr. W.F. Tanner and later Dr. George Wheeler fed groups of women patients the standard diet of the South, adding to this a single item like carrots or tomatoes or turnip greens. In both locations the researchers were looking for the pellagra-preventive factor, preferably in inexpensive foods readily available in the South. They obtained their best results with Brewer's yeast, which worked almost like magic.[39] This discovery came in time to save thousands of lives when the Mississippi River flooded in 1927, driving people from their homes and destroying crops. The Red Cross distributed tons of yeast to pellagra victims. Along with the yeast, the Red Cross workers dispensed advice: always set aside enough land for a food crop as well as an economic crop.[40]

Goldberger did not live to isolate the vitamin which would prevent pellagra. In research at the University of Wisconsin in 1937,[41] nicotinic acid, or niacin, was found to be the specific preventive factor. But Goldberger did begin the search, and perhaps more important, he was among the first to recognize that a social revolution would be required to wipe out the new scourge of the South.

Less than a year after Goldberger died in January 1929, his associate Dr. George Wheeler, who succeeded him as director of the pellagra studies, read a paper on pellagra prevention at the meeting of the Southern Medical Association. The gist of the paper was that people could prevent pellagra if they ate pellagra-preventing foods like turnip greens, tomatoes, and yeast. Among those present was one of Goldberger's most consistent critics, Dr. Hayne of South Carolina, who had once asked him how to cure a disease caused by economics. Hayne challenged Wheeler's thesis and especially his idea that a change of diet might somehow be engineered. "There is only one man, and that is Mussolini, who can say 'Come,' and he cometh; or 'Go,' and he goeth, and he has said corn must not be used in any form in Italy . . . because, he believed, from the Italian situation, that maize is the primary cause of pellagra. . . . We have tried brewer's yeast, we have tried tomatoes and other dietary measures suggested, without results."[42]

The argument seemed to have come full circle. But even as

Hayne spoke, forces were at work in society which, coupled with advances in science in the next decade, would make pellagra a disease of the past. The social revolution which wiped out pellagra came, oddly enough, in the form of widespread depression. As the South, along with the nation, became poorer and poorer in the early 1930s, pellagra, although always linked with poverty, began to disappear. The reason was simple: people with time on their hands had an incentive to grow food for themselves, and with this change, their health began to improve.

The drought of 1929–30 prodded southerners to produce in 1931 one of the largest food and feed crops in the region's history. County and home demonstration agents put a new emphasis on gardening in the 1930s. The Red Cross distributed yeast and garden seeds. Several New Deal programs after 1933 were effective in reducing incidence of the disease. The Farm Security Administration, in particular, made some real progress in teaching people to live better. The coming of World War II reinvigorated the region's economy and bolstered the health of the South and of the nation with the new program of enriching bread, flour, and cornmeal with synthetic vitamins, including the pellagra-preventive niacin. Soon it became difficult to get pellagra if you ate enough to stay alive.[43]

Pellagra was the distinctive mark of hunger in the South, and it set the hungry of that region apart from the hungry elsewhere in America. Its passing thus reduced the monuments of regional distinctiveness. Pellagra vanished along with other landmarks to which it was directly or indirectly related, such as the one-horse farmer, one-crop agriculture, one-party politics, the sharecropper, the poll tax, the white primary, the Jim Crow car, and the lynching bee.[44] Laziness, often cited as a "fundamental aspect of Southern distinctiveness,"[45] has sometimes been attributed to pellagra and a list of parasites. With the waning of pellagra, southerners appeared to be no lazier than other Americans.

Pellagra remains something of a mystery still. The biochemical processes which cause the disease or prevent it, as the case may be, are very complex. Nicotinic acid will prevent the disease, but so will tryptophan, an amino acid which the body converts to niacin. The peculiar association of corn and pellagra is still an enigma. Mexicans, who surely ate as much corn as southerners, rarely if ever had pellagra, probably because they soaked their corn in hot lime water before making it into tortillas. Through hydrolysis, lime releases the niacin from the corn and makes it available to the body.[46] Still unexplained is the relationship of pellagra to exposure to the sun. And why a particular dietary pattern should lead to profound mental disturbances and depression also remains unknown.[47] Two and a half centuries of study and research have not unraveled all the riddles of this mysterious disease. It remains as complex and elusive as the South itself.

National efforts conquered pellagra in the South. The work of the U.S. Public Health Service, the programs of several New Deal agencies, and the success of bread enrichment made it virtually impossible for pellagra to exist. The transformation of the postwar South into the Sunbelt erased this and many other marks of southern distinctiveness. Pellagra is all but forgotten. The southern landscape looks more and more like that of the rest of America, and so does the roster of diseases to which its citizens fall prey. There may be those who regret the loss of so much regional distinctiveness, but no-one, not even the most ardent proponent of the "southern way of life," would mourn the disappearance of the meat, meal, and molasses diet and the disease which came in its wake.

NOTES

Abbreviations:

GPO	Government Printing Office
JAMA	Journal of the American Medical Association
NA	National Archives, Washington, D.C.
PHR	Public Health Reports
TNASP	Transactions of the National Association for the Study of Pellagra
VMCL	Vanderbilt Medical Center Library, Nashville, Tennessee

1. The proceedings of this conference are published in *Transactions of the National Conference on Pellagra* (Columbia, S.C.: The State Co., Printers, 1910).

2. Casal's classic book was *Historia Natural y Médica de la Principado de Asturias* (Madrid: Manuel Martín, 1762). Thiéry's account appeared in *Journal de Médecine, Chirugie et Pharmacie* 2 (1755):337–46. The most complete account of the association of pellagra with corn is Daphne Roe,

A Plague of Corn: The Social History of Pellagra (Ithaca, N.Y.: Cornell Univ. Press, 1973).

3. F.M. Sandwith, "Introductory Remarks," *Transactions of the National Conference on Pellagra*, 19. It was subsequently learned that pellagra was no newcomer to the South. Cases has occurred as early as 1834. See also Kenneth F. Kiple and Virginia H. King, *Another Dimension to the Black Diaspora: Diet, Disease, and Racism* (Cambridge, England: Cambridge Univ. Press, 1981), 123–33.

4. George C. Mizell, "Etiologic Factor and Recurrent Attacks of Pellagra," *TNASP* (Columbia, S.C.: R. L. Bryan Co., 1914), 297–304; Charles Morrow Wilson, *Ambassadors in White* (New York: Henry Holt, 1942), 156–83; J.H. Taylor, "Sambon the Man and His Later Investigations of Pellagra," *TNASP*, 291–96; M.L. Ravitch, "A Plea for Earlier Diagnosis of Pellagra," *JAMA* 59 (6 July 1912):33–35.

5. Among these was "Ez-X-Ba River, the Stream of Life." See "Pellagracide and Ez-X-Ba," *JAMA* 58 (2 Mar. 1912):648–49.

6. C.H. Lavinder, "The Prevalence and Geographic Distribution of Pellagra in the United States," *PHR* 27 (13 Dec. 1912):2076–81.

7. *The* (Columbia, S.C.) *State*, 3 Oct. 1912, 6 Oct. 1912.

8. Paul M. Gaston, *The New South Creed: A Study in Southern Mythmaking* (New York: Knopf, 1970), 18.

9. Quoted in ibid., 1.

10. These characteristics of the New South are cited in ibid., 191.

11. C. Vann Woodward, *Origins of the New South, 1877–1913* (Baton Rouge: Louisiana State Univ. Press, 1951, 1971), 396–97.

12. Quoted in Gaston, *New South Creed,* 199.

13. *Eighty-Fifth Annual Report of the South Carolina State Hospital for the Insane for the Year 1908* (Columbia: Gonzales and Bryan, 1908–1909), 7, 10.

14. Elizabeth W. Etheridge, *The Butterfly Caste: A Social History of Pellagra in the South* (Westport, Conn.: Greenwood, 1972), 16–17; *Eighty-Seventh Annual Report of South Carolina State Hospital for the Insane for the Year 1910* (Columbia: Gonzales and Bryan, 1910–1911), 12, 13.

15. *Eighty-Ninth Annual Report of South Carolina State Hospital for the Insane for the Year 1912* (Columbia: Gonzales and Bryan, 1913), 10; Joseph Goldberger, "Address," Conference of the Louisiana State Board of Health, 16 July 1915, in the Joseph Goldberger–W.W. Sebrell Collection, VMCL I–5; "Report on Committee on Pellagra," *Proceedings*, 29th Annual Meeting of the Conference of State and Provincial Boards of Health of North America, Washington, D.C., 19–20 June 1914 (Raleigh, N.C.: E.M. Uzzell, 1914), 70–72.

16. The most complete biography of Goldberger is Robert Percival, *Trail to Light: A Biography of Joseph Goldberger* (Indianapolis: Bobbs-

Merrill, 1943); Goldberger, "Memorandum on Pellagra," 2 Mar. 1914, in U.S. Public Health Service General File, No. 1648, Boxes 150–51, NA; "The Etiology of Pellagra," PHR 29 (26 June 1914):1683–86.

17. W.O. Atwater and Charles D. Woods, Dietary Studies with Reference to the Food of the Negro in Alabama in 1895 and 1896 (Washington, D.C., GPO, 1897).

18. Rupert B. Vance, Human Geography of the South: A Study of Regional Resources and Human Adequacy (Chapel Hill: Univ. of North Carolina Press, 1932), 417.

19. Joseph Goldberger, Notebook, 26 Apr.–12 May [1914], VMCL I–13.

20. Goldberger, Memo, 19 Nov. 1914, VMCL I–4.

21. Joseph Goldberger, C.H. Waring, and D.G. Willets, "The Prevention of Pellagra," PHR 30 (22 Oct. 1915):3119–24; W.F. Lorenz to Goldberger, 8 Sept. 1914, VMCL I–4; Goldberger, "Cutter Lecture," VMCL I–5.

22. [G.C. Trimble], "Report on Pellagra and Treatment in Georgia Baptist Orphan Home in Hapeville, Georgia," [Oct. 1914], VMCL I–26.

23. A convenient collection of the most important of Goldberger's Papers is Milton Terris, ed., Goldberger on Pellagra (Baton Rouge: Louisiana State Univ. Press, 1964).

24. Joseph Goldberger, G.A. Wheeler, and Edgar Sydenstricker, "A Study of the Relation of Family Income and Other Economic Factors to Pellagra Incidence in Seven Cotton-Mill Villages of South Carolina in 1916," PHR 35 (12 Nov. 1920):2693–2701.

25. "Minutes of Third Triennial Meeting," [1915], 143–44, James Woods Babcock Papers, South Caroliniana Library, Columbia, S.C.

26. Goldberger to Dr. Schereschewsky, 9 July 1921, NA, U.S. Public Health Service General File 1648, Box 151.

27. New York Times, 25 July 1921, p. 1; President Warren G. Harding to Surgeon General Hugh Cumming, 25 July 1921; Harding to Livingston Farrand, 25 July 1921, Warren G. Harding Papers, Ohio Historical Society, Columbus, Ohio.

28. Charles H. Stoll to President Harding, 27 July 1921, VMCL I–55.

29. George B. Tindall, The Emergence of the New South, 1913–1945 (Baton Rouge: Louisiana State Univ. Press, 1967), 70–79.

30. Ibid., 278 n112; Etheridge, Butterfly Caste, 103, 240n14.

31. Tindall, Emergence of the New South, 70.

32. Congressional Record, 67th Cong., 1st Sess. (July 1921):4428.

33. Clipping marked "Saginaw," 29 July 1921, Harding Papers.

34. George B. Tindall, "Mythology: The New Frontier in Southern History," in The Idea of the South: Pursuit of a Central Theme, ed. Frank Vandiver (Chicago: Univ. of Chicago Press, 1964), 5–6.

35. Quoted in George B. Tindall, "The Benighted South: Origins of a Modern Image," Virginia Quarterly Review 40 (1964):290.

36. Many southern newspapers denounced the report showing an increase in pellagra. See, e.g., Savannah (Ga.) *Morning News,* 27 July 1921; Athens (Ga.) *Banner,* 30 July 1921; Atlanta (Ga.) *Constitution,* 28 July 1921. The South's reaction may have had some validity. George B. Tindall has written that the repeated attacks on the South served as a national catharsis, the South becoming "a convenient scapegoat upon which the sins of all may be symbolically laid and thereby expiated—a most convenient escape from problem solving." See Tindall, "Mythology: The New Frontier in Southern History," 14.

37. Gaston, *New South Creed,* 190.

38. Frank Tannenbaum, *Darker Phases of the South* (New York: G.P. Putnam's Sons, 1924), 64–139.

39. Etheridge, *Butterfly Caste,* 170–186. Turnip greens proved to be one of the richest vegetable sources of the pellagra-preventive factor. If the orphanages in Jackson, Miss., had served enough greens, pellagra might not have been such a problem. Goldberger discovered, however, that the difference between a pellagra-causing diet and a pellagra-preventive one was narrow. Beans, which he originally thought would solve the South's dietary problem, proved ineffective in preventing pellagra.

40. W.R. Redder (Red Cross) to Goldberger, 9 Mar. 1928, VMCL II–11.

41. C.A. Elvehjem, R.J. Madden, F.M. Strong, D.W. Wooley, "Relation of Nicotinic Acid and Nicotinic Acid Amide to Canine Black Tongue," *Journal of American Chemical Society* 59 (1937):1767–68; C.J. Koehn, Jr., and C.A. Elvehjem, "Further Studies of the Concentration of the Antipellagra Factor," *Journal of Biological Chemistry* 118 (1937):693–99.

42. "Discussion," *Southern Medical Journal* 23 (Apr. 1930):304.

43. Etheridge, *Butterfly Caste,* 195–196, 204–205, 210.

44. These monuments of distinctiveness, with the exception of pellagra, are cited in C. Vann Woodward, *The Burden of Southern History* (Baton Rouge: Louisiana State Univ. Press, 1968), 5.

45. C. Vann Woodward, "The Southern Ethic in a Puritan World," *William and Mary Quarterly,* 3d series, 25 (1968):343. This theme is developed in David Bertelson, *The Lazy South* (New York: Oxford Univ. Press, 1967).

46. Kenneth Carpenter, "Effects of Different Methods of Processing Maize on its Pellagragenic Activity," in Federation of American Societies for Experimental Biology, *Proceedings,* 40 (Apr. 1981):1531.

47. S.G. Srikanta, "Endemic Pellagra," in *Human Nutrition: Current Issues and Controversies,* ed. A. Neuberger and T.H. Jukes (Lancaster, England: MTP Press, 1982), 213. Urocanic acid, which acts as a trap for ultraviolent light, is found in lower amounts in the skin of pellagrins than in normal controls. Thus, this reduction may be responsible for the photosensitive rash. Mental disturbances may be related to an alteration in serotonin metabolism.

6

Slave Health and Southern Distinctiveness

•

TODD L. SAVITT

Slavery was a fundamental element of southern life and society, one of several factors that made the region distinctive. Nowhere else in America did two large disparate racial populations live side by side in such intimate contact. The presence in the Old South of enslaved blacks with health care needs and group medical experiences often differing from those of whites helped set that region apart from the North and West in the minds of contemporary Americans. In the South whites had control over, but were inevitably affected by, black health matters. Two medical issues specific to American Negro slavery ultimately related health affairs to politics and economics: first, whites, who were responsible for slave medical care, in large part dictated the living and working conditions that promoted or destroyed blacks' health; and second, some white southerners claimed (and many others believed) that blacks were medically different from whites and so in need of special treatment. This essay will look at the three groups of southerners most directly involved in issues of black health and care—masters, physicians, and the slaves themselves—and show that matters of slave health contributed to the distinctiveness of southern society.[1]

The first section of this chapter discusses how southern physicians used their own and others' observations of black medical differences to develop both a partial rationale for enslaving blacks in the American South, and a special approach to medical care and treatment of Negroes. The second section describes ways in which the living and working conditions of plantation slaves, generally different from the conditions of agricultural workers in other regions of the country, affected black health. A final section deals with the various forms of black medical care which masters, physicians, and slaves themselves provided under this unique labor system known as "the peculiar institution." Each section points to ways in which the presence of the slavery system and of a large black population resident in a white-dominated society contributed to southern distinctiveness.

WERE BLACKS MEDICALLY DIFFERENT FROM WHITES?

"Scarcely any observant medical man, having charge of negro estates, fails to discover, by experience, important modifications in the diseases and appropriate treatment of the white and black race respectively."[2] Thus wrote the editor of a prominent Virginia medical journal in 1856, in an attempt to impress upon the state's physicians the importance of providing adequate health care to slaves. He could very well have been speaking to all southern doctors, many of whom believed that medical differences existed between blacks and whites. The issue was of both practical and political importance; it involved not only the health care of an entire racial group in the South, but also the partial justification for enslaving them.

Physicians who treated slave diseases had a pecuniary and a professional concern with the subject. Their recorded opinions in medical, commercial, and agricultural journals, as well as in personal correspondence, attest to the seriousness with which they approached issues of black health. The politically-minded physicians (all of whom practiced medicine) were also resolutely committed to explaining the southern position on slavery. They, too, published for the medical, commercial, and lay public. Men like Josiah Clark Nott of Mobile and Samuel A. Cartwright of New Orleans utilized their knowledge of black medicine to rationalize the necessity and usefulness of slavery. These apologists for the peculiar institution, in order to prove that slavery was humane and economically viable in the South, argued that blacks possessed immunity to certain diseases which devastated whites. Slaveowners, they said, did not sacrifice blacks every time they sent them into the rice fields or canebrakes. Nor could physicians

Loudon County, Virginia, slave (aged fifty-one) with tumor of jaw-bone, before and after surgical excision in Baltimore. From *American Journal of the Medical Sciences*, n.s. 4 (1842), 277, 280.

adequately treat blacks without knowledge of their anatomical and physiological peculiarities and disease proclivities. Blacks were medically different and mentally inferior to whites, they asserted.

In certain obvious physical ways Negroes did differ greatly from Caucasians. Old South writers particularly commented on facial features, hair, posture, gait, skin color, and odor. One school of American scientists spent much time and effort investigating cranium and brain size, as well as other characteristics, in part to discover whether blacks were inferior to whites. Physicians, slaveowners, and other interested persons also detected distinctions in the physical reactions of the two races, both to diseases and to treatments. Their observations were often accurate, but at times racial prejudice clouded their views. These observers remarked particularly about the relative immunity of blacks to southern fevers, especially intermittent fever (malaria) and yellow fever, susceptibility to intestinal and respiratory disease, and tolerance of heat and intolerance of cold. Black children, they noted, died more frequently of marasmus (wasting away), convulsions, "teething," and suffocation or overlaying than did whites.[3]

One of the most fascinating subjects about which Old South medical authors wrote was black resistance to malaria, the focus of constant comment during the antebellum period because blacks' liability to it appeared to vary from region to region, plantation to plantation, and individual to individual. In dispute was the degree of susceptibility and the virulence of the disease in Negroes. Could slaves acquire some resistance to malaria by living in constant proximity to its supposed source? Were some slaves naturally immune? Did slaves have milder attacks of the disease than whites?

Modern science has answered many of the questions about immunity and prevention of malaria with which doctors and planters struggled in the antebellum period. Several factors contributed to the phenomenon of malarial immunity. As will be discussed below, many blacks did possess an inherited immunity to one or another form of malaria. But for Caucasians and those Negroes without natural resistance to a particular type of plasmodium (the organism that causes malaria), it was possible to acquire malarial immunity or tolerance only under the conditions stated by the author of an article in the *New Orleans Medical News and Hospital Gazette* (1858–59)—by suffering repeated infections of the disease over a period of several years. For this to occur, one of the four species of plasmodium—falciparum, vivax, malariae, and ovale—had to be present constantly in the endemic region, so that with each attack a person's supply of antibodies was strengthened against further parasitic invasions. Interruption of this process, such as removal to nonendemic areas for the summer (when exposure to the parasite was useful in building immunity) or for several years (during schooling or travel), prohibited the aggregation of sufficient antibodies to resist infection. In truly endemic areas, acquiring immunity this way was a risky affair: unprotected children struggled for their lives, adults suffered from relapses of infections contracted years before, and partially immune adults worked through mild cases. It is no wonder, then, that slaves sold from, say, Virginia, where one form of malaria was prevalent, to a Louisiana bayou or South Carolina rice plantation, where a different species or strain of plasmodium was endemic, had a high incidence of the disease. Even adult slaves from Africa had to go through a "seasoning" period, because the strains of malarial parasites in this country differed from those in their native lands.

Generally speaking, most malaria in the upper South and in inland piedmont areas was of the milder vivax type, while vivax and the more dangerous falciparum malaria coexisted in coastal and swampy inland portions of both the lower and upper South. Rare pockets of the malariae type (quartan fever) were scattered across the South. Ovale malaria appears not to have been present in the United States. Of course, epidemics of one type or another could strike any neighborhood, resulting in sickness and death even to those who had acquired resistance to the endemic variety. *Plasmodium falciparum* usually caused such epidemics, especially in the temperate regions of the South.[4]

The major reason for black immunity to vivax or falciparum malaria relates not to acquired resistance, but to selective genetic factors. At least three hereditary conditions prevalent among blacks in parts of modern Africa appear to confer immunity to malaria upon their bearers. Recent medical research indicates that the red blood cells of persons lacking a specific factor called Duffy antigen are resistant to invasion of *Plasmodium vivax*. Approximately 90 percent of West Africans lack Duffy antigens, as do about 70 percent of Afro-Americans. This inherited, symptomless, hematologic condition is extremely rare in other racial groups. All evidence points to the conclusion that infection by *Plasmodium vivax* requires the presence of Duffy-positive red blood cells. Since most Negroes do not possess this factor, they are immune to vivax malaria. It can safely be assumed that the vast majority of American slaves and free blacks were likewise resistant to this form of the disease.

Some antebellum blacks had additional protection against malaria as a result of two abnormal genetic hemoglobin conditions, sickle cell disease (a form of anemia) and sickle cell trait (the symptomless carrier state of the sickling gene). People with either of these conditions had milder cases of, and decreased risk of mortality from, the most malignant form of malaria, falciparum. Many of those who had sickle cell *disease* died from its consequences before or during adolescence; however, blacks who had sickle cell *trait* lived entirely normal lives and could then transmit the gene for sickling to their offspring. Since people with the trait had one normal gene and one abnormal gene for sickling (in contrast to those with the disease, who had two of the abnormal genes), their offspring could inherit sickle cell anemia only when each parent contributed a gene for sickling. Because the sickle cell condition was not discovered until 1910, physicians in the antebellum South were unaware that this was one reason why some slaves on plantations appeared to be immune to malarial infections. One other genetic condition with a high incidence within the former slave-trading region probably affords some malarial resistance: deficiency of the enzyme glucose-6-phosphate dehydrogenase (G-6-PD deficiency).

It is impossible to provide an exact calculation of sickle cell and G-6-PD deficiency gene prevalence among antebellum southern blacks. However, an estimate might be ventured based on known gene frequencies among present-day Afro-Americans and those Africans residing in former slave-trading areas. One leading medical authority on abnormal hemoglobins has estimated that at least 22 percent of Africans first brought to this country possessed genes for sickling. Other medical scientists have determined that approximately 20 percent of West Africans have genes for G-6-PD deficiency. Overall, then, using conservative figures, approximately 30-40 percent of newly arrived slaves had one or both of these genes. Recent evidence points to a higher-than-expected frequency of the G-6-PD gene in patients with sickle cell disease, which might reduce this estimate by a few percent. Thus a large proportion of Negroes were immune to the severe effects of falciparum malaria and to the less virulent vivax malaria, facts which planters and physicians in the South could not help but notice and discuss openly.

As with malaria, planters and physicians speculated publicly on blacks' intolerance of cold climates but could never adequately prove their contentions. It was the confirmed opinion of many white southerners that, because of their dark skin and equatorial origins, blacks could not withstand cold weather to the same degree as whites. Their major concern was that blacks seemed to resist and tolerate respiratory infections less well then whites. Since the germ theory of disease was years in the future, these men and others explained their observations with a combination of then-current though not universally accepted medical, anthropological, and scientific logic—and occasionally with unfounded theories. Blacks, natives of a tropical climate, were physiologically ill-suited for the cold winter weather and cool spring and fall nights of the temperate zone. They breathed less air, dissipated a greater amount of "animal heat" through the skin, and eliminated larger quantities of carbon via liver and skin than whites. In addition, blacks were exposed to the elements for much of the year, placing a strain on heat production within the body. One medical extremist, Samuel A. Cartwright of New Orleans, even claimed that Negroes' lungs functioned inefficiently, causing "defective atmospherization of the blood." Some noted that slaves often slept with their heads (rather than their feet) next to the fire and entirely covered by a blanket; this was seen as proof that they required warm, moist air to breathe and to survive in this climate. Blacks were, these men concluded, physiologically different from whites.

Even today there is some confusion among medical authorities regarding the susceptibility of Negroes to severe pulmonary infections. Some claim a racial or genetic predisposition, while others deny it. Historically, blacks have shown a higher incidence and more severe manifestations of respiratory illness than have whites. Explanations for this phenomenon are numerous. First, Negroes did not experience bacterial pneumonias until the coming of the Caucasian. The entire newly-exposed population was thus exquisitely sensitive to these infections, and developed much more serious cases than whites, who had had frequent contact with the bacteria since childhood. Second, black African laborers who today move from moist tropical to temperate climates (e.g., to the gold mines of South Africa) contract pneumonia at a much higher rate than whites. Though the incidence of disease decreases with time, it always remains at a more elevated level than among Caucasians. The same phenomenon probably operated during slavery. At first the mortality rate from pneumonia among newly-arrived slaves was probably inordinately high, but with time the figure decreased somewhat, though it remains higher than in Caucasians. Third, there appears to be a close relationship between resistance to pulmonary infection and exposure to cool, wet weather. Slaves, who worked outdoors in all seasons and often lived in drafty, damp cabins, were therefore more likely to suffer from respiratory diseases than their masters. Fourth, poor diet, a common slave problem, predisposes people to infections like pneumonia and other respiratory problems[5] Finally, overcrowding and unsanitary living conditions caused an increased incidence of respiratory diseases. Slaves living in small cottages or grouped together in a large community at the quarters, where intimate and frequent visiting was common, stood a greater chance of contracting airborne infections than did the more isolated whites. Undoubtedly, all these factors combined to increase the occurrence of respiratory illness among southern blacks.

The most serious nonfatal manifestation of cold intolerance was frostbite. At least one proslavery apologist claimed that the Negro race was more susceptible than whites to this condition: "Almost every one has seen negroes in Northern cities, who have lost their legs by frost at sea—a thing rarely witnessed among whites, and yet where a single negro has been thus exposed doubtless a thousand of the former have."[6] The condition was a serious one, especially for slaveowners who stood to lose the labor of valuable workers.

Blacks are in fact more susceptible to cold injury than whites. Studies conducted during and after the Korean War indicate that blacks have a poorer adaptive response to cold exposure than whites in the following ways: their metabolic rates increase more slowly and not as much as whites'; their first shivers (one of the body's defensive responses to cold) occur at a lower skin temperature than for whites; and their incidence of frostbite is higher and their cases more severe than those of whites. Even after blacks have acclimated to cold (and they do so in a manner physiologically similar to whites), they are then only slightly less liable to sustain cold injury than they had been previously. Those antebellum observers who warned against overexposure of slaves to cold were essentially correct.

Racial differences in tolerance to heat also exist but may be modified under certain conditions. Again, antebellum observers agreed that blacks, having originated in an area known for its heat and humidity, were ideally suited for labor in the damp, warm South. One northern physician, John H. Van Evrie, explained blacks' resistance to heat in both religious and physiological terms:

> God has adapted him, both in his physical and mental structure, to the tropics. . . . His head is protected from the rays of a verti-cal sun by a dense mat of woolly hair, wholly impervious to its fiercest heats, while his entire surface, studded with innumera-ble sebaceous glands, forming a complete excretory system, re-lieves him from all those climatic influences so fatal, under the same circumstances, to the sensitive and highly organized white man. Instead of seeking to shelter himself from the burning sun of the tropics, he courts it, enjoys it, delights in its fiercest heats.[7]

Modern medical investigators would not agree with Van Ev-rie's reasoning. But they have discovered that under normal living conditions, Negroes in Africa and the United States are better equipped to tolerate humid heat than whites. However, both races possess the same capacity to become acclimatized to hot, humid conditions. The physiological mechanisms by which the human body acclimatizes itself to heat can be readily observed and measured. Increased external temperature causes the body to perspire more, resulting in a greater evaporative heat loss, a decline in skin and rectal temperatures, and a drop in the heart rate from its initially more rapid pace. When whites and blacks are equally active in the same environment over a period of time, there is little difference in heat tolerance.

From this information it can be assumed that in the Old South slaves and free blacks possessed a higher *natural* tolerance to humid heat stress than did whites. In addition, Negroes quickly became acclimatized to performance of their particular tasks under the prevailing climatic conditions of the region. This natu-ral and acquired acclimatization enabled black laborers to withstand the damp heat of summer better than whites, who were unused to physical exertion under such severe conditions. White farm and general laborers, however, also must have adjusted to the heat and fared as well as blacks. One physiological difference between Caucasians and Negroes which might have affected work performance in the hot, humid South was the latter's inherent ability to discharge smaller amounts of sodium chloride and other vital body salts (electrolytes) into sweat and urine. Excessive loss of these salts leads to heat prostration and heatstroke. Thus conservation of needed electrolytes provided slaves with an advantage over laboring whites, whose requirements for replacement of the substances were greater. In the case of heat tolerance, then, white observers were correct in noting a racial difference, but they tended to ignore the fact that many whites did become acclimatized to the hot, humid environment.

Whites detected, or thought they detected, distinctive susceptibility in blacks to several other medical conditions common in the antebellum South. Many believed that slave women developed prolapsed uteri at a higher rate than white women, though modern anatomists have shown that Negroes are actually less prone to this affliction than Caucasians. Observers also noted that slaves were frequent sufferers of typhoid fever, worms, and dysentery, though we now know that the reason for this high prevalence was environmental rather than racial or genetic. Blacks did, however, have a greater resistance to the yellow fever virus than whites.[8]

One disease that drew great attention because of its frequency and virulence was consumption (pulmonary tuberculosis), a leading cause of death in nineteenth-century America for members of both races. A particular form of the disease—characterized by extreme difficulty in breathing, unexplained abdominal pain around the navel, and rapidly progressing debility and emaciation, usually resulting in death—struck blacks so commonly that it came to be known as "Negro consumption" or *Struma Africana*. In all likelihood, most of the cases which white southerners described as Negro consumption were miliary tuberculosis, the most serious and fatal form of the disease known, in which tubercles are found in many body organs simultaneously, overwhelming what natural defenses exist. The reason that rapidly fatal varieties of the disease (so-called galloping consumption) afflicted Negroes more frequently than Caucasians may be related to the fact that Caucasians (like Mongolians) had suffered from tuberculosis for many hundreds of years and had developed a strong immune response to the infection, whereas Africans (and American Indians and Eskimos) had been exposed to tuberculosis only since the coming of the white man and had not yet built up this same effective resistance. Others have discounted racial immunity as an explanation and argued that, as a "virgin" population, blacks were highly susceptible to serious first attacks of tuberculosis. Additional factors such as malnourishment, preexisting illness, or general debility also contributed to the apparent black predisposition to tuberculosis.

Neonatal tetanus (also called *trismus nascentium*) was a common cause of death among newborn slaves throughout the South. Slaveowners and physicians, who recognized its origin in the improper handling of the umbilical stump, often discussed it in their writings. It still kills large numbers of children in undeveloped countries. *Clostridium tetani*, the same bacterium which caused tetanus in older children and adults, also infected newborns through the unwashed and frequently touched umbilical stump. In a typical antebellum case, related by Dr. Albert Snead of Richmond to his colleagues at a medical society meeting in 1853, an eight-day-old black child first refused her mother's breast and gave a few convulsive hand jerks. Soon the baby's entire muscular system was rigid, with her head bent back, fists and jaws clenched, and feet tightly flexed, as the bacterial toxin affected central nervous system tissue. In this case death from suffoction owing to respiratory muscle paralysis did not intervene until the eighteenth day (though it usually occurred within seven to ten days).

One cause of death not considered a disease which seemed to occur almost exclusively among the slave population was "smothering," "overlaying," or "suffocation." Observers assumed that sleeping mothers simply rolled onto or pressed snugly against their infants, cutting off the air supply, or that angry, fearful parents intentionally destroyed their offspring rather than have them raised in slavery. Modern medical evidence strongly indicates that most of these deaths may be ascribed to a condition presently known as Sudden Infant Death Syndrome (SIDS) or "crib death" which, for reasons yet unexplained, affects blacks more frequently than whites.[9]

The diseases and conditions discussed above represent only

some of the several which whites noted affected blacks and whites differently. Others are difficult to trace back to slavery times, either through direct records or by implication through comparative West African medicine. Among those not mentioned, the most important is hypertension (high blood pressure). Others include polydactyly (six or more fingers per hand); umbilical hernia; cancers of the cervix, stomach, lungs, esophagus, and prostate; and toxemia of pregnancy. At the same time, Negroes are much less susceptible to hookworm disease, cystic fibrosis, and skin cancer than Caucasians.

Though blacks are not the only racial or ethnic group possessing increased immunity and susceptibility to specific diseases, they were the only group whose medical differences mattered to white residents of the Old South. Reports of black medical "peculiarities" appeared regularly in periodicals and pamphlets, presumably to alert southern physicians of problems they might encounter in practice. Agricultural and medical journal articles and medical student dissertations also discussed racial differences in responses to medical treatments. Most writers agreed that blacks withstood the heroic, depletive therapies of the day (bleeding, purging, vomiting, blistering) less well than whites.

Despite many writings on the subject of black diseases and treatments, no comprehensive discussion existed in any standard textbook for student doctors or practitioners. Some articles on the subject of treatment provided vague information, such as: "The Caucasian seems to yield more readily to remedies . . . than the African," or "It is much more difficult to form a just diagnosis or prognosis with the latter [African] than the former [white], consequently the treatment is often more dubious."[10] In 1855 an editor of the *Virginia Medical and Surgical Journal* suggested that a Virginian write a book on "the modifications of disease in the Negro constitution." The subject, he proclaimed, stood "invitingly open"; no medical student, "fresh from Watson or Wood [textbooks of the day], with his new lancet and his armory of antiphlogistics," had been properly trained to treat many of the diseases to which the black man was subject: "Has he been taught that the African constitution sinks before the heavy blows of the 'heroic school' and runs down under the action of purgatives; that when the books say blood letting and calomel, the black man needs nourishment and opium?"[11] Other southern medical writers put forth similar pleas for medical school courses and books

on black medicine. Northern textbook authors and professors at
northern medical schools, they asserted, could not and did not
accurately or adequately discuss diseases afflicting blacks in the
South.

John Stainbach Wilson, a Columbus, Georgia, physician who
had spent years practicing medicine in southern Alabama, came
closest to actually producing a textbook on black health. Its advertised title indicated the wide scope of the proposed contents: *The
Plantation and Family Physician; A Work for Families Generally and
for Southern Slaveowners Especially; Embracing the Peculiarities
and Diseases, the Medical and Hygienic Management of Negroes,
Together with the Causes, Symptoms, and Treatment of the Principal
Diseases to Whites and Blacks*. But apparently the outbreak of
hostilities in 1861 interrupted Wilson's plans. It was not until
more than one hundred years later, in 1975, that the first *Textbook
of Black-Related Diseases* was finally published, written this time
by black physicians. [12]

For southern whites, black medical problems and health care
had political as well as medical ramifications. Men like Cartwright, Nott, and Wilson, advocates of what historians have
labeled "state rights medicine," were writing for a sectional audience who wished to hear that blacks were distinct from whites.
This theme was, after all, a part of the proslavery argument.
Medical theory and practice were still in such a state of flux in the
late eighteenth and early nineteenth centuries that there was little
risk of any true scientific challenge to a medical system based on
racial differences. Observers were correct in noting that blacks
showed differing susceptibility and immunity to a few specific
diseases and conditions. They capitalized on these conditions to
illustrate the inferiority of blacks to whites, to rationalize the use
of this "less fit" racial group as slaves, to justify subjecting Negro
slaves to harsh working conditions in extreme dampness and
heat in the malarious regions of the South, and to prove to their
critics that they recognized the special medical weaknesses of
blacks and took these failings into account when providing for
their human chattel. But in terms of an overall theory of medical
care predicated on racial inferiority, the issue was a false one. It is
instructive to note here, for example, that no writer ventured
beyond vague and cautious statements about bleeding or purging
blacks less than whites. None presented an account of the
amount of blood loss or the dose of medicine which was optimal

for blacks. Remarks on the subject were always couched in terms that placed whites in a position of medical and physical superiority over Negroes, perfect for southern sectional polemics and useless to the practitioner.

LIVING AND WORKING CONDITIONS

The state of slave health depended not only on disease immunities and susceptibilities but also on living and working conditions. In the latter two matters, the South stood apart from the rest of the nation. Nowhere else did one group exert such great control over most aspects of their workers' lives as slaveowners and overseers had over the daily routines of their black slaves. How whites in the slave South provided for sanitation, housing, food, clothing, and children's and women's special needs, and how they worked and disciplined their human chattel, necessarily affected the health of their black work force.

Most slaves on plantations or farms lived in a well-defined area known as the quarters. Here was a setting ideal for the spread of disease, similar to the situation which existed in antebellum villages and urban areas. What might have been considered a personal illness in the isolated white rural family dwelling became in a three- or ten- or thirty-home slave community a matter of public health and group concern.

At the slave quarters, sneezing, coughing, or contact with improperly washed eating utensils and personal belongings promoted transmission of disease-causing micro-organisms among family members. Poor ventilation, lack of sufficient windows for sunshine, and damp earthern floors added to the problem by aiding the growth of fungus and bacteria on food, clothing, floors, and utensils, and the development of worm and insect larvae. Improper personal hygiene (infrequent baths, hairbrushings, and haircuts, unwashed clothes, unclean beds) led to such nuisances as bedbugs, body lice (which also carried typhus germs), ringworm of skin and scalp, and pinworms. In a household cramped for space, these diseases became family, not individual, problems. And when two or more families shared homes and facilities, the problem of contagion was further aggravated.

Contacts outside the home also facilitated the dissemination of disease. Children who played together all day under the supervision of a few older women, and then returned to their cabins in the evening, spread their day's accumulation of germs to other family members. Even mere Sunday and evening socializing in an ill neighbor's cabin was enough to "seed" the unsuspecting with disease. Contaminated water, unwashed or poorly cooked food, worm larvae–infested soil, and disease-carrying farm animals and rodents also contributed their share to the unhealthfulness of the quarters.

The two major types of seasonal diseases—respiratory and intestinal—that afflicted southern blacks reflected living conditions within most slave communities. Respiratory illnesses prevailed during the cold months, when slaves were forced to spend much time indoors in intimate contact with their families and friends. Several important contagious diseases were spread through contact with respiratory system secretions: tuberculosis, diphtheria, colds and upper respiratory infections, influenza, pneumonia, and streptococcal infections (including sore throats and scarlet fever). The community life of the slave quarters also provided excellent surroundings for dissemination of several year-round diseases contracted through respiratory secretions. People today tend to regard these illnesses—whooping cough, measles, chicken pox, and mumps—as limited to the younger population, but adult slaves who had never experienced an outbreak of, say, measles, in Africa or the United States were quite susceptible to infection and even death. Measles and whooping cough are still important causes of fatality in developing countries, as they were in the antebellum South.

As warm weather arrived and workers spent more time outside, intestinal diseases caused by poor outdoor sanitation and close contact with the earth became common. Respiratory diseases decreased in frequency and insects became culprits important in the spread of disease—particularly maladies of the digestive tract and various "fevers." What more could a mosquito or housefly wish than a large concentration of human beings, decaying leftover food scraps, scattered human feces, or a compost heap? Mosquitoes discharged yellow fever or malaria parasites while obtaining fresh blood from their victims. Flies transported bacteria such as *Vibrio* (cholera), *Salmonella* (food poisoning and typhoid), and *Shigella* (bacillary dysentery), the virus which causes infectious hepatitis, and the protozoan *Entameba histolytica* (amoebic dysentery), from feces to food. Trichina worms, embedded in the muscles of hogs inhabiting yards often shared with bondsmen, were released into a slave's body when the meat was not completely cooked. Finally, there were the large parasitic worms, a concomitant of primitive sanitation.

Intestinal disorders were at least as common among Virginia's antebellum blacks as were respiratory diseases. The human alimentary tract is distinguished among all other body systems in that it receives daily large amounts of foreign material, usually in the form of food, which it must sort and assimilate into a usable form. In the Old South, where living conditions were generally unhygienic, seemingly good food and drink often concealed pathogenic organisms ranging from viruses to worm larvae. Hands entering mouths sometimes contained the germs that others had cast off in feces, urine, or contaminated food. It is not surprising to find that dysentery, typhoid fever, food poisoning, and worm diseases afflicted large numbers of southerners, especially those living in the poorest, most crowded circumstances without sanitary facilities or time to prepare food properly. Slaves often fit into this category.

Though their major medical problems were communicable diseases, blacks, in the course of a day, also faced health challenges unrelated to contagion or parasites. Inadequate clothing and food, poor working conditions, harsh physical punishment, pregnancy, and certain bodily disorders also made slaves sick or uncomfortable, at times rendering them useless to their masters and burdensome to friends and family.

Though adequate clothing was important for slaves, it did not play as crucial a role in the maintenance of health as did housing. Of course clothing covered and protected the body from exposure to wind, sun, rain, snow, cold, and insects. It also limited the severity of many minor falls to cuts, scrapes, and bruises, and of some accidents to smaller areas of the body. But only a few disorders are spread by contact with infected clothing (smallpox, body lice, impetigo, typhus) or by contact of exposed skin with other objects (tetanus, yaws, hookworm, brucellosis).

Except in cases where slaves were truly underclothed in winter, possibly causing decreased resistance to respiratory ailments, the danger of contracting disease owing to inadequate or dirty wearing apparel was relatively small. Of articles of clothing which masters provided their bondsmen, shoes were probably the most important in terms of health and disease. Not only did

they provide warmth in the winter to feet and toes highly susceptible to frostbite, but they also protected slaves against hookworm
penetration, scrapes, scratches, burns, and some puncture
wounds which would otherwise have caused tetanus.

Did slaves receive a diet adequate to keep them healthy, laboring, and producing vigorous offspring? Opinions vary on this
question, for diets differed from individual to individual, and our
understanding of nutritional needs has changed often. Based on
today's dietary standards, the daily typical ration—one quart
of whole ground, dry, bolted cornmeal, prepared from white
corn (the South's favorite); and half a pound of cured, medium-
fat ham with no bone or skin—could not have provided enough
essential nutrients to sustain a moderately active twenty-two-
year-old male or female, much less a hardworking laborer or a
pregnant or lactating woman. Fieldhands fed this diet alone (with
water) would soon have become emaciated and sickly and would
have shown symptoms of several nutrient deficiencies. It is
highly unlikely that any slave could have survived very long on a
diet consisting solely of pork and cornmeal.

Most masters provided supplements to the basic hogmeat and
cornmeal, a practice most urgently recommended by agricultural
writers throughout the South. Vegetables topped the list of required additional foods. Planters could, if they planned ahead,
have a ready supply of at least one or two varieties throughout the
year. These writers also suggested adding to slave diets, when
available, fish, fresh meat, molasses, milk, and buttermilk.

Many agricultural authors and slavemasters indicated in their
writings that blacks often raised vegetables, poultry, and even
pigs on their own plots of land near the quarters. The assumption
was that extra food from this source would supplement rations
supplied by the master. Surprisingly, however, some of these
same writers pointed out that slaves usually sold what they raised
to the master or at the marketplace, thereby defeating the major
purpose of the plan. In all likelihood the slaves did not dispose of
all their produce, but saved some for future needs. The fact that
there were bondsmen who sold rather than kept food indicates
that, in addition to those who saved every available penny to
purchase their freedom, there were some slaves who received
sufficient nutrition from their regular rations, supplemented by
homegrown food, to feel quite comfortable relying on their masters for proper nutrition.

Kenneth Kiple and Virginia H. King, in their book, *Another Dimension to the Black Diaspora*, assess the adequacy of a slave diet consisting primarily of pork and cornmeal supplemented occasionally with other foods.[14] Using recently discovered knowledge of human nutritional needs and nutrient actions and interactions in the body, they conclude that slaves received sufficient amounts of carbohydrates and calories but generally lacked some essential amino acids, vitamin C, riboflavin, niacin, thiamine, vitamin D, calcium, and iron. And slave children, who all too often began life with nutritional deficiencies owing to their mothers' poor pre- and postnatal diets, also lacked sufficient magnesium, calories, and protein in their diets. Not surprisingly, Kiple and King assert, slave adults and children suffered higher morbidity and mortality than whites, because of lower resistance to infection and disrupted basic metabolic pathways. Among the most common resultant black health problems were respiratory and intestinal diseases, skin and eye afflictions, "teething," tetanus, "fits and seizures," and rickets. Diet, controlled to a large degree by the master, greatly affected slave health.

In addition to providing food, clothing, and housing, slave-owners also directed working conditions, punishments, and care of women and children. Though warm weather helped the crops grow, it did not always have the same effect on the black laborers who tended them. Planters recording the effects of excessive heat on their fieldhands made it clear that even though Negroes originated in tropical Africa, they were not immune to sunstroke. Hill Carter of Shirley Plantation, for instance, wrote during the 1825 wheat harvest, "Hotest day ever felt—men gave out & some fainted."[15]

Slaveowners also recognized the potential hazards of overexertion and exposure. Some indulged their slaves by easing their tasks; others found this impossible, especially at certain times of the year. Hill Carter and no doubt many others worked their blacks in intense heat when necessary to harvest a crop. Charles Friend of Prince George County, Virginia, on the other hand, had second thoughts when the ditching operation to which he had assigned many slaves evolved into a messy and unhealthy job: "We have the ditchers knee deep in water and mud. If I had known how bad it was I should not have put them to work at it but hired labor to do it."[16]

Farm accidents also took their toll on slaves. Falls, overturned

carts, runaway wagons, drownings, limbs caught in farm ma-
chines, kicks from animals, and cuts from axes or scythe blades
were the commonest types. Occasionally slaves suffered more
remarkable mishaps, as when a 260-pound Culpepper County
fieldhand jumped eight feet from a hay loft onto a pile of hay in
which a wooden pitchfork lay concealed. The point punctured
the man's scrotum and passed into his abdominal cavity, but
miraculously pierced no internal organs. Thanks to prompt surgical attention he was doing "light work" around the plantation
about three weeks later.

The whip was an integral part of slave life in the Old South.
Those bondsmen who had not experienced its sting firsthand
were acquainted with persons, usually friends or relatives, who
had. Whites held out the threat of whipping as a means of
maintaining order. When strong discipline was called for, so,
very often, was the lash. Even the mildest and most God-fearing
of masters permitted application of this painful instrument in
extreme cases, though some insisted that the slave's skin not be
cut or that there be a responsible witness present when punishment was administered.

From a medical point of view, whipping inflicted cruel and
often permanent injuries upon its victims. Laying stripes across
the bare back or buttocks caused indescribable pain, especially
when each stroke dug deeper into previously opened wounds.
During the interval between lashes, victims anticipated the next
in anguish, wishing for postponement or for all due speed,
though neither alternative brought relief. In addition to multiple
lacerations of the skin, whipping caused loss of blood, injury to
muscles (and internal organs, if the lash reached that deep), and
shock. (Rubbing salt into these wounds, often complained of as a
further mode of torture, actually cleansed the injured, exposed
tissues and helped ward off infection). An alternative, the paddle, jarred every part of the body by the violence of the blow, and
raised blisters from repeated strokes. In addition to the possibility
of death (uncommon), there was the danger that muscle damage
inflicted by these instruments might permanently incapacitate or
deform a slave. An Old Dominion slave who experienced the
sting of the paddle recalled years later: "You be jes' as raw as a
piece of beef an' hit eats you up. He loose you an' you go to house
no work done dat day."[17] No work done that day or, in many
cases, for several days. Ellick, a rebellious member of Charles

Friend's White Hill Plantation slave force, was slapped one day "for not being at the stable in time this morning," and "soundly whipped" the next day for running away and for not submitting to a flogging earlier that morning. He spent the next week recovering in bed, only to receive another whipping upon his return to work. This time he ran off for two days before settling back into the plantation routine.

The daily routines of slave women and children were often upset by health conditions peculiar to these groups.[18] Female slaves probably lost more time from work for menstrual pain, discomfort, and disorders than for any other cause. Planters rarely named illnesses in their diaries or daybooks, but the frequency and regularity with which women of childbearing age appeared on sick lists indicates that menstrual conditions were a leading complaint. A Fauquier County, Virginia, physician considered the loss of four to eight workdays per month not unusual for slave women. Among the menstrual maladies which afflicted bondswomen most often were amenorrhea (lack of menstrual flow), abnormal bleeding between cycles (sometimes caused by benign and malignant tumors), and abnormal discharges (resulting from such conditions as gonorrhea, tumors, and prolapsed uterus).

Some servants took advantage of their masters by complaining falsely of female indispositions. One unnamed Virginian who owned numerous slaves complained to Frederick Law Olmsted about such malingering women:

> The women on a plantation will hardly earn their salt, after they come to the breeding age; they don't come to the field, and you go to the quarters and ask the old nurse what's the matter, and she says, "oh she's not well, master; she's not fit to work, sir;" and what can you do? You have to take her word for it that something or other is the matter with her, and you dare not set her to work; and so she lays up till she feels like taking the air again, and plays the lady at your expense.[19]

Masters found it difficult to separate the sick from the falsely ill; as a result they often indulged their breeding-aged women rather than risk unknown complications. Thomas Jefferson, for instance, ordered his overseer not to coerce the female workers into exerting themselves, because "women are destroyed by exposure to wet at certain periodical indispositions to which nature has subjected them."[20]

If whites treated women's gynecological complaints with a certain delicacy, they regarded pregnancy as almost holy. In addition to receiving time off from work and avoiding whippings, expectant women in Virginia were protected from execution in capital offenses until after parturition.[21] At least three cases arose between the Revolution and the Civil War in which slave women obtained execution postponements for this reason, though all were presumably put to death following delivery.

Children, like women, were exposed to certain unique disorders which caused illness or death. Though their labor did not usually account for much, young slaves' serious illnesses did mean time lost from work for mothers watching over them at home or distractedly worrying about them while performing daily tasks. Owing to poorer living conditions and diet, slave children suffered more frequently from most illnesses than their white counterparts, especially diarrhea, neonatal tetanus, convulsions, "teething" (not really a disease, but considered a cause of sickness and death prior to the twentieth century), diphtheria, respiratory diseases, and whooping cough. And their mortality rate far exceeded that of whites, especially in infancy.[22]

Worms occurred frequently in black children. The poor sanitary conditions at many slave quarters were conducive to the development of these parasites in the soil. Children playing in the dirt inevitably picked up worm larvae as they put fingers in mouths. Failure to use, or lack of, privy facilities only served to spread worm diseases to other residents of the quarters and to visiting slaves, who then carried these parasites to their own plantation quarters.

Some black children had overt sickle cell disease (noted above) with irregular hemolytic crises, severe joint pains, chronic leg ulcers, and abdominal pains. The medical records relating to antebellum Virginia do not provide any clear descriptions of the disease, probably because its symptoms resemble so many other conditions and because the sickness was not known until 1910. These children were often the "sickly" ones, useless for field work or heavy household duties, expensive to maintain because of frequent infections, and, if female, often unable to bear children if they survived puberty. Their lot was a poor and painful one.

Slave children also developed diseases which no-one could identify or treat. John Walker's young servants appeared one day

with "head ach sweled faces & belly diseases"; Col. John Am-
bler's evinced swollen feet and faces, and bones cutting through
the skin; and Landon Carter's had "swelling of the almonds of
. . . [their] ears which burst inward and choaked . . . [them]."
The white tutor at Nomini Hall, Philip Vickers Fithian, noticed
that one slave mother on this Westmoreland County, Virginia,
estate had lost seven children successively, none of whom
had even reached the age of ten: "the Negroes all seem much
alarm'd. . . ."[23] Childhood was generally the least healthy
period of a slave's life.

In many ways, then, the state of southern blacks' health depended on the living and working conditions whites provided.
The self-conscious writings of southern whites and the frequent
negative comments of northern whites, in magazines, journals,
newspapers, letters, and public documents of the period, about
the manner in which slaves were maintained, affected Americans' concern over the subject and their awareness of that feature
of southern life as one setting the region apart from the rest of the
nation.

SLAVE MEDICAL CARE

Bondage placed slaves in a difficult position with regard to health
care. When taken ill, they had a limited range of choices. Masters
wished their slaves, legally articles of property, immediately to
inform the person in charge about any sickness, so the malady
might be arrested before it worsened. But some blacks felt reluctant to submit to the often harsh prescriptions and remedies of
eighteenth- and nineteenth-century white medical practice. They
preferred self-treatment or reliance on cures recommended by
friends and older relatives. They depended on Negro herb and
root doctors, or on influential conjurers among the local black
population. This desire to treat oneself, or at least to have the
freedom to choose one's mode of care, came into direct conflict
with the demands and wishes of white masters, whose trust in
black medicine was usually slight and whose main concern was
keeping the slave force intact.

To compound the problem, unannounced illnesses did not
entitle slaves to time off from work. To treat their own illnesses,
slaves had to conceal them or pass them off to the master as less

serious than they actually were. Masters who complained that
blacks tended to report sickness only after the disease had pro-
gressed to a serious stage often discovered that slaves had treated
illnesses at home first. The blacks' dilemma, then, was whether to
delay reporting illnesses and treat those diseases at home, risking
white reprisal; or to submit at once to the medicines of white
America and, in a sense, to surrender their bodies to their masters. The result was a dual system in which some slaves received
treatment from both whites and blacks.

When illness afflicted a slave, whites responded in several
ways. They almost always applied treatments derived from
European experience. Most often the master, mistress, or overseer first attempted to treat the ailment with home remedies. If
the patient failed to respond to these home ministrations, the
family physician was summoned. Some slaveowners distrusted
"regular" doctors and instead called "irregular" practitioners:
Thomsonians, homeopaths, hydropaths, empirics, eclectics, etc.
Masters who hired out their bondsmen to others for a period of
time arranged for medical care when signing the hiring bond.
Whatever the situation, white southerners often displayed concern for the health of blacks in bondage. The reasons were
threefold: slaves represented a financial investment which required protection; many masters felt a true humanitarian commitment toward their slaves; and whites realized that certain
illnesses could easily spread to their own families if not properly
treated and contained.

Those responsible for the care of sick slaves made home treatment the first step in the restorative process. They knew that
physicians, though possessed of great knowledge of the human
body and the effects of certain medicines on it, were severely
limited in the amount of good they could perform. Because
no-one understood the etiology of most diseases, no-one could
effectively cure them. Astute nonmedical observers could make
diagnoses as well as doctors, and could even treat patients just as
effectively. Physicians played their most crucial roles in executing
certain surgical procedures, assisting mothers at childbirth, and
instilling confidence in sick patients through an effective bedside
manner. At other times their excessive use of drugs, cups,
leeches, and lancets produced positive harm, depleting the body
of blood and nourishment and exhausting the already weakened
patient with frequent purges, vomits, sweats, and diuretics.

Laymen often merely followed the same course of treatment that they had observed their physicians using or that they had read about in one of the ubiquitous domestic medical guides. With a little experience, anyone could practice bloodletting or dosing. And a physician's services cost money, even when no treatment or cure resulted from the consultation.

Home care, of course, stemmed from people's natural instincts to relieve their own or their families' illnesses as quickly as possible. The unavailability of physicians, the inaccessibility of many farms to main highways, and the lack of good roads and speedy means of transportation reinforced such impulses among rural southerners. Even when a doctor was summoned, hours or even a day passed before his arrival, during which time something had to be done to ease the patient's discomfort. People learned to tolerate pain and to cope with death, but the mitigation of suffering was still a primary goal. To that end, most people stocked their cabinets with favorite remedies (or the ingredients required for their preparation) in order to be well equipped when relief was demanded. On large plantations with many slaves, this was a necessity, as Catharine C. Hopley, tutor at Forest Rill near Tappahannock, Essex County, Virginia, noted: "A capacious medicine chest is an inseparable part of a Southern establishment; and I have seen medicines enough dispensed to furnish good occupation for an assistant, when colds or epidemics have prevailed."[24] Some physicians made a living selling medicine chests and domestic health guides designed specifically for use on southern plantations. Self-sufficiency in medical care was desirable on farms and even in urban households, especially when financial considerations were important.

An additional feature of home medical care for slaves was the plantation hospital or infirmary. Existing primarily on the larger slaveholdings, its form varied from farm to farm. It was quicker and more efficient to place ailing slaves in one building, where care could be tendered with a minimum amount of wasted movement and where all medicines, special equipment, and other necessary stores could be maintained. Of course, infectious diseases could spread quite rapidly through a hospital, subjecting those with noncontagious conditions to further sickness.

Armed with drugs from the plantation or home dispensary, one person, usually white, had the responsibility of dosing and treating ill slaves. The master, mistress,[25] or overseer spent time each day with those claiming bodily disorders and soon developed a certain facility in handling both patients and drugs. The approach was empirical—if a particular medication or combination of drugs succeeded in arresting symptoms, it became the standard treatment for that malady in that household until a better one came along. Overseers and owners inscribed useful medical recipes into their diaries or journals and clipped suggestions from newspapers, almanacs, and books.

An overseer's or owner's incompetence or negligence was the slave's loss. New and inexperienced farm managers, unskilled in the treatment of illness, necessarily used blacks as guinea pigs for their "on-the-job" training. As a consequence of living on the wrong plantation at the wrong time, some slaves probably lost their lives or became invalids at the hands of new, poorly trained, or inhumane overseers or masters.

Despite many masters' policy of delaying a call to the physician until late in the course of a slave's disease, there were times when owners desperately wished for the doctor's presence. More practitioners should have retained in their files the numerous hastily scrawled notes from frantic slaveowners begging for medical assistance, or kept a record of each verbal summons to a sick slave at a distant farm or village household. For physicians did play important roles, both physiological and psychological, in the treatment of illness. Dr. Charles Brown of Charlottesville, Virginia, for instance had a thriving country practice during the early nineteenth century. He handled many types of problems: James Old wanted him to determine whether his slave woman, then "in a strange way," was pregnant or not; Bezaleel Brown needed his opinion "if I must bleed her [Jane, who had a pain in her side and suppression of urine] either large or small in quantity"; and Jemima Fretwell wished Brown to "cutt of[f] the arm" of a four-month-old slave which had been "so very badly burnt" that "the [elbow] joint appears like it will drap of[f]."[26] Sometimes physicians made daily visits to dress slaves' wounds or to keep track of household epidemics. In emergencies some owners panicked and fretted away many hours after learning of their physician's temporary absence.

Between the remedies of the household and the standard treatments of the physicians stood "irregular" medicine. The impact of alternative movements on the medical care of blacks in at least one southern state, Virginia, was greater than historians have recognized. Most slaveowners there either treated with conventional medicines or called in regular doctors, rejecting the new cults as quackery; but a sizable minority, difficult to estimate, became enthusiastic proponents of the system known as Thomsonianism. This self-help botanic medicine movement, with followers in areas of heavy slave concentrations (64 percent of the Tidewater counties and 66 percent of the Piedmont counties during the 1830s and 1840s), appealed to masters who were fed up with the ineffective and expensive treatments of their regular physicians. One Tidewater resident, after experienced Norfolk physicians had unsuccessfully managed a household scarlet fever outbreak, turned to Thomsonianism; all twenty cases, the happy slaveowner reported to the editors of a Thomsonian journal, had been cured. Another man, in Goochland County, stated that a local Thomsonian practitioner had cured his slave of a disease which one of the most respected regular physicians of the area had found intractable to the usual blister and salivation treatments. And a Prince Edward County Thomsonian doctor claimed to have cured a ten-year-old slave who had been suffering from rabies (a misdiagnosis, no doubt). With adherents to the sect so widely diffused throughout the state, the services or success stories of practitioners no doubt reached at least a portion of the slaveholding class and influenced its thinking. [27]

Beyond the master's and the overseer's eyes, back in the slaves' cabins, some blacks took medical matters into their own hands. When under surveillance of whites, slaves usually (but not always) accepted their treatments. Some even administered them in the name of the master. But others developed or retained from an ancient African heritage their own brand of care, complete with special remedies, medical practitioners, and rituals. The result was a dual system of health care, the two parts of which often conflicted with each other.

Masters did not appreciate slaves overusing the plantation infirmary, medicines, or family doctor, but for several reasons they preferred this to black self-care. Their quarrel with slaves was the same as the physicians' with the masters: they waited too long before seeking medical assistance and often misdiagnosed illnesses. Owners permitted blacks a small amount of freedom in treating minor ailments at home, but lost their patience when sickness got out of hand. James L. Hubard, in charge of his father's lands during the latter's vacation at Alleghany Springs,

Virginia, reported that Daphny had treated her own son with vermifuges (worm medicines) for several days before realizing that the boy was suffering not from worms but from dysentery. Hubard quickly altered the medication and summoned a doctor, blaming the entire affair on "the stupidity of Daphny." An enraged Landon Carter found a suckling child with measles at the slave quarters. "The mother," he wrote in his diary, "let nobody know of it until it was almost dead."[28]

Whites also accused slaves of negligence or incompetence in the care of their fellow blacks. Dr. G. Lane Corbin of Warwick County, Virginia, for instance, promoted slaves' use of collodion, a syrupy dressing, because it required so little attention, once applied: "This I consider of moment in regard to our slave population, whose negligence and inattention to such matters [as the proper dressing of wounds] must have attracted the notice of the most superficial observer."[29] Negroes frequently were charged with irresponsibility, ignorance, slovenliness, and indifference in the management of other blacks' illnesses. "They will never do right, left to themselves," declared one Franklin County planter.[30]

Furthermore, some whites argued, slaves did not even care for their own personal health properly. Recovery was retarded and even reversed, Dr. W.S. Morton of Cumberland County remarked, "by their [the slaves'] own stupid perversity in refusing confinement to bed, and to follow other important directions when in a very dangerous condition."[31] Masters and physicians often confirmed this but were powerless to combat it. It was difficult for whites, unless they were present at all times, to force ailing blacks to take medicines or to remain constantly in bed. A most spectacular instance of death following defiance of medical orders occurred in Portsmouth when a black male patient of Dr. John W. Trugien, confined to bed with a stab wound of the heart, sustained a massive effusion of blood from that organ upon exerting himself by rising from his pallet.[32]

To offset the failures and harshness of white remedies or the negligence of masters, or perhaps to exert some control over their lives, some slaves treated their own diseases and disorders or turned to other trusted blacks for medical assistance, with or without the master's knowledge.[33] Black home remedies circulated secretly through the slave quarters and were passed down privately from generation to generation. Most of these cures were derived from local plants, though some medicines contained ingredients that had magical value only. Occasionally whites would learn of a particularly effective medicine and adopt it, as when Dr. Richard S. Cauthorn announced in the *Monthly Stethoscope* (1857) that an old folk remedy (milkweed or silk weed, *Asclepias syriaca* in the United States Dispensatory) which had been used for years by blacks in the counties north of Richmond worked almost as well as quinine for agues and fevers.[34] Otherwise most whites simply ignored or tolerated the black medical world until something occurred to bring their attention to it— either a great medical discovery or a slave death caused by abuse.

Because blacks practiced medicine in virtually every portion of the Old Dominion and because their methods were based partially on magic, problems occasionally arose. The main source of trouble was usually not the misuse of home remedies, but the "prescriptions" and activities of so-called "conjure doctors," whose system existed in the South only because slaves brought it with them from Africa and the West Indies. These men and women used trickery, violence, persuasion and medical proficiency to gain their reputations among local black communities. They were viewed as healers of illness that white doctors could not touch with their medicines, and as perpetrators of sicknesses on any person they designated—all through "spells."

Superstition was a powerful force within the slave community, and a difficult one for white non-adherents to understand or overcome. For instance, the older brother of a slave patient of Dr. A.D. Galt of Williamsburg observed to the doctor that his medicines were useless because Gabriel "had been tricked" and "must have a Negro Doctor" to reverse the progress of the illness. Galt soon claimed to have cured the man, though he did admit that Gabriel suffered frequent relapses, "probably from intemperance in drink."[35] In another case, a slave woman took sick and eventually died on a plantation near Petersburg from what her fellow bondsmen believed were the effects of a conjurer. Some slaves speculated that the young man whom she had refused to marry "poisoned or tricked" her, though the overseer attributed her death to consumption.[36] Virginia Hayes Shepherd, a former slave interviewed in 1939 at 83, described an incident to illustrate how superstitious her stepfather had been: "He believed he had a bunch something like boils. White doctor bathed it. After a few days it burst and live things came out of the boil and crawled on the floor. He thought he was conjured. He said an enemy of his put something on the horse's back and he rode it and got it on his buttocks and broke him out."[37]

Whites did permit blacks to fulfill certain medical functions. Some planters assigned "trusted" slaves to the task of rendering medical assistance to all ailing blacks on the farm. In most cases, these people simply dispensed white remedies and performed venesection and cupping as learned from the master. Though not complete black self-care, this activity did represent a transitional stage in which slaves had the opportunity to apply some of their own knowledge of herbs and so on, gained from elders, in addition to white remedies. These nurses, predominantly women, usually won the respect of both blacks and whites for their curative skills. "Uncle" Bacchus White, an eighty-nine-year-old former slave interviewed in Fredericksburg in 1939, attested: "Aunt Judy uster to tend us when we uns were sic' and anything Aunt Judy couldn't do 'hit won't worth doin.'"[38] A white lady writing at about the same time provided a similarly romantic view of the black plantation nurse: "One of the house-servants, Amy Green—'Aunt Amy' we children called her—was a skilled nurse. My father kept a store of medicines, his scales, etc., so with Aunt Amy's poultices of horseradish and plattain-leaves and her various cuppings and plasters the ailments of the hundred negroes were well taken in hand."[39] Given such high testimony and devotion from plantation folk, one could hardly dispute the novelist Louise Clarke Pyrnelle's depiction of Aunt Nancy, a fictional antebellum household nurse who claimed, while dosing several young slaves, "Ef'n hit want fur dat furmifuge [vermifuge—worm medicine], den Marster wouldn't hab all dem niggers w'at yer see hyear."[40]

To Negro women often fell another task as well: prenatal and obstetrical care of whites and blacks, especially in rural areas.[41] At least one slave on most large Virginia plantations learned and practiced the art of midwifery, not only at home but throughout the neighborhood. Masters preferred to employ these skilled accouchers in uncomplicated cases rather than pay the relatively high fees of trained physicians. Doctors, remarked one member of the medical profession, attended at less than half of all births in the state. He estimated that nine-tenths (another physician said five-sixths) of all deliveries among the black population were conducted by midwives, most of whom were also black. He further asserted that midwives attended half the white women. Physicians often saw obstetrical cases only when problems arose. As a result of this demand for competent nonprofessional obstetrical services, Negro midwives flourished in the countryside.

Blacks did play a significant role in the health care system of the South. They assisted whites and blacks in delivering children, letting blood, pulling teeth, administering medicines, and nursing the sick. The techniques and drugs they used were overtly derived from white medical practices. But unknown to masters, overseers, health officers, or physicians, blacks also resorted to their own treatments, derived from their own heritage and experience. Occasionally the white and black medical worlds merged or openly clashed, but usually they remained silently separate.

The health and medical needs of slaves added another important dimension that distinguished the antebellum South from the rest of the nation. Whites were legally required to see to the proper medical care of, by 1860, some four million enslaved people who, these same whites believed (sometimes accurately, sometimes not, we now know), differed physically and medically from themselves. Whites focused on these differences both to understand the best treatments of "black diseases" and to justify slavery to the rest of the nation and world. Furthermore, the living and working conditions of slaves, dictated in the main by whites and by the South's agricultural economy, directly affected these blacks' health. Southern blacks received medical care from white masters, mistresses, overseers, and several sorts of physicians, but also used various healing practices on each other, some of which found their way into common usage. In these ways, slave medical affairs contributed to the region's distinctiveness.

NOTES

N.B. This essay is extracted in large part from Todd L. Savitt, *Medicine and Slavery: The Diseases and Health Care of Blacks in Antebellum Virginia* (Urbana: Univ. of Illinois Press, 1978), 1–184. The author acknowledges the very helpful suggestions of James Breeden, Paul Escott, David Goldfield, Kenneth Kiple, Ronald Numbers, and James Harvey Young.

A slightly different version of this paper was prepared for publication in Ronald L. Numbers and Todd L. Savitt, eds., *Science and Medicine in the Old South* (Baton Rouge: Louisiana State Univ. Press, forthcoming), and is reprinted here with the editors' permission.

1. Except in the first section, where a general overview of black-related diseases is presented, the focus is on Virginia, from the Revolution to the Civil War. Health conditions in the Old Dominion at that time were in many respects typical of those prevailing throughout the antebellum South. Residents suffered from malaria, parasitic worm diseases, and dysentery just as Mississippians and Georgians did. Yellow fever struck Virginia's major ports, though not so severely or so frequently as it did Charleston, Mobile, or New Orleans. Virginia's position on the northern fringe of the slave South perhaps lessened the intensity and duration of warm-weather diseases, but not enough to render its diseases significantly different from those in the lower South.

During the timespan under consideration, the black population and the health picture in Virginia were relatively stable. The slave trade had ended, there was little black immigration into the state, and tropical diseases brought from Africa and unable to survive in the new environment had all but disappeared.

2. Editorial, *The Monthly Stethoscope and Medical Reporter* 1 (1856), 162–63.

3. These and other diseases and conditions are discussed in an important book on black medical differences, Kenneth Kiple and Virginia H. King, *Another Dimension to the Black Diaspora: Diet, Disease and Racism* (Cambridge, England: Cambridge Univ. Press, 1981). On the life and thought of one southern medical thinker, see Reginald Horsman, *Josiah Nott of Mobile: Southerner, Physician, and Racial Theorist* (Baton Rouge: Louisiana State Univ. Press, 1987).

4. For a discussion of the southern disease environment from colonial times to the present, see Albert Cowdrey, *This Land, This South: An Environmental History* (Lexington: Univ. of Kentucky Press, 1983).

5. Kiple and King, *Another Dimension*, emphasizes dietary considerations to explain many slave health problems.

6. John H. Van Evrie, *Negroes and Negro "Slavery"* (New York: Van Evrie, Horton and Co., 1861), 25.

7. Van Evrie, *Negroes and Negro "Slavery,"* 251, 256.

8. See Jo Ann Carrigan's essay in this volume for examples of the political use some white southerners made of the relative immunity of blacks to yellow fever and of blacks' ability to labor in humid heat.

9. Recent historical discussions of SIDS include Kiple and King, *Another Dimension*, 107–110, and Michael P. Johnson, "Smothered Slave Infants: Were Slave Mothers at Fault?", *Journal of Southern History* 47 (1981):493–520.

10. E.M. Pendleton, "On the Susceptibility of the Caucasian and African Races to the Different Classes of Disease," *Southern Medical Reports* 1 (1849):336–37.

11. Editorial, "The Medical Society of Virginia," *Virginia Medical and Surgical Journal* 4 (1855):256–58.

12. Richard Allen Williams, ed., *Textbook of Black-Related Diseases* (New York: McGraw-Hill, 1975). On the matter of southern medical nationalism, see James O. Breeden, "States-Rights Medicine in the Old South," *Bulletin of the New York Academy of Medicine* 52 (1976):348–72; John Duffy, "Medical Practice in the Antebellum South," *Journal of Southern History* 25 (1959):53–72; John Harley Warner, "The Idea of Southern Medical Distinctiveness: Medical Knowledge and Practice in the Old South," in *Science and Medicine in the Old South* ed. Numbers and Savitt; John Harley Warner, "A Southern Medical Reform: The Meaning of the Antebellum Argument for Southern Medical Education," *Bulletin of the History of Medicine* 57 (1983):364–81.

13. For examples of typical planters' writings on the management of slaves, see James O. Breeden, ed., *Advice Among Masters: The Ideal in Slave Management in the Old South* (Westport, Conn.: Greenwood, 1980).

14. Kiple and King, *Another Dimension*. See also Robert A. Margo and Richard H. Steckel, "The Heights of American Slaves: New Evidence on Slave Nutrition and Health," *Social Science History* 6 (1982):516–38; Steckel, "A Peculiar Population: The Nutrition, Health, and Mortality of American Slaves from Childhood to Maturity," *Journal of Economic History* 46 (1986):721–41.

15. Shirley on the James Farm Journals, 23 June 1825, Library of Congress Manuscript Division.

16. Quoted in Wyndham B. Blanton, *Medicine in Virginia in the Eighteenth Century* (Richmond: Garrett and Massie, 1931), 161 (Blanton cites no source).

17. Interview of William Lee, n.d., WPA Folklore File, Manuscript Room, Alderman Library, Univ. of Virginia.

18. On slave women's and children's health conditions, see also Kiple and King, *Another Dimension*; Richard H. Steckel, "A Dreadful Childhood: The Excess Mortality of American Slaves," *Social Science History* 10 (1986):427–65; J. Campbell, "Work, Pregnancy, and Infant Mortality Among Southern Slaves," *Journal of Interdisciplinary History* 14 (1984):793–812; Deborah Gray White, *Ar'n't I A Woman?: Female Slaves in the Plantation South* (New York: Norton, 1985), 79–87, 124–126.

19. Frederick Law Olmsted, *A Journey in the Seaboard Slave States, with Remarks on Their Economy* (New York: Mason Brothers, 1856), 190.

20. Thomas Jefferson to Joel Yancey, 17 Jan. 1819, reproduced in *Thomas Jefferson's Farm Book*, ed. Edwin M. Betts, (Princeton, N.J.: Princeton Univ. Press, 1953), 43.

21. There were, of course, exceptions to these statements. See, e.g., Johnson, "Smothered Slave Infants," 511–20.

22. Steckel, "A Dreadful Childhood," 427–29.

23. John Walker Diary, 23 Apr. 1853, Southern Historical Collection, Univ. of North Carolina at Chapel Hill; Jack P. Greene, ed., *The Diary of Colonel Landon Carter of Sabine Hall, 1752–1778* (Charlottesville: Univ. Press of Virginia, 1965), I:377 (31 Mar. 1770); Hunter Dickinson Farish, ed., *Journal and Letters of Philip Vickers Fithian, 1773–1774: A Plantation Tutor of the Old Dominion* (Williamsburg, Va.: Colonial Williamsburg, 1957), 182.

24. Catharine C. Hopley, *Life in the South: From the Commencement of the War* (London, England: Chapman and Hall, 1863), I:103.

25. On the healing roles of white women on the plantation, see Catherine Clinton, *The Plantation Mistress: Woman's World in the Old South* (New York: Pantheon, 1982), 28, 43, 187.

26. For more examples of such notes, see Todd L. Savitt, ed., "Patient Letters to an Early Nineteenth Century Virginia Physician," *Journal of the Florida Medical Association* 69 (1982):688–94.

27. The best treatment of Thomsonianism in a southern state is James O. Breeden, "Thomsonianism in Virginia," *Virginia Magazine of History and Biography* 82 (1974):150–80.

28. James L. Hubard to Robert T. Hubard, 4 Aug. 1857, Robert T. Hubard Papers, Manuscript Room, Alderman Library, Univ. of Virginia; Greene, ed., *Carter Diary*, II:812 (20 May 1774).

29. G. Lane Corbin, "Collodion on Stumps of Amputated Limbs," *The Stethoscope and Virginia Medical Gazette* 1 (1851):489.

30. L.G. Cabell to Bowker Preston, 8 Oct. 1834, John Hook Collection, Manuscript Room, Alderman Library, Univ. of Virginia.

31. W.S. Morton, "Causes of Mortality Amongst Negroes," *The Monthly Stethoscope and Medical Reporter* 1 (1856):290.

32. John W.H. Trugien, "A Case of Wound of the Left Ventricle of the Heart.—Patient Survived Five Days;—with Remarks," *American Journal of the Medical Sciences*, N.S., 20 (1850):99–102.

33. See, for more information and references, Lawrence W. Levine, *Black Culture and Black Consciousness: Afro-American Folk Thought from Slavery to Freedom* (New York: Oxford Univ. Press, 1977), 55–80; Elliott J. Gorn, "Folk Beliefs in the Slave Community," in *Science and Medicine in the Old South*, ed. Numbers and Savitt.

34. Richard S. Cauthorn, "A New Anti-Periodic and a Substitute for Quinia," *The Monthly Stethoscope and Medical Reporter* 2 (1857):7–14.

35. A.D. Galt, *Practical Medicine: Illustrated by Cases of the Most Important Diseases*, ed. John M. Galt (Philadelphia: Barrington and Haswell, 1843), 295–96.

36. [William McKean to James Dunlap], 17 July 1810, Roslin Plantation Records, Virginia State Library.

37. Interview of Virginia Hayes Shepherd, 1939, WPA Folklore File, Manuscript Room, Alderman Library, Univ. of Virginia.

38. Interview of Uncle Bacchus White, 1939, WPA Folklore File, Manuscript Room, Alderman Library, Univ. of Virginia.

39. White Hill Plantation Books, I:8, Southern Historical Collection, Univ. of North Carolina at Chapel Hill. See also White, *Arn't' I A Woman?*, 125.

40. Louise Clark Pyrnelle, *Diddie, Dumps, and Tot; or Plantation Child-Life* (New York: Harper, 1882), quoted in Blanton, *Medicine in Virginia in the Eighteenth Century*, 49.

41. See also White, *Ar'n't I A Woman?*, 111–24. Free black women also practiced midwifery in parts of the Old South. See, for example, Suzanne Lebsock, *The Free Women of Petersburg: Status and Culture in a Southern Town, 1784–1860* (New York: Norton, 1984).

Patent Medicines:
An Element in Southern Distinctiveness?

.

JAMES HARVEY YOUNG

Some years after the Civil War had ended, a northern nostrum manufacturer promoted a deafness cure with a testimonial from Henry Farrar. His hearing had so declined, Farrar lamented, that he could no longer hear the "Beloved Bugle" with which he once had led Union troops on many a glorious assault. This distressed him greatly. Learning of the antideafness remedy, he had tried it, with amazing success. His hearing had been completely restored, so he sent the medicine maker not only a letter of gratitude but also a photograph. Farrar's bearded portrait, replete with G.A.R. insignia, medals, and Union army hat, appeared in newspapers throughout the northern states.[1]

But what of the South? Did not aging men grow deaf there also? Indeed they did. And from the advertising columns of the southern press, the same Henry Farrar spoke forth. Here he was not a "Civil War veteran" but a "Veteran Musician." His "Beloved Bugle" had become a "Beloved Cornet," which, rather than leading "troops to . . . victory," had merely "helped in his career." Henry had nonetheless grown deaf, been cured, and gratefully provided a portrait to gaze out at ex-Confederates, still bearded but deprived of hat, medals, and insignia.

Farrar's bifurcated fate presents an example of regional distinctiveness respecting patent medicines. But is this anything but an isolated and freakish incident arising from an advertiser's desire to extract profit by waving the bloody shirt in one section and concealing it in another? Are there matters more substantial involving nostrums that distinguish between North and South? This query warrants exploration.

Let us, therefore, examine this matter from two perspectives. First we look at the *taking* of patent medicines in the South, to see whether or not patterns of usage differed from those in the North, so that there may have been distinctiveness with respect to therapy. Second, let us study the *making* of patent medicines in the South, to observe whether manufacturing and marketing of nostrums differed there from northern practices, so that there may have been distinctiveness with respect to economics. Before turning to self-administered therapy through proprietary remedies, however, it may be useful to set the stage by considering therapy as administered by physicians.

THERAPY ADMINISTERED BY PHYSICIANS

Before the germ theory came to be established and generally accepted at the close of the nineteenth century, explanations of disease were conjectural, and therapies flowed largely from theory. Yet, despite conflicting interpretations bombastically debated by physicians, as, for example, between those espousing contagion and those favoring miasmas as the causes of sickness, virtually all physicians, and their patients too, shared a set of convictions about illness and treatment, the product of a long tradition extending back to the rationalistic speculations of classical antiquity.[2]

The human body, this traditional doctrine held, sailed like a frail bark upon an uncertain sea amidst stormy winds, always at risk. Its state of health at any given moment depended on the degree of equilibrium maintained among a host of forces, some relating to constitutional endowment, some to personal conduct and misconduct, others linked to environment—such factors as air, food, water, climate, topography, working conditions.

To maintain good health, a person required a balanced vital economy, a proper income of breath and nourishment, a proper outgo of energy expenditure and wastes. Each individual strove to lead the mode of life most conducive to equilibrium, but too often revealed a balance disturbed. Then, often after self-treatment, the patient sought a physician to play his customary role. The doctor might modify intake by dietary counsel, but

An example of Confederate cultural nationalism in the patent medicine field. Van Schaack & Grierson drugstore advertisement. From the *Charleston Daily Courier*, 4 January 1862.

regulating excretions was deemed his essential task, striving to alter the course of the ailment and to restore the body's balance and hence its health by promoting perspiration, urination, and defecation, and by removing blood. Such procedures provided both physician and patient with visible evidence that something significant was happening. When balance had been righted, tonics built up the patient's strength.

Since each individual possessed a constitution different from that of every other person, and also encountered varying environmental circumstances through time, each patient required a different combination of prescribed therapies. Indeed, prescription files reveal, the physician tended to reassess the condition of a patient frequently, changing prescriptions, often radically, day by day as circumstances seemed to warrant.[3] These events, taking place with solemn ceremony, usually in the home, directed by a concerned and confident physician, provided reassurance to the patient and his family. More often than not, the therapy seemed to prove its efficacy, sustaining faith in the system, because the patient survived.

Drugs, then, were not considered specifics to treat particular disease entities, but rather tools to achieve calculated physiological effects. In treatises on the *materia medica*, the classification of drugs testifies to this perspective, for they were arranged in such categories as astringents, cathartics, emetics, diaphoretics, sedatives, stimulants.[4]

During the first half of the nineteenth century, under these prevailing concepts drugging, as prescribed by regular physicians, reached "heroic" levels. Led by Dr. Benjamin Rush of Philadelphia, a signer of the Declaration of Independence and the most respected medical professor in the new nation, physicians resorted to massive purging and extensive bloodletting in their efforts to conquer disease.[5]

"How could a people," queried Dr. Oliver Wendell Holmes, a later critic of heroic medicine, "which has a revolution once in four years, which has contrived the Bowie-knife and the revolver, . . . which insists on sending out yachts and horses and boys to out-sail, out-run, out-fight . . . all the rest of creation; how could such a people be content with any but 'heroic' practice? What wonder that the stars and stripes wave over doses of ninety grains of sulphate of quinine, and that the American eagle screams with delight to see three drachms of calomel given at a single mouthful."[6]

Rush's heroic therapy spread throughout the union, North and South, persisting stubbornly despite critics who called for giving Nature a larger role in therapy. Holmes and other northern opponents of excessive bleeding and purging brought their moderate views back to American shores from studying clinical medicine in Parisian hospitals, where the numerical method of Pierre Louis was revealing the inefficacy of heroic regimens. The same lessons of mildness influenced French Creole medical practice in New Orleans. Criticism of the heavy-dosing regulars also came from a range of sectarian practitioners—Thomsonians, hydropaths, and homeopaths—who appealed to the populace with therapeutic regimens less severe. Some among the orthodox, in order to keep patients, reduced their dosages, but many, confronted with the severe sectarian challenge, reacted by insisting even more defiantly upon the rightness of their heroic cause.[7]

Heroic or mild as to dosage levels, contagionist or anticontagionist as to etiological persuasion, American physicians North and South relied on essentially the same therapeutic arsenal. During the late colonial period, John Duffy sums up, "drastic therapy" reigned in both sections. In the antebellum years, southern physicians (and planters, too), while recognizing that blacks were more susceptible than whites to some diseases and less so to others, used the same drugs that were standard in the North—calomel, quinine, opium, ipecac, castor oil, jalap, camphor—plus heavy bleeding, even though it was generally recognized that slaves could not stand well the loss of much blood. In the main, physicians prescribed the same drugs for the planter and his family as for slaves. John C. Gunn, a Knoxville physician, published in 1830 an immensely popular volume on *Domestic Medicine*. While Gunn described therapeutic uses of folk botanicals, he also relied substantially on the heroic stalwarts, mercury, opium, and ipecac, and referred to Rush frequently and admiringly as his most respected authority. Inventories of physicians' estates, drugstore bills, plantation account books—all repeat the same list of drugs. In the Confederacy during the Civil War, an almost frantic search for substitute drugs went on in southern fields and forests, with Surgeon General Samuel Preston Moore leading the way. Native medicines, wrote a hospital orderly, "sit like a nightmare upon the brain of the

surgeon-general." Despite this crusade, prompted by both a fear
of drug shortages and Confederate cultural nationalism, the
gray-clad troops relied heavily on calomel, opium, quinine, castor oil, and alum.[8]

Thus, over the decades, throughout the nation, North and
South, physicians depended to a great extent upon the same
armamentarium. Their wielding of these therapeutic weapons
against disease, however, might vary considerably from patient
to patient, because each patient's illness depended on his own
unique personal and environmental circumstances. And from
region to region, environments were bound to differ. The ancient
concept that the characteristic attributes of location modified
disease and changed the requirements for treatment had been
given a distinctive American form by the nationalism of the
Revolutionary generation, with its urge to throw off colonial
dependence on the former mother country and its outraged pride
sparked by European criticism of American culture. Benjamin
Rush, his associates, and his students were leading exponents of
the medical differences between America and Europe, insisting
that the American environment made diseases more energetic
than they were across the Atlantic and therefore demanding
more forceful, more heroic treatment.[9]

The same kind of gulf that separated America from Europe,
Rush and his followers held and taught in their medical school
lectures, also, if to a lesser degree, divided regions in America.
Many southern physicians trained in the North accepted as a
matter of course the medical distinctiveness of the South, recognizing that much of what they had been taught would be irrele-
vant to practice below the Mason-Dixon line. Southern climate,
miasmatic exhalations, diet, dress, work habits, class structure,
racial composition—all would, they believed, change disease
symptoms and modify requisite therapy. Young physicians entering the South, observed a medical professor in Louisiana, were
"utter strangers to the diseases of the climate."[10]

As sectional tensions increased in the years preceding secession and war, southern medical distinctiveness as a concept itself
changed, intensifying, hardening, generating major institutional
imperatives. The differences in this new thrust, John Harley
Warner observes, came "not in its content, or assumptions about
medical knowledge and practice, but in the emotion, the force,
the stridency that informed the way it was argued . . . , the tenor

of the rhetoric" which "evoked the crusading sense of a socio-political movement." A northern critic of the trend dubbed it "states-rights medicine."[11]

Both broad and narrow factors prodded the southern doctors on. They shared with other southerners an awareness of the region's differences from the North—the South's agrarian econ-omy, slavery, colonial economic status, shrinking political power, and sensitivity to expanding northern criticism of its backwardness and immorality. Thoughtful southern physicians also chafed over problems within their own region: the lack of adequate training and skill of the majority of doctors, the low regard in which the public held the profession, the rising tide of sectarianism threatening the incomes of doctors already barely able to survive.[12]

Articulate proponents of states-rights medicine defended slav-ery as the only adequate protection for blacks, who, the physi-cians' researches demonstrated to their own satisfaction, were inferior human beings. Further, stressing the indispensability of southern medical education to equip physicians practicing under distinctive southern conditions, champions of states-rights med-icine sought to establish schools and create journals that would improve southern practice and dispel the anxieties arising from the low status of the profession.[13]

To propel the gospel of southern medical distinctiveness for-ward, one of its leading exponents, Samuel A. Cartwright, who, after studying with Rush, practiced in Natchez and then in New Orleans, created a myth. The art of medicine, he asserted, had originated with Hippocrates in the southern climate of Greece, and had been advanced in Rome, only to be dismembered by barbarian invaders from the north, who carried home with them the looted remnants. In the climate of the north, these elements had been revamped to meet distinctive local needs. The medicine from chilly Edinburgh, transplanted to Philadelphia, did not suit southerly climes. As an Alabama physician phrased it, northern medicine was "too frigid for the ardent temperature and more relaxed system of our 'Sunny South.' " Cartwright counseled: "We must . . . begin *de novo*, or go back to Hippocrates and to the ancient southern writers . . . in order to profit by experience in southern diseases. . . ." Beginning anew meant creating an American southern medicine grounded in bedside observation. The myth, Warner suggests, was a way of making the confused and demoralized medical situation meaningful in order that purposeful action could be launched. [14]

States-rights medicine occasionally exhibited distinctive therapy. Southern diseases, Cartwright held, required more stimulating and fiery drugs than did northern ailments, like lobelia and cayenne pepper. Because, it was believed, a malarial influence, a dangerous miasma, underlay the character of diseases in the South, quinine was prescribed in greater quantities. Dosage schedules of other standard drugs also differed between the regions during the heyday of states-rights medicine, as they long had done under prevailing theory. Venesection was probably practiced on a smaller proportion of patients in the South than in the North. [15]

The more important generalization, however, is that, despite the sound and fury of states-rights rhetoric, the same basic list of medications stocked drugstore shelves and doctors' saddlebags in both South and North. Southern distinctiveness, even during the years when it was proclaimed most loudly, did not mean a major difference between the two sections in the therapeutic arsenal of regular physicians.

Indeed, although a tendency toward moderation of dosage continued after the Civil War, heroic practice had not yet come to an end in postbellum days, either North or South. [16]

TAKING PATENT MEDICINES

If physician therapy did not display as glaring a difference between the sections in practice as it did in rhetoric, what about self-therapy with proprietary medicines? In the *taking* of patent medicines, did self-dosers in the South reveal a pattern of usage distinguishing them from those who treated themselves with nostrums in the North?

The extent and nature of disease is a factor relevant to confronting this question. The disease situation in the Old South, Richard H. Shryock concluded, was on the whole "more serious" than in the Old North. The South was largely rural and tardier than the North in draining swamps; hence malaria retreated southward. Yellow fever, which once threatened northern cities, also became in time only a southern disease. The longer, hotter summers fostered insect life, hastened food spoilage, complicated sanita-

tion, encouraged barefootedness. Half the South's children contracted hookworm. Life insurance companies charged a premium
larger by one percent on southern than on northern risks.[17]

During the antebellum period, slaveowners deemed nostrums
worthy of use in treating the illnesses of slaves. As early as 1802,
the makers of Doctor Lee's Patent New-London Pills aimed at this
market, advertising: "Owners of plantations will find . . . [these
Pills] the most Useful Domestic Medicine of any extant." Later
the proprietor of the northern-made Potter's Vegetable Catholi-
con, addressing "Southern Planters," reported that the medicine
had "saved many a valuable slave" and was especially effective
for diseases common to blacks. In the 1820s, the manager of four
plantations on the Georgia Sea Islands treated both the slaves
under his charge and himself with Swaim's Celebrated Panacea,
made in Philadelphia. Three decades later *DeBow's Review* carried a long advertisement for this same nostrum, addressed "To
Planters of the South & West." The Panacea, the text boasted,
had cured cases of scrofula in which "the patients had been
almost eaten up" by that disease. Planters should regard that
news as welcome, because "Negroes who are confined in large
numbers on plantations in hot climates, are peculiarly liable to
such forms of disease, arising from a vitiated state of the blood
and want of cleanliness and a variety of food. These diseases so
frequently set regular practice at defiance, and render their miserable victims both useless and expensive to their masters, that
planters would study their own interest as well as that of humanity, by keeping always a supply of Swaim's Panacea, which
appears to be the only thing which can be relied on in such
cases."[18]

The Civil War worsened health conditions. Confederate veter-
ans carried aches and pains homes with them, and on the home
front deprivations undermined constitutions. Poverty was widespread among both blacks and whites. The recent debate over
slave diets has been resolved, by Kenneth and Virginia Kiple and
by Richard H. Steckel, on the gloomy side.[19] Nutritional in-
adequacies, augmented by genetic factors, led to serious malnu-
trition, frequent illness, and elevated mortality, especially among
children. During Reconstruction, diets did not improve markedly
for either blacks or whites. In time, indeed, nutritional levels
declined—for rural tenant and sharecropper families, who abandoned gardens as they grew cotton ever closer to their cabin

walls; for mill workers, subsisting mainly on food bought at the company store; and for children, the elderly, the insane, and prisoners, dwelling in institutions with stringent budgets.[20] The traditional "white diet" (the three Ms of the frontier—meat, meal, and molasses), which the South had maintained while the North improved nutritional levels beginning in the 1840s, lacked many food factors necessary for good health. Toward the end of the nineteenth century, conditions worsened, as new mill procedures eliminated the nutrient-bearing husks and germs from wheat flour and cornmeal. The ledgers of countless country stores, which Thomas D. Clark examined in retrospect, revealed the "monotonous and harmful" diet of rural southerners. The ledgers of mill village stores presented the same dismal picture when examined during the pellagra "epidemic." A whole dictionary full of symptoms could develop from reliance on such nutritionally restricted diets, symptoms included among the lists of conditions which patent medicine promoters advertised their products to cure.

Loneliness, boredom, and fatigue could foster the patent medicine habit. In an article entitled "The Great Rural Tragedy," appearing in the *Kansas City Star*, the reporter let southern women tell of their "Heart Weariness." "I have never been to a lecture, nor play, nor show since marriage," said a woman from Texas, "have been trying to buy a home. It has been a very monotonous road to travel." A Virginia woman echoed the sentiment: "Isolation, stagnation, ignorance, loss of ambition, the incessant grind of labor, and lack of time for improvement by reading, social intercourse, or by recreation of some sort are all working against the farm woman's happiness and will ultimately spell disaster for the Nation." Less articulate women also led dreary lives. Many store ledgers gave ample evidence of one response to such a plight, the once-a-week purchase of morphine, or laudanum, or of opiate nostrums, sometimes bartered for eggs or chickens. David T. Courtwright has recently concluded: "With the possible exception of the Chinese, southern whites [in the years 1860–1920] had the highest [opium] addiction rate of any regional racial group in the country, and perhaps one of the highest in the world."[21]

Poor diets, hot summer climate, and drab rural lives were not unique to the South. Yet, within the nation, the difference in degree might approximate a distinctiveness of kind. No other section shared the South's turn-of-the-century "trilogy of 'lazy diseases,' " malaria, hookworm, and pellagra.[22]And no other section had such a low level of education and such inadequate medical care.

Two of these diseases, the chronic malaria and pellagra, along with the epidemic yellow fever, gave a distinctive pattern to nostrum-taking in the South. In this realm may lie the greatest measure of sectional differentiation with respect to patent medicines.

When the malaria that had afflicted the entire frontier became restricted to the South, it stimulated not only the inclusion of that illness in labeling of panaceas but also the creation of chill tonics. The first proprietary to aim quinine at malaria, Dr. Sappington's Celebrated Anti-Fever Pills, "an unrivaled cure for Ague & Fever," was made in Missouri and could be bought as early as 1837 in Woodville, Mississippi. A number of other brands, some northern-made, others products of the South, entered the southern market. Rich's Tasteless Chill Tonic came from Nashville; Grove's Chill Tonic from Paris, Tennessee; and Marshall's Dead-Shot for Chills and Fever from Macon, Georgia.[23]

One of the most persistent quinine-containing antimalarial proprietaries bore the name 666 (perhaps derived from Revelations 13:18). Devised by a physician in Monticello, Florida, and later moved to Jacksonville, this remedy sold widely until World War II. Then, its supply of quinine cut off, the company encountered trouble but managed to survive that crisis and the later decline of malaria by changing 666, first to a treatment for colds and then to a spring tonic.[24]

The fear generated by epidemics has always sent the panicked scrambling for purported preventives and cures opportunistically marketed by unscrupulous promoters. Nineteenth-century cholera spawned quack nostrums; twentieth-century influenza pushed proprietors into exaggerated claims.[25] The great Philadelphia yellow fever epidemic of 1793 prompted its share of quick-cure nostrums, and so did later attacks of yellow jack upon the South, from Savannah to New Orleans. Even before newspapers had begun editorially to admit the fever's presence, nostrums would be advertised with their preposterous claims. A presumed preventive vaccine promoted by the alleged nephew of Alexander von Humboldt had to be debunked in 1856 by a Louisiana physician.[26]

In Pensacola in the 1880s, a dubious doctor named Bosso vended Bosso's Blessing for Mankind as a yellow fever preventative. He himself, contracting the disease, sought from his attending physician a pledge that, should he die, the doctor would sign a certificate attributing death to some other cause. "If I die of yellow fever," Bosso explained, "people will not buy my medicine anymore!" Bosso did die. The physician did not honor the fervent deathbed plea. Nonetheless, Bosso's dire prediction did not prove true. Shrewdly promoted by his heirs, Bosso's Blessing survived into the twentieth century.[27]

Indeed, after the mosquito vector mode of yellow fever transmission became known, other nostrums for the yellow peril besides Bosso's Blessing continued. "Disinfective," a soap, was guaranteed to heal mosquito bites and thus prevent yellow fever. So too did G.H. Tichenor's Antiseptic. A 1905 advertisement read: "Mosquito Bites Rendered Harmless . . . Rub in Well."[28]

When pellagra became identified as a specific disease entity at the beginning of the twentieth century, pellagra patent medicines entered the marketplace. Three such nostrums, all southern, achieved considerable prominence: Baughn's Pellagra Remedy, Pellagracide, and Ez-X-Ba.[29]

Baughn's concoction, the production of two local bank officials, surfaced in sensational style in 1912 in Jasper, Alabama. A promotional pamphlet called *Pellagra Cured!* evoked fear in the reader before offering hope. The disease was termed a "grim spector, stalking unseen up and down the land, touching with the icy hand of death the young child playing in the sun, the devoted mother crooning o'er her babe, the father toiling in the field." The pamphleteer then startled the reader by asking if he might already be grasped in pellagra's grip. "Have you a feeling of exhaustion and lassitude? Have you unusual bowel disturbance and diarrhoea? Have you pains and aches for which there seems no cause? Have you headaches and vertigo difficult to explain?" If the reader could answer yes to any of these questions, he stood on the threshold of pellagra's final stage, "the MAD HOUSE and DEATH."

Baughns' Pellagra Remedy, however, offered escape. "Like a guardian spirit my remedy stands between you and this hitherto unconquered disease—thrusting off its hideous grasp, healing your body and filling you again with the JOY of living."

This sovereign remedy came in two bottles, one of capsules for internal use, the other of powder for external application. Sent to the American Medical Association by the Alabama state health officer, Prescription No. 1 turned out to consist of iron sulphate, quinine sulphate, charcoal, straw, and dirt. Prescription No. 2 contained iron sulphate and sodium chloride.

The other two nostrums, Pellagracide and Ez-X-Ba, may well have been manufactured by the same concern in Spartanburg. The composition of the medicines was the same. But it was Ez-X-Ba that shot off the more dazzling fireworks, appearing in South Carolina mill towns in 1911. Sales soon expanded phenomenally. The discoverer and promoter, Ezxba W. Dedmond, claimed that the secret of his medicine had been imparted to him by God himself.

When the Public Health Service's Hygienic Laboratory analyzed Ez-X-Ba, which came in two forms, the laboratory director thought that a solution very like the liquid version might be made by mixing dilute sulphuric acid with low-grade iron-bearing ores plentiful in the region. The tablet form consisted of sulphur trioxide, aluminum oxide, calcium oxide, cane sugar, and starch.

An investigation of testimonials and a survey of physicians countered Dedmond's boastful curative claims. One doctor cited the case of a nine-day cure advertised in a Columbia paper, saying that, instead of recovering, the man giving the testimonial had died. Dedmond, investigation revealed, had not the slightest background for medical innovation: he was a millhand devoid of education and something of a religious crank. Under the impact of unfavorable publicity, Dedmond withdrew his medicine from the marketplace. In 1921 he and Ez-X-Ba made a brief reprise.

When the plague of hookworm came to be identified, it seems safe to assume, agile promoters would behave as Ezxba Dedmond did when sensing public concern over pellagra and concoct for hookworm a rapid and painless cure. None has so far been discovered by this researcher in patent medicine advertising. Nor has there been found an enterprising vendor from the various marketers of vermifuges and worm syrups who expanded the labeled indications for use to include hookworm infestation. A 1917 list of proprietaries contained sixteen such products, two of them southern: Sweet's Honey Vermifuge, made in Memphis, and Thacher's Worm Syrup, made in Chattanooga.[30] But the word "hookworm" has not so far been found

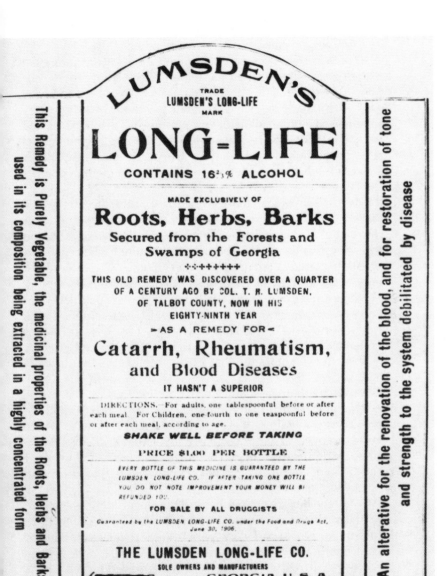

Lumsden's Long-Life, a Georgia-made proprietary featuring on its label that state's native botanicals. Application to Georgia secretary of state to have label copyrighted as a trademark: 1910. From Trade Mark Books, vol. 2, Office of the Secretary of State Records, Georgia Department of Archives and History, Atlanta.

on any nostrum label. Perhaps the vigor of the Rockefeller Sanitary Commission checkmated such an initiative.

If all southerners were potential victims of nostrums promoted
for the diseases peculiar to the region, black southerners continued to be a population at special risk. As slaves they had been
dosed with patent medicines by their masters. Once free, they
were pressed and persuaded to spend some of their hard-earned
cash for quackish wares. Inasmuch as the South contained a
higher proportion of blacks than the North, the cheating of blacks
by patent medicine proprietors possesses an element of distinctiveness.

"Even the skin of the Ethiop is not exempt from the attention of
quacks." So wrote Samuel Hopkins Adams, leading muckraker
in the patent medicine field, early in 1906. He had been spurred to
addressing this theme by a black correspondent who requested
that Adams "give a paragraph to these fiends who cater to the
vanity of those of my race who insult their Creator in attempting
to change their color and their hair." The correspondent sent
Adams advertisements for Lustorene, which "straightens kinky,
nappy, curly hair," and for Lustorone Face Bleach, which
"whitens the darkest skin." "Nothing," commented Adams,
"could better illustrate to what ridiculous lengths the nostrum
fraud will go."[31]

Soon after Adams' article, a North Carolina congressman made
the same point at a House committee hearing. "The credulity of
the colored population of America," asserted Edwin Y. Webb,
"has been appealed to by speciously advertised medicines promising to straighten their hair and whiten their faces, and the poor
negro, who needs his money, has been duped into buying these
worthless lotions and salves."[32]

Already the Bureau of Chemistry of the Department of Agriculture had analyzed a number of such nostrums for the Post Office
Department, which had a law permitting it to attack fraudulent
mail promotions. A concoction made in Virginia, which flatly
promised to turn blacks white, had been removed from the market. A similar proprietary, Bureau analysts found, contained
corrosive sublimate mixed with glycerine.[33]

Such products received advertising play in the black press. A
historian of the black-controlled media in Atlanta has noted the
bitter irony inherent in this circumstance: "Commitment to the
'cause' demanded that these papers promote race pride; but the

economic imperatives demanded that they promote products as 'skin whiteners,' patent medicine 'cures,' dream books and 'love charms.' Such were the meager advertisements available to them."[34] Even *The Crisis*, edited by W.E.B. DuBois accepted an occasional dubious ad.[35]

Products of this sort proved lucrative. The Skin Whitener marketed by Joseph Jacobs, an Atlanta druggist, sold more briskly than any other of his many proprietaries. A similar concoction, Black & White ointment, made in Memphis, also did well. Jacobs' product was eventually seized under the 1906 law for false and fraudulent claims. Black & White Ointment met a similar fate soon after the 1938 law went into effect.[36]

As *takers* of patent medicines, it can be concluded, southerners acquired and maintained an ardent appetite for nostrums, fueled by a mix of inadequate diet, wide range of warm climate diseases, rural boredom, respect for tradition, low level of education, and inadequate medical care. The most prominent areas of distinction in the consumption of proprietary products related to malaria, yellow fever, pellagra, and cosmetics for black residents of the region.

MAKING PATENT MEDICINES

During the eighteenth century, both the American North and the South shared literal colonial status under the British crown, and with respect to commercial self-medication shared virtually complete economic subservience. Proprietary pills and elixirs, the product of English therapeutic ingenuity, primed by the advent of newspaper advertising, came alike to both northern and southern ports. The nostrums were packed in containers of distinctive shape, sealed in wrappers printed with bold curative promises and glowing testimonials. Godfrey's Cordial, Turlington's Balsam, Hooper's Female Pills, Sir Walter Raleigh's Cordial—these brands and three score more or so, just imported on the latest ships from London, were listed in apothecary and general store advertising up and down the Atlantic coast, in Boston, New York, and Philadelphia; in Williamsburg, Charleston, and Savannah. Zabdiel Boylston sold them in Massachusetts; Button Gwinnett sold them in Georgia. North and South, the market had no detectable difference.[37]

Until the Revolution, these English imports dominated the American patent medicine scene. In the faint stirrings of American inventiveness that occurred, neither North nor South seemed to gain sectional advantage. A self-styled Frenchman, Francis Torres, showed up in Philadelphia in 1745 selling "Chinese Stones" to cure toothache, cancer, and the bites of mad dogs and rattlesnakes. Where had M. Torres been before arriving in the City of Brotherly Love? He had vended his powerful pebbles in Charleston.[38]

In Charleston, too, certain ladies advertised a "Choice Cure for the Flux, Fevers, Worms, bad Stomach [and] Pains in the Head," just as in Philadelphia the Widow Read, Benjamin Franklin's mother-in-law, advertised in his gazette her "well-known Ointment for the ITCH," which also killed or drove away lice.[39] Neither in the activity of outright mountebanks like Torres, nor in the field of folk remedies modestly entering the marketplace, as with the women, does any clear differentiation appear in colonial days between the North and South.

The disruption of trade preceding and accompanying the Revolution dealt the English patent medicine proprietors a fatal blow.[40] In postwar years they sought vigorously to regain their lost American markets, but with only scant and temporary success. The imports faced too great competition from new American brands, born amidst the cultural nationalism of the Revolutionary generation. And there was competition from America in another way. American apothecaries had begun to imitate the English remedies, retaining the traditional names and bottle shapes, and by so doing deprived them of proprietary status and turned them into generic drugs. As such some of them survived into our own day. In these trends a sectional difference may be noted. Mention of the English patent medicine names fades from northern drugstore advertising before it disappears from advertising in the South. In the 1940s the Food and Drug Administration seized some British Oil and Dalby's Carminative, both made in Charleston.[41] A quarter of a century ago, a nurse in the Georgia State Department of Health told the author that she had the week before observed the use of Godfrey's Cordial in a Georgia country home. Perhaps the relative slowness of the rural South to change long-established habits helped to perpetuate use of the old English patent medicines.

Another reason why the British nostrums hung on longer in

Dixie, no doubt, is that they were not shouldered aside so soon by brash new American brands, even though such brands entered the South early. The first American-made nostrums to achieve commercially significant success were fabricated in the North.

The North produced packaged commercial remedies in far greater numbers than did the South, and successful northern entrepreneurs far outstripped their southern rivals in scope of market and extent of sales. An indicator of the greater northern productivity may come from the records of medicines patented. In 1793 the Congress enacted its second law under the Constitutional provision to grant patents in order to "promote the Progress of Science and the useful Arts." Despite the laxness of the law's terms, only some 75 patents were granted for medicinals before a tougher law was passed in 1836. By 1874, when a list was published by the Patent Office, 788 patents for medicines, pills, liniments, ointments, and salves had been granted through the first eight decades.[42] To be sure, shrewd marketers of medicines avoided the Patent Office, preferring secrecy of formula to the modest revelations the process of patenting imposed. Thus, by and large, applications came from simpleminded folk not used to the clever ways of the commercial world. Nonetheless, this smaller sample may not be too much different in sectional proportion from the total universe of American nostrum production.

An analysis of the residence of those who secured patents shows the North to have exceeded the South. Residents of the eleven states that constituted the Confederacy received 109 of the 788 medical patents granted between 1796 and 1873. Southern patents ranged from a single one from Arkansas to Georgia's twenty. New York State, whose citizens garnered the largest share, totaled 165. If to the Confederate eleven be added the border states of Maryland, Kentucky, and Missouri, the South claimed 176 patents to the North's 612, less than a quarter.

Inventiveness involves a great deal of individual caprice, and its patterns are difficult to explain. The South had a smaller population than the North, and less urbanization. Even though invention as a calculated facet of industrialization had, in the period of these statistics, barely begun to affect the making of drugs, some correlation between urbanization and drug patenting seems apparent. Over half of the New York State patentees came from New York City (70) and Brooklyn (15); a third of Pennsylvania patentees resided in Philadelphia (27 of 75); a quarter of Illinois patentees lived in Chicago (12 of 48). In the South, the established city of New Orleans dominated patenting from Louisiana (13 of 17), but in no other state did a single city come close to such a preponderance. In Virginia, Richmond residents acquired 4 of the state's 18 patents; in Tennessee, Nashville citizens got 3 of 10; in Georgia, Atlantans secured 4 of 20. A concentration of patents seem to require a metropolis, and the South had few cities.

The geographical range of inventiveness, both North and South, seems a most impressive feature. In New York, besides medium-sized cities such as Albany, Buffalo, Rochester, and Syracuse, villages such as Cherry Valley, Gallupville, Hebron, and Java were represented. In Georgia, besides Atlanta, patentees came from Americus, Athens, Augusta, Bainbridge, Columbus, Hancock, Jackson, Rattlesnake Springs, Savannah, Van Wirt, Washington, and Waynesborough.

From the earliest days of native patent medicine manufacturing, northern nostrum makers sought out markets in the South and found that region receptive. Samuel Lee, Jr., of Connecticut, the first American to patent a drug, Bilious Pills, in 1796, and his early rival, Samuel H.P. Lee, also of Connecticut, who in 1799 also patented Bilious Pills, quickly carried their intense competition to Georgia and to Louisiana.[43] Thomas W. Dyott of Philadelphia, one of the new nation's pioneering proprietary entrepreneurs, during the early years of the nineteenth century vended his large assortment of nostrums throughout the country. His advertisements featured drawings of large Conestoga wagons being loaded from his capacious warehouse with remedies destined for the South and West.[44] Dyott set up a substation in New Orleans. Other largescale northern nostrum promoters invaded the South during the antebellum years, their advertising outweighing in extent that of proprietors native to the section.[45]

Meanwhile, very few patent medicines of southern origin penetrated northern markets. Two which so succeeded to a modest extent were Gray's Ointment and Dr. John Bull's King of Pain. A physician in a Virginia village, W.W. Gray developed his Ointment formula in 1820 and soon took it with him to Raleigh.[46] From there he engineered a coup that helped his remedy outlast a century. After sending a jar to Andrew Jackson in the White House in 1831, Dr. Gray received in reply a quasi-testimonial. "I will, with much pleasure, use the ointment," wrote Old Hickory, "which I doubt not will prove highly beneficial." Dr. Gray and his son, who moved manufacturing operations to Nashville, relied on Jackson's optimistic anticipations for years. Gray's Ointment is said to have enjoyed a steady market among emigrants to the West. In 1852 it was listed among the wares available from a large patent medicine entrepreneur in New York City.[47]

Coming to Louisville as a boy, John Bull grew up there, having sequential connections with various pharmacies and launching his first patent medicine, a Sarsaparilla, prior to 1850.[48] Other nostrums followed: a Bitters, a Cough Syrup, a Spring Tonic, a Worm Destroyer, and the King of Pain, "TENTH WONDER OF THE WORLD, and the greatest blessing ever offered to afflicted humanity." Bull diligently worked both sides of the Ohio River and aspired to a national market. He set up an office in New York, probably moving there in 1856 to remain for two or three years before returning to Louisville, where production of his nostrums had continued. After the Civil War, Bull's business boomed, and the sale of his medicines survived their proprietor, who died in 1875.

Unlike Bull's assorted remedies and Gray's Ointment, however, most nostrums generated in the antebellum South, no matter how high the hopes of their inventors, garnered only a local or a regional market. For example, a medicine that has survived to the present day, once known as Swift's Syphilitic Specific, was later changed to Swift's Sure Specific and is now called S.S.S.[49] Purchased by Colonel C.T. Swift after the Civil War, the original formula, according to company chronicle, had been secured by a Captain Denard from the Creek Indians in the mid-1820s. Concocted by boiling botanical ingredients in a wash pot, the remedy gained a following in Georgia and Alabama before the war. A twentieth-century scholar, presuming that the original ingredients were sarsaparilla, smilax, and sassafras, fit the formula into the tradition begun in early exploration days, that these New World plants could cure the New World disease of syphilis, brought to Europe by Columbus' returning sailors.[50] A more recent scholar suggested that, if the original formula was that still used in 1914, consisting of chionanthus root, sumac, and swamp sumac, then the first two of these three plants did indeed have established usages in Indian medicine, chionanthus as a promoter of wound healing, sumac as a hemostatic and treatment for urinary retention.[51]

Cherokee Indian theme, as used by a twentieth-century southern proprietor. Cherokee Chief, Sagawah Remedy Company, Bryson City, North Carolina. Bottle in author's collection. Used courtesy of Margaret Leake.

Whether antebellum promotion featured Indian origin is not known. A postwar trade card shows a group of Indians gathered around a pot which boils over an outdoor fire, their wigwams in the background emblazoned with the letters S.S.S. In the foreground a stalwart brave hands a bottle of the medicine to a debilitated white man seated under a tree. Testimonials on the card remain within the South, ranging from Georgia to Arkansas.[52]

Indian origin provided one of the stock promotional devices for patent medicines during the nineteenth century, most of the tales being more fanciful and less plausible than that reported purchase of the original S.S.S. formula from the Creeks.[53] Another popular southern remedy was Cleman's Indian Tonic.[54] Southern proprietors, however, had no monopoly on southern Indians as sources for commercial remedies. It was a New York concern that, in promoting its Southern Balm, pictured an Indian giving herbs to Aesculapius and Hygeia. Clement's Genuine Osceola Indian Liniment came from Philadelphia; the Florida Balm, or Seminole Cough Balsam, from New York; and Dr. W.R. Merwin's Cherokee Remedy also originated in that northern metropolis.[55] Merwin explicitly exploited the Columbian origin of syphilis theme.

The Civil War provided northern vendors with abundant opportunity to turn patriotism into profitable appeals, which they carried forward with great zest. Confederate cultural nationalism also came into play eventually, but never with the vigor displayed in Union patent medicine advertising.[56] By 1863 most of the ads for northern remedies had disappeared from the southern press, and ads for Confederate medicines somewhat replaced them. The spirit of sectional patriotism influenced the promotion of new-born Dixie proprietaries. A Charleston druggist announced the Memphis-made Cherokee Remedy and other "SOUTHERN PREPARATIONS" for sale at the Sign of the Negro and Golden Mortar. In Augusta, the makers of Broom's Anti-Hydropic Tincture used bold type to proclaim: "DROPSY CURED! NO YANKEE HUMBUG!" A Nashville-made Ambrosial Oil was offered to cure twenty-eight listed human ailments, plus ten equine ones. Early in 1865, an Augusta concern marketed a proprietary version of a substitute much resorted to by regular physicians, advertising "Dennis' Compound Dogwood Bitters, A Substitute for Quinine."[57]

Despite such examples, patent medicine advertising in the Confederate press was sparse, short, and lacking in flamboyance. Many papers, in the middle and last years of the war, included in their shrunken advertising columns no pills or potions at all.

When the war ended, northern nostrum merchants were glad to get their southern markets back. The year 1865 was not yet over before a Charleston druggist was shipping roots of southern plants to Massachusetts in payment for the packaged remedies of J.C. Ayer. The next year a Columbia editor complained that southern publishers were selling advertising space at cut rates to "patent blood-suckers" manufactured by Yankee concerns. Northern proprietors might denigrate the South in advertising at home, but they were not averse to catching a southern reader's eye with the cut of a man resembling "Stonewall" Jackson.[58]

Northern dominance of the southern market continued thereafter. Despite an upsurge in patent medicine production as a significant phase of New South economic development, and a larger than prewar entrance of Dixie-made remedies into the North, the challenge of established, big-name, heavily advertised northern brands could not be met.

One insight into northern dominance of the southern market may be found in the nearly one thousand unbroken medicine bottles from bygone days taken from the moat at Fort Pulaski National Monument near Savannah. The two southern brands brought up from the water—P.P.P. of Savannah and Mother's Friend of Atlanta—are far outnumbered by their northern competitors.[59]

More persuasive, a perusal of advertising for proprietary medicines in almost any southern newspaper from Reconstruction to the New Deal—and beyond—reveals a higher proportion placed by northern than by southern concerns. For example, a survey of Atlanta newspapers between 1900 and 1920 reveals that 20 percent of the patent medicines advertised were products of the states that had formed the Confederacy, while 70 percent came from elsewhere in the nation.[60] The origin of 10 percent could not be determined. Northern nostrums also dominated the advertising columns of the readyprint pages which many southern country newspaper editors came to rely on.

Northern advertising agencies played a role in placing both northern and southern ads in the southern press. Scott & Scott of New York, for example, had arrangements with forty prominent

southern dailies, into all of whose columns it was prepared, for a
fee, to put the same ad, thus saving the nostrum promoter much
time and trouble. Nor was this the only reliance on northern
talent that southern medicine proprietors paid for. Northern
pharmaceutical manufacturers sometimes made the patent medicines that southern firms sold, mass-producing formulas mailed
north from Dixie. Parke, Davis & Company in Detroit, for example, prepared Panhorst's Indigestion Powder for the East Tennessee Medicine Company in Johnson City. Packages to contain
this medicine came from a factory in Aurora, Illnois.[61]

Proprietors from both North and South employed multiple
media to promote their wares. Besides the ubiquitous newspaper
advertising, they painted their appeals on barns and country
stores and attached their signs to trees. Manufacturers loaded
store counters with almanacs and calendars crowded with advertising, and besought storekeepers and ministers to furnish lists of
customers and parishioners to whom direct mail circulars might
be sent. Peddlers with stocks of nostrums invaded rural areas at
time for crop settlement, when tenant farmers might have ready
cash.[62]

Such agents might be given an additional assignment, gathering a collection of testimonials. Not all the testimony that appeared in print, to be sure, could be taken at face value.[63] Outright fakery was sometimes resorted to, with testimonials fabricated out of whole cloth. Praise also might be bought or pried
from the reluctant by various shrewd devices. But many, even
prominent citizens, seemed to enjoy seeing their names in print.
The Ohio proprietor of Peruna, a high-alcoholic nostrum, managed to sign up fifty members of the Congress. So many of his
colleagues had been "rejuvenated by Peruna," a Texas representative remarked ironically, that "Peruna seems to be the favorite
congressional drink." When one of those lofty testifiers, William
Bankhead, appeared for a political debate at the University of
Alabama, he could hardly launch his speech because of the
rhythmic student chant booming through the chamber: "Peruna!
Peruna! Peruna!"[64]

Praise from notables patent medicine promoters presented
when they could, but they believed that the common touch also
prospered business. A New Orleans editor explained the process:
testimonials "have a tremendous influence in small communities, and those signed by plain, everyday working people

are at present regarded as more valuable than the indorsement of celebrities." Letters from "factory hands, firemen, railroad engineers and humble clerks . . . are vastly more convincing, they cost nothing to get, and the average man feels at liberty to write to the signers for further particulars." Such endorsements "are secured, as a rule, by an agent who is selected especially for his tact and suavity and who makes a tour of small towns. . . . He gets the names of purchasers from the druggists, and tries to learn which, if any, have made favorable comments on the remedy. They are visited, and the round trip is certain to be productive of a big sheaf of flattering testimonials."⁶⁵ Medicine makers sought to heighten their impact by showing the faces of the testifiers, usually in line drawings based on photographs.

An early-twentieth-century pamphlet put out by the makers of Swift's Specific illustrates the presentation of testimonials.⁶⁶ In *Blood and Skin Diseases: How to Cure Them,* the Atlanta concern, while explicitly asserting that S.S.S. is "Sold everywhere," concentrates upon the South. Two-thirds (45) of the 68 testimonials with place names given come from the territory of the ex-Confederacy. All eleven of these states are represented, Georgia most heavily (15). The fourteen states outside the South from which 23 testifiers praise S.S.S. range from Massachusetts to California, with the Midwest predominating. Georgians speak forth from all corners of the state, from the capital of Atlanta to small villages and farms identified only by county.

Most of the S.S.S. testifiers seem to live in small towns, and for a majority no occupation is given, although the portraits suggest that all are dressed in Sunday best. When jobs are mentioned, they suggest not national or even regional structure, but the elite of Main Street: a bank president, a druggist, an alderman, a dry goods merchant, a music dealer, a judge, a town health officer, a passenger train conductor. Men sometimes present the case histories of their wives or daughters, but women also give their own. No regional sentiment predominates: a Florida veteran of the Army of the Tennessee is balanced by a former U.S. Navy captain.

The broad curative compass then being recommended for S.S.S. can be suggested by the pamphlet's sections: rheumatism, scrofula, catarrh, malaria, cancer, eczema, acne, tetter, blood poison, sores and ulcers, carbuncles, erysipelas, general tonic. Even the discussion of malaria lacks special southern emphasis:

any bad air anywhere, including sewer gas, can cause the disease.

Lingering Victorian restraint and reticence did not apply to patent medicine testimonials. In this genre of subliterature, the most intimate aspects of health history received candid and gruesomely detailed exposure. Terse narratives with such headings as "Covered with Sores," "Holes in the Tongue," "Poisoned by Acid," and "Surgeon's Cruel Knife" could be expected to disturb the reader beset with his own worrisome or painful symptoms, and yet to reassure him, too. For if his village neighbors and their like in other towns could suffer so and yet be cured, buying a nostrum was worth a try. Patent medicine testimonials constituted a form of horror literature that always ended happily.

Swift's Sure Specific got new and more vigorous ownership soon after the Civil War and challenged the reinvasion of the South by northern nostrum makers. In time, indeed, S.S.S. made its own forays into the North. Colonel Swift acquired ownership of the remedy in 1870, and with the help of friends in the wholesale drug business, launched S.S.S. on its more prosperous course.[67] During this campaign some of the testimonials came from distinguished Georgians: General John B. Gordon, Governor W.J. Northen, Senator Hoke Smith, Joel Chandler Harris. The washpot gave way to steam-jacketed percolators. Changes in ingredients and in the scope of therapeutic promises came with time and with regulatory legislation.[68] No other New South proprietary exceeded S.S.S. in longevity.

Many other southern entrepreneurs hoped for fame and fortune from patent medicines marketed in the ambitious economic climate of the New South. Always a risky business, the odds for success lengthened in the fiercely competitive postbellum years, as more and more proprietaries sought to win American public favor. Regulation began during the same years. The Federal Food and Drugs Act of 1906 sought to ban false and misleading labeling. Checkmated by an adverse Supreme Court decision, regulators faced a tougher legal task under the 1912 Sherley Amendment: therapeutic claims in labeling, to be actionable, had to be both false and fraudulent. The 1938 Food, Drug, and Cosmetic Act increased the rigor of controls.[69] All through the difficult years, nonetheless, the Bureau of Chemistry of the Department of Agriculture, and its successor, the Food and Drug Administration, sought to enforce the law. Thousands of Notices of Judgment, plus critical articles in American Medical Association publications, sketch a national gazeteer of patent medicine production and of the transgressions of proprietors.

These sources reveal that every state of the ex-Confederacy, in its major cities and random villages, exhibited New South venturesomeness in the launching of patent medicines. From Richmond to Little Rock; from Mineral Wells, Texas, to Miami, Florida, entrepreneurs entered the market with such names as Samaritan Nervine, McGraw's Liquid Herbs of Youth, Peerless Crystals, and Ponce de Leon Cream.[70] Cities that became significant centers of production included Atlanta, Birmingham, Chattanooga, Greensboro, Knoxville, Louisville, Memphis, Nashville, New Orleans, Salisbury, and Vicksburg. Chattanooga and Atlanta stood out.

Two Union soldiers, mustered out of the army at war's end in Chattanooga, set up a stationery store, then acquired ownership of two prewar local patent medicines—Thedford's Black Draught, laxative; and McElree's Wine of Cardui, a remedy for women's ailments.[71] For many years the Chattanooga Medicine Company developed its market within the South, promoting vigorously with outdoor advertising and a lavish distribution of almanacs and calendars. In 1914 the American Medical Association, in its *Journal,* blasted Wine of Cardui as "a vicious fraud."[72] Its alcoholic content high, AMA's *Journal* charged, the remedy contained no ingredient capable of lifting up a fallen womb. The article also disparaged company officials, one of whom, John A. Patten, was a leading layman nationally in the Methodist Church. The company countered the AMA attack with two libel suits—a personal suit by Patten, which lapsed during trial when Patten died; and a partnership suit. After thirteen tempestuous weeks of testimony, the jury returned a verdict against the AMA, the only libel case ever lost by that association in its continuing campaign of criticizing nostrums. Damages, however, fell far short of the $100,000 that had been sought. Indeed, the award came to only a single cent, and the Chattanooga Medicine Company had to pay its own court costs. The AMA was satisfied, reporting the verdict as "Technically guilty; morally justified!" The trade association of medicine proprietors deemed most of the national newspaper coverage of the trial "prejudiced and biased to the extreme." Some southern papers, however, had taken the manufacturer's side.

The Chattanooga Medicine Company, sustained by its legal victory, continued imaginative merchandising. Aided by such "hot" salesmen as Huey Long, who served a turn as company representative,[73] the firm became one of the South's most successful marketers. Black Draught promised to "Uncork 25 Feet of Stomach Tubes," and Wine of Cardui became bolder in fighting Lydia E. Pinkham's Vegetable Compound on her home ground.[74] These medicines continue on the market.

Atlanta, self-styled Gate City of the South, also became the region's patent medicine capital. Profits from its proprietary industries helped to fuel the city's rise to New South leadership. By 1890 Atlanta derived a larger proportion of its manufacturing income from patent medicines than did any other city in the nation.[75] Such remedies accounted for 6.7 percent of Atlanta's total production. This surpassed the share for Lowell, Massachusetts, at 5 percent. The figure for New Haven and for Rochester was 2 percent; for Baltimore and Buffalo, between 1 and 2 percent; and for St. Louis, Pittsburgh, Philadelphia, and Chicago, in descending order, less than 1 percent.

Scores of Atlanta-made patent medicines—not all of them accounted for in census reckoning—show up in city directories, newspaper advertising, Notices of Judgment, and volumes recording trademarks kept by the Georgia Secretary of State. Dr. S.T.B. Biggers, president of the Eclectic Medical College, devised a Huckleberry Cordial, "The Great Southern Remedy for all Bowel Troubles and Children Teething," that won a testimonial from no less a New South luminary than Henry W. Grady himself.[76]

Three druggists moved from smaller Georgia towns to Atlanta and went on to bigger things. John S. Pemberton came from Columbus and spent the rest of his life concocting patent medicines, several of which he patented.[77] From his French Wine of Coca evolved his Coca-Cola, promoted as a pick-me-up and "brain tonic." Purchased by Asa G. Candler, who had moved from Cartersville to Atlanta to enter the drug business, Coca-Cola was transformed from a medicine, its original tiny trace of cocaine removed, to a soda fountain beverage.[78] Shrewdly marketed, Coca-Cola became the New South's greatest national commercial success. Because of its caffeine, Coca-Cola did not escape Bureau of Chemistry scrutiny and legal action. Candler, before concentrating on Coca-Cola, had sold Dr. Biggers' Huckleberry Cordial, and, while confessing skepticism about remedies whose formulas he did not know, had given a testimonial for the Atlanta-made Dr. Cheney's Expectorant and Croup Preventive.[79] His family, Candler said, would "not put out our lights at night without knowing that" a bottle of the Expectorant rested "on the mantel of the nursery." He had never known it "necessary to give a second dose in order to arrest this dangerous enemy to the little ones."

Joseph Jacobs came to Atlanta from Athens, Georgia, where he had apprenticed in the drugstore operated by Dr. Crawford W. Long.[80] While still in Athens, Jacobs had begun to devise and sell proprietary formulas. In Atlanta Jacobs expanded by invention and purchase his stable of proprietaries. In 1904, when he sold his personal rights in these preparations to a corporation which he headed, the contract listed eighty-two names. Jacobs did not escape unscathed the scrutiny of the Bureau of Chemistry. He pleaded guilty and paid $25 fines for falsely and fraudulently labeling Dr. Fred Palmer's Skin Whitener and Jacobs' Liver Salt.[81]

Patent medicines went forth into the market from at least twenty-five smaller cities and towns in Georgia. For example, Savannah's P.P.P.—Prickly Ash, Poke Root, and Potassium—vended by a woman, Florence Virginia Lippman, developed extensive sales and encountered considerable difficulty with the law because of its broad claims as a cure for syphilis, blood poisoning, rheumatism, and malaria.[82] Avoiding such trouble but probably suffering from minimal sales, Fitzhugh Lee in 1903 began his career as proprietor in Winder, with Aunt Dinah's Blue Flag Liver Medicine, to which he soon added a Female Remedy and a Sweet Shrub.[83] Moving to Covington, Lee marketed under the Kill-Germ name a Cough Balsam and a Salve, as well as Sap-a-rilla Teething Powders and True-Tone Liver Medicine. Some years later, three promoters in Warm Springs, trading on President Franklin D. Roosevelt's connection with the town, put out a Warm Springs Crystal Compound, alleging that the medicine came from the Georgia resort, when in fact it consisted of the simple laxative Glauber's salts. For this deception, two of the trio received two-year prison sentences and the other a one-year term.[84]

Occasionally a black citizen entered the nostrum business, concentrating his sales efforts on those of his own race. One such promoter, William F. Edwards, began business in Orangeburg,

South Carolina, in 1909 and later moved to Vidalia, Georgia. His
Dy-O-Fe, The Great Blood Remedy, claimed well-nigh panacea
prowess in treating lung, liver, kidney, skin, and nervous diseases; chills and fever; rheumatism; and female complaints.[85]
Three decades later, Robert Lee Brightwell dispensed from his
home in White Plains, Georgia, and sold by mail, an assortment
of remedies which he claimed to prepare from native barks and
roots. Among them were a "Rattle Snake Medicine" good for
blood poisoning; an unnamed cure-all with claims of effectiveness running the gamut from asthma to worms; and a third
concoction made from snake weed purportedly "Good for crazy
people."[86]

Despite all of this southern therapeutic creativity, however, the
region did not mount a significant challenge to the proprietary
outpouring in the rest of the nation. Statistics in the 1890 and 1900
censuses make this fact plain. From the relatively small number of
concerns included in the tabulations, it is obvious that total output of patent medicines is underrepresented, the production of
smaller firms most likely accounting for omissions. This inaccu-
racy, however, probably applies to figures from all the states. The
1890 data show that the value of patent medicine production from
the eleven states of the former Confederacy accounted for only 6
percent of the entire nation's output.[87] New York State alone
manufactured four times as much. If the considerable production
of Maryland, Kentucky, and Missouri is added to that of the
ex-Confederacy, the South in 1890 still made only a fifth of the
nation's nostrums. The three border states each outproduced
Georgia, the leading ex-Confederate state, in the value of its
patent medicine manufacturing. Georgia's share of the eleven
surpassed 40 percent.

A decade later Georgia had lost its lead to Tennessee.[88] Production in the ex-Confederate South had doubled since 1890, expanding a little faster than in the nation as a whole, and accounting for
7 percent of the value of United States output. Still, New York
production alone possessed four times the value of the eleven
southern states, and that of both Massachusetts and Illinois also
individually surpassed it. In 1900, the Deep South states, plus
Maryland, Kentucky, and Missouri, represented just under 17
percent of the national total, a decline from 20 percent in 1890.

Were the names of southern-made nostrums distinct? Inasmuch as occasionally patent medicines from all sections of the

country bore names signifying their place of origin, no uniqueness marked the practice of now and then giving a southern
proprietary a southern name. In this tradition there came on the
market Mansfield's Southern Matchless Sanative Pills, Louisiana
Creole Hair Restorer, Mississippi Diarrhea Cordial, Georgia Sarsaparilla, Hot Springs Improved Sarsaparilla Compound, and a
host of Texas remedies: Texas Universal Pills, Texas Tonic Syrup,
Texas Mineral Crystals.[89] The maker of Hall's Texas Wonder
proved to be one of the Bureau of Chemistry's, and then the Food
and Drug Administration's, most litigious opponents.[90] Perhaps
geography can carry overtones of sectional pride, as in Dixie
Fever and Pain Powder, or of some special merit possessed by the
region's flora, as in Georgia Aromatic Pure Long Leaf Pine Oil.[90]
Overall, however, place-named medicines were few and far between in the South. Did Dixie's nostrum-makers seek to attract
sectional customers by exploiting southern symbols? This did
occur, but, again, only infrequently. The lingering luster of the
Lost Cause played a small but vivid role. An antipain medicine
marketed in New Orleans soon after the Civil War bore the name
and an equestrian portrait of "Stonewall" Jackson. An Atlanta
marketer issued a promotional pamphlet entitled *The Confederate
Souvenir*. And G.H. Tichenor of New Orleans placed on the label
of his Antiseptic Refrigerant a battle scene prominently display-
ing the Stars and Bars.[92]

Indian naming continued in the South as well as in the North,
often without specifying tribe, as in Old Indian Fever Tonic,
Indian Champion of Pain, and PreWit's Indian Liniment.[93] For
generations, the cover of *The Ladies Birthday Almanac*, issued by
the Chattanooga Medicine Company, showed a kneeling Indian
woman pointing out to a standing white woman a flourishing
plant of healing potency.[94] Southern Indian tribes explicitly entered the names of Taylor's Cherokee Remedy of Sweet Gum and
Mullein, Cherokee Chief, and Re-Leave-It Liniment, a Seminole
Indian Formula.[95] If northern marketers could borrow southern
Indians to promote their wares, one southern proprietor, at least,
returned the compliment. A resident of DeKalb County, Georgia,
recorded a trademark for Hiawatha Indian Herb Tonic.[96]

A complexity of appeals characterized the label of Fitzhugh
Lee's Aunt Dinah's Blue Flag Liver Medicine. The United States
flag was featured, printed in blue, because the "Iris or Blue Flag"
had furnished southern Indians a valuable medicinal. This heal-

ing secret had been passed on to old Aunt Dinah, a slave owned by Lee's family. Lee himself had adapted the ancient formula in accord with "the learning of the present day." With patriotism of the reunited nation, Indian lore, black folk wisdom, modern science, and even punning all conjoined, Lee no doubt hoped to capture a significant share of the proprietary market.[97]

Sweeping symbolism and bold therapeutic claims characterized the promotion of proprietary medicines, northern and southern, through decades of endeavor, even though the impact of the 1906 law brought some retrenchment, especially on the part of large marketers with much at stake. Panacea advertising, besides naming many diseases, tended to list symptoms which almost anyone could be expected to encounter—upset stomach, diarrhea, constipation, cough, weariness, sluggishness, gloominess, nervousness, fever, vague aches and pains, spots before the eyes—and to make these symptoms sound like harbingers of dread disease, portents of imminent death. Northern and southern proprietors shared this tendency.

Some promoters preferred the particular to the panacea, especially as the germ theory sharpened the specificity of disease entities. Nostrums for cancer, tuberculosis, and epilepsy appeared, again without regional differentiation. Even for the diseases in which the South had the dubious distinction of possessing a near-monopoly in the nation, southern proprietors had to compete with northern manufacturers, during epidemics of yellow fever and recurring seasons of malaria. Pellagra patent medicines may constitute an exception.

All in all, southern nostrums for southern diseases did not enable the section's proprietary industry to challenge that of the North. In the years immediately following the Revolution, the North began making nostrums much more quickly than did the South, and northern vendors entrenched themselves in the receptive southern market. Considerable southern inventiveness did occur, as the plethora of trade names, patented and unpatented, reveals. But few proprietors, even during the vigorous New South years, could muster the capital and ingenuity to mount a serious challenge to the established northern merchants of medicine. Despite individual southern successes, as a region the South did not win independence in the realm of commercial self-dosage, but remained subservient to the North. The role of southern nostrum distinctiveness was narrow indeed.

NOTES

1. The theme of this chapter I first addressed in a paper given before the South Carolina Historical Association in 1960. In the chapter I draw somewhat on my *The Toadstool Millionaires* and *The Medical Messiahs* (Princeton, N.J.: Princeton Univ. Press, 1961, 1967, respectively). The opening example comes from American Medical Association (AMA), *Nostrums and Quackery*, 3 vols. (Chicago: AMA, 1911, 1921, 1936) II:119.

2. Charles E. Rosenberg, "The Therapeutic Revolution: Medicine, Meaning, and Social Change in Nineteenth-Century America," in *The Therapeutic Revolution: Essays in the Social History of Medicine,* ed. Morris J. Vogel and Charles E. Rosenberg (Philadelphia: Univ. of Pennsylvania Press, 1979), 3–25.

3. David L. Cowen, Louis D. King, and Nicholas Lordi, "Nineteenth Century Drug Therapy: Computer Analysis of the 1854 Prescription File of a Burlington Pharmacy," *Journal of the Medical Society of New Jersey* 78 (1981):760–61. The South revealed a similar complexity and diversity of prescribing. John Harley Warner, "The Idea of Southern Medical Distinctiveness: Medical Knowledge and Practice in the Old South," in *Sickness and Health in America,* ed. Judith Walzer Leavitt and Ronald L. Numbers, 2d ed. (Madison: Univ. of Wisconsin Press, 1985), 57.

4. Rosenberg, "The Therapeutic Revolution," 7–8.

5. William G. Rothstein, *American Physicians in the Nineteenth Century: From Sects to Science* (Baltimore: Johns Hopkins Univ. Press, 1972), 41–55.

6. Oliver Wendell Holmes, *Medical Essays* (Boston: Houghton, Mifflin, 1891), 193.

7. John S. Haller, Jr., *American Medicine in Transition, 1840–1910* (Urbana: Univ. of Illinois Press, 1981), 79–81; John Duffy, *The Rudolph Matas History of Medicine in Louisiana,* 2 vols. (Baton Rouge: Louisiana State Univ. Press, 1958, 1962), I:269–71; II:7–8; Duffy, *The Tulane University Medical Center: One Hundred and Fifty Years of Medical Education* (Baton Rouge: Louisiana State Univ. Press, 1984), 3–4; John Harley Warner, "Medical Sectarianism, Therapeutic Conflict, and the Shaping of Orthodox Professional Identity in Antebellum American Medicine," in *Medical Fringe and Medical Orthodoxy, 1750–1850,* ed. W.F. Bynum and Roy Porter (London: Croom Helm, 1987), 234–60.

8. John Duffy, *The Healers: The Rise of the Medical Establishment* (New York: McGraw-Hill, 1976), 29–30, 219, 225–26; Todd L. Savitt, *Medicine and Slavery: The Diseases and Health Care of Blacks in Antebellum Virginia* (Urbana: Univ. of Illinois Press, 1978), 12–13, 18, 35, 40–47, 150, 155, 232, 253; John C. Gunn, *Gunn's Domestic Medicine, or Poor Man's Friend* (Knoxville: John C. Gunn, 1830; facs. ed. with "Introduction to the New Edition" by Charles E. Rosenberg, Knoxville: Univ. of Tennessee Press,

1986); Duffy, *Matas History of Medicine in Louisiana,* I:155–57 and II:28–30; H.H. Cunningham, *Doctors in Gray* (Baton Rouge: Louisiana State Univ. Press, 1958), 148–50.

9. Rosenberg, "The Therapeutic Revolution," 3–25; John Harley Warner, "A Southern Medical Reform: the Meaning of the Antebellum Argument for Southern Medical Education," *Bulletin of the History of Medicine* 57 (1983):364–81; Warner, "The Idea of Southern Medical Distinctiveness," 53–70.

10. Warner, "The Idea of Southern Medical Distinctiveness," 53–70; Duffy, *Tulane University Medical Center,* 27.

11. Warner, "The Idea of Southern Medical Distinctiveness," 60, 68.

12. Ibid., 61, 62.

13. Ibid., 62; John Duffy, "A Note on Ante-bellum Southern Nationalism and Medical Practice," *Journal of Southern History* 34 (1968):266–76; James O. Breeden, "States-Rights Medicine in the Old South," *Bulletin of the New York Academy of Medicine* 52 (1976):348–72.

14. Breeden, "States-Rights Medicine in the Old South," 354, 360–62; Warner, "The Idea of Southern Medical Distinctiveness," 62–64.

15. Warner, "The Idea of Southern Medical Distinctiveness," 54, 57, 63; Warner, "A Southern Medical Reform," 368.

16. Duffy, *The Healers,* 232.

17. Richard H. Shryock, "Medical Practice in the Old South," *South Atlantic Quarterly* 29 (1930):160–78.

18. Young, *Toadstool Millionaires,* 58–74, 99; Richard H. Shryock, ed., *Letters of Richard D. Arnold, 1808–1876,* Papers of the Trinity College Historical Society, Double Series XVIII–XIX (Durham, N.C., 1929), 33n; *DeBow's Review* 14 (1853):634; Roswell King, Jr., to Thomas Butler, 19 June 1823, and to Frances Butler, 11 Apr. 1824, in Wister Family Papers, and King to Thomas Butler, 7 Oct. 1827, and 21 Nov. 1830, in Butler Family Papers, Historical Society of Pennsylvania, Philadelphia. I am indebted to Mart Stewart for the information from the King letters.

19. Kenneth F. Kiple and Virginia H. Kiple, "Slave Child Mortality: Some Nutritional Answers to a Perennial Puzzle," *Journal of Social History* 10 (1977):284–309; and "Black Tongue and Black Men: Pellagra and Slavery in the Antebellum South," *Journal of Southern History* 43 (1977):411–28; Kenneth F. Kiple and Virginia Himmelsteib King, *Another Dimension to the Black Diaspora: Diet, Disease, and Racism* (Cambridge, England: Cambridge Univ. Press, 1981); Richard H. Steckel, "A Peculiar Population: The Nutrition, Health, and Mortality of American Slaves from Childhood to Maturity," *Journal of Economic History* 46 (1986):721–41.

20. Sam Bowers Hilliard, *Hog Meat and Hoecake* (Carbondale: Southern Illinois Univ. Press, 1972), 62–69; Thomas D. Clark, *Pills, Petticoats and Plows: The Southern Country Store* (Indianapolis: Bobbs-Merrill,

1944), 258–63; Elizabeth W. Etheridge, *The Butterfly Caste* (Westport: Greenwood, 1972); Edward H. Beardsley, *A History of Neglect: Health Care for Blacks and Mill Workers in the Twentieth Century South* (Knoxville: Univ. of Tennessee Press, 1987).

21. Clark, *Pills, Petticoats and Plows*, 237; *Kansas City Star*, 28 Mar. 1915, Clippings 1915, Records of the Office of the Secretary of Agriculture, Record Group 16, National Archives, Washington, D.C.; David T. Courtwright, "The Hidden Epidemic: Opiate Addiction and Cocaine Use in the South, 1860–1920," *Journal of Southern History* 49 (1983):57. Courtwright, 63–64, holds patent medicines less responsible for this situation than prescribing by physicians.

22. George B. Tindall, *The Emergence of the New South, 1913–1945* (Baton Rouge: Louisiana State Univ. Press, 1967), 277.

23. E.L. Hammond, Kenneth Redman, and J.G. Wickstrom, Jr., "Drug and Medical Advertising in Woodville, Miss., 1823–1843," *Journal of the American Pharmaceutical Association (Practical Pharmacy Edition)* 9 (1948):164; Thomas B. Hall, "John Sappington," *Missouri Historical Review* 24 (1930):177–99; W.A. Strickland, Jr., "Quinine Pills Manufactured on the Missouri Frontier (1832–1862)," *Pharmacy in History* 25 (1983):60–68; Clark, *Pills, Petticoats and Plows*, 235–36; Georgia Trade Marks Books, I, Office of the Secretary of State Records, Georgia Dept. of Archives and History, Atlanta [hereafter cited as Georgia Trade Marks Books].

24. L.G. Gramling, *A History of Pharmacy in Florida* (Gainesville: privately printed, 1973), 205; Albert Deutsch, "The Strange Case of the Three Sixes," *PM* (New York, N.Y.), 23 Apr. 1944; Karen Brune, "It's Business as Usual at Monticello Drug Co.," *Florida Times-Union* (Jacksonville), 23 June 1982, courtesy of John E. Tilford, Jr.

25. Young, *Toadstool Millionaires*, 38–39, 299.

26. J.H. Powell, *Bring Out Your Dead* (Philadelphia: Univ. of Pennsylvania Press, 1949), 257; Evelyn Ward Gay, *The Medical Profession in Georgia, 1773–1983* (Fulton, Missouri: Ovid Bell Press, 1983), 403; "The Plague in the South-West," *DeBow's Review* 15 (1853):625; Jo Ann Carrigan, "The Saffron Scourge: A History of Yellow Fever in Louisiana, 1795–1905" (Ph.D. diss., Louisiana State Univ., 1961), 438–41; Duffy, *Matas History of Medicine in Louisiana*, II:41.

27. Elizabeth Dwyer Vickers and F. Norman Vickers, "Notations on Pensacola's Medical History, 1873–1923," *Journal of the Florida Medical Association* 61 (1974), 99.

28. Carrigan, "The Saffron Scourge," 438–41.

29. The discussion of the three pellagra proprietaries is drawn from "Pellagracide and Ez-X-Ba," *Journal of the American Medical Association* 58 (1912):648–49; "Baughn's Pellagra Remedy," ibid., 61 (1913):1828–30; "Exploitation of the Sick—Alleged Cures for Pellagra Being Advertised and Sold," *Public Health Reports* 29 (1914):1065–66; Etheridge, *The But-*

terfly Caste, 38–39; Daphne A. Roe, *A Plague of Corn* (Ithaca: Cornell Univ. Press, 1973), 95–98; Ann Springall, "Three Pellagra Remedies" (seminar paper, Univ. of Wisconsin, 1975).

30. John Phillips Street, comp., *The Composition of Certain Patent and Proprietary Medicines* (Chicago: AMA, 1971), 238, 242.

31. Samuel Hopkins Adams, *The Great American Fraud* (Chicago: AMA, 1906), 53.

32. *Hearings on H.R. 13086,* 59th Cong., 1st sess., 10.

33. Adams, *The Great American Fraud,* 53; "Report of Work Done [1896–1899] by the Division of Chemistry . . . for the Various Executive Departments," Miscellaneous Papers, II, Bureau of Chemistry Records, Record Group 97, National Archives; *Investigations of Adulterated Foods, Etc.,* 58th Cong., 1st sess., Sen. Document 270 (1904), 2–4.

34. Gloria Blackwell, "Black-Controlled Media in Atlanta, 1960–1970: The Burden of the Message and the Struggle for Survival" (Ph.D. diss., Emory Univ., 1973), 13.

35. *The Crisis* 3 (Feb. 1912):130; 4 (Oct. 1912):202; 13 (Nov. 1916):44.

36. Notice of Judgment (NJ) 4495. Section 4 of the Food and Drugs Act of 1906 stated: "After judgment of the court [in cases brought under the law], notice shall be given by publication. . . ." In May 1908 the Board of Food and Drug Inspection of the Department of Agriculture published Notice of Judgment 1. The final Notice of Judgment under the 1906 law, number 31156, was issued by the Food and Drug Administration, then a part of the Federal Security Agency, in Feb. 1943. In March 1940 new series of Notices of Judgment separately for foods and drugs began to be issued, reporting actions under the Food, Drug, and Cosmetic Act of 1938. The NJ set consulted for this chapter is in the library of the Emory Univ. School of Law. Atlanta Station Report, in Eastern District Report, Aug. 1939, Decimal file 606ED, Food and Drug Administration Records, Record Group 88, Washington National Records Center, Suitland, Maryland.

37. George B. Griffenhagen and James Harvey Young, "Old English Patent Medicines in America," *Contributions from the Museum of Science and Technology,* United States National Museum Bulletin 218 (Washington: Smithsonian Institution, 1959), 155–83; Young, *Toadstool Millionaires,* 3–15; Roger A. Hambridge, " 'Empiricomany, or an Infatuation in Favour of *Empiricism* or *Quackery':* The Socio-economics of Eighteenth Century Quackery," in *Literature and Science and Medicine* (Los Angeles: William Andrews Clark Memorial Library, Univ. of California at Los Angeles, 1982), 45–102.

38. *Pennsylvania Gazette,* 17 Oct. 1745; *South Carolina Gazette,* 21 Nov. 1743.

39. *South Carolina Gazette* 7 Mar. 1743; *Pennsylvania Gazette* 19 Aug. 1731.

40. Griffenhagen and Young, "Old English Patent Medicines."

41. NJ 31134.

42. These calculations are made from U.S. Patent Office, *Subject-Matter Index of Patents for Inventions Issued for the United States Patent Office from 1790 to 1873, Inclusive*, comp. M.D. Leggett (Washington, D.C.: Patent Office, 1874), 863–64, 912–18, 975, 1046–47, 1240, and 1936–38. Medical devices and animal drugs were excluded, and a few scattered references to drugs under such names as "Panacea" and "Elixir of Life" were omitted. The number of southern patents by states was: Missouri, 31; Kentucky, 23; Georgia, 20; Virginia, 18; Louisiana, 17; Maryland, 13; Tennessee, 11; Alabama, North Carolina and Texas, 10; Mississippi, 7; South Carolina, 3; Florida, 2; Arkansas, 1. The leading states were New York, 165; Pennsylvania, 75; Ohio, 65; Illinois, 48; Massachusetts, 40; California, 36; Indiana, 31. For commentary on patent granting for medicines up to 1849, see House Report 52, 30th Cong., 2d sess. (1849). Also see Lyman F. Kebler, "United States Patents Granted for Medicines during the Pioneer Years of the Patent Office," *Journal of the American Pharmaceutical Association* 24 (1935):485–89.

43. Robert Cumming Wilson, *Drugs and Pharmacy in the Life of Georgia, 1733–1959* (Athens, Ga., privately printed, 1959), 113, 116; *Columbian Museum & Savannah Advertiser*, 29 Sept. 1802; *Louisiana Gazette*, 16 Apr. 1805, cited in Duffy, *Matas History of Medicine in Louisiana*, I:344.

44. Young, *Toadstool Millionaires*, 31–43; Helen McKearin, *Bottles, Flasks and Dr. Dyott* (Philadelphia: Crown, 1970).

45. Hammond et al., "Drug and Medical Advertising in Woodville," 160–65.

46. "Gray's Ointment Is Now 102 Years Old," *Standard Remedies* 8 (June 1922):8, 9; Clark, *Pills, Petticoats and Plows*, 232.

47. Radway & Co.'s Patent Medicine Circular sent to Birchall and Owen, Springfield, Ill., 1852, in author's collection.

48. Henry W. Holcombe, *Patent Medicine Tax Stamps* (Lawrence, Mass.: Quarterman, 1979), 68–70; Richard F. Riley, "New Historical Light on Dr. John Bull," *American Philatelist* 88 (1974):142–44; correspondence between John Bull & Co., and Birchall and Owen, 1850–1852, author's collection; Madge E. Pickard and R. Carlyle Buley, *The Midwest Pioneer: His Ills, Cures & Doctors* (New York: Henry Schuman, 1946), 284; *Republican Citizen* (Frederick, Md.), 26 Feb. 1875; Dr. John Bull's King of Pain poster, copyrighted 1855, Prints and Photographs Division, Library of Congress; James Harvey Young, "The Marketing of Patent Medicines in Lincoln's Springfield," *Pharmacy in History* 27 (1985):98–102.

49. "Bottle of S.S.S. Sold Every Eight Seconds," *Standard Remedies* 7 (Sept. 1921):8, 10.

50. Chauncey Leake, "The History of Self-Medication," in "Home Medication and the Public Welfare," ed. Harold E. Whipple, *Annals of the New York Academy of Science* 120 (1965):819–20.

51. Varro E. Tyler, "Three Proprietaries and Their Claim as American 'Indian' Remedies," *Pharmacy in History* 26 (1984):146–49.

52. Bella C. Landauer Collection, New York Historical Society.

53. Young, *Toadstool Millionaires*, 176–79.

54. Duffy, *Matas History of Medicine in Louisiana*, II:40.

55. All of these items are in Prints and Photographs Division, Library of Congress.

56. Young, *Toadstool Millionaires*, 93–96.

57. *Charleston Daily Courier*, 18 Jan. 1862; Augusta *Daily Chronicle & Sentinel*, 4 Jan. 1862; Augusta *Daily Constitutionalist*, 1 Jan. 1865.

58. John Bennett, *Apothecaries' Hall, A Unique Exhibit at the Charleston Museum* (Charleston, 1923), 16; *Columbia Phoenix*, 27 June 1866; Thomas D. Clark, *The Southern Country Editor* (Indianapolis: Bobbs-Merrill, 1948), 70.

59. These observations were made in 1959.

60. The 1 Feb. and 1 July issues of the *Atlanta Constitution* for 1900, 1910, and 1920, and of the *Atlanta Journal* for 1905 and 1915 were examined. Of the total of 187 proprietary advertisements encountered, 38 of the medicines were manufactured in the eleven states of the ex-Confederacy, 130 elsewhere in the nation, and 19 could not be determined. On the readyprint industry, see Clark, *Southern Country Editor*, 75, and Young, *Toadstool Millionaires*, 100.

61. Blake D. Applewhite to W.J. Cass, 11 July 1921; [Cass] to Parke, Davis & Co., 1 July 1912; Pictorial Paper Package Corporation to East Tennessee Medicine Co. [1920], East Tennessee Medicine Company Collection, Archives of Appalachia, Sherrod Library, East Tennessee State Univ., Johnson City.

62. Clark, *Pills, Petticoats and Plows*, 186, 223, 230; Edward A. Gaston, "A History of the Negro Wage Earner in Georgia, 1890–1940," (Ph.D. diss., Emory Univ., 1957), 103.

63. Young, *Toadstool Millionaires*, 187–88; Clark, *Pills, Petticoats and Plows*, 246.

64. *National Druggist* 33 (Jan. 1903):xxvi; Congressman James L. Slayden, *Congressional Record*, 59th Cong., 1st sess., 8987; the Bankhead incident of 1904 furnished by Walter J. Heacock.

65. *New Orleans Times-Democrat*, cited in *Druggists Circular and Chemical Gazette* 45 (Jan. 1901):xi.

66. Pamphlet in author's collection.

67. "Bottle of S.S.S. Sold Every Eight Seconds."

68. *FDA Reports* 16 (6 Nov. 1954):9; Tyler, "Three Proprietaries and Their Claim As American 'Indian' Remedies."

69. Young, *Medical Messiahs*, 3–190.

70. NJs 6673 and 19492; AMA, *Nostrums and Quackery*, III:77, 102.

71. Clark, *Pills, Petticoats and Plows*, 247–59.

72. Young, *Medical Messiahs*, 142; Morris Fishbein, "Libel Suits

Against the American Medical Association," *Food Drug Cosmetic Law Quarterly* 2 (1947):180–82; James G. Burrow, *AMA: Voice of American Medicine* (Baltimore: Johns Hopkins Univ. Press, 1963), 124–25; AMA, *The Wine of Cardui Suit* (Chicago: AMA, 1916); *Standard Remedies* 2 (Apr. 1916):5–8; (May 1916):12–13; (June 1916):23; (July 1916):8–13; (Sept. 1916):9. The quotation appears in *Journal of the American Medical Association* 63 (1914):262.

73. *Drug Trade News,* 20 Mar. 1933, p. 25.

74. Ad in *Grier's Almanac,* 1957; *Chattanooga News,* 14 Jan. 1936.

75. Census Office, Dept. of Interior, *Eleventh Census of the United States, 1890,* vol. 6, *Report on Manufacturing Industries in the United States* (Washington: Government Printing Office, 1895), pt. 2, Statistics of Cities.

76. *Grier's Almanac,* 1888, imprinted with name of Asa G. Candler, Asa Griggs Candler Papers, Special Collections, Robert W. Woodruff Library, Emory Univ.

77. Monroe Martin King, "Pemberton, John Stith," in *Dictionary of Georgia Biography,* ed. Kenneth Coleman and Charles Stephen Gurr, 2 vols. (Athens: Univ. of Georgia Press, 1983), II:785–86; King, "Dr. John S. Pemberton: Originator of Coca-Cola," *Pharmacy in History* 29 (1987):85–89; James Harvey Young, "Three Southern Food and Drug Cases," *Journal of Southern History* 49 (1983):5–6; Pat Watters, *Coca-Cola* (Garden City, N.Y.: Doubleday, 1978), 1–8, 12–20.

78. Mark K. Bauman, "Candler, Asa Griggs," in *Dictionary of Georgia Biography,* ed. Coleman and Gurr, I:163–66; Charles Howard Candler, *Asa Griggs Candler* (Emory University: Emory Univ., 1950); Young, "Three Southern Food and Drug Cases," 3–19; Watters, *Coca-Cola,* 12–121.

79. *Grier's Almanac,* 1888, imprinted with Candler's name; carton label for Dr. Cheney's Expectorant, recorded in 1898, Georgia Trade Marks Books, I.

80. James Harvey Young, "Jacobs, Joseph," in *Dictionary of Georgia Biography,* ed. Coleman and Gurr, I:516–17; 1904 contract in author's collection.

81. NJs 4495 and 4992.

82. NJs 4113, 5824, 6524, 6333.

83. Georgia Trade Marks Books, II and III.

84. Food and Drug Administration 1935 Report, in Food Law Institute Series, *Federal Food, Drug and Cosmetic Law: Administrative Reports, 1907–1949* (Chicago: Commerce Clearing House, 1951), 843–44; NJs 22613 and 25126; AMA, *Nostrums and Quackery,* III:74, 77.

85. Georgia Trade Marks Books, II.

86. C. Fleming, Post Office Inspector, Philadelphia, to J.J. McManus, FDA, Atlanta, 21 Oct. 1937, Decimal file 540B for 1939, FDA Records, Washington National Records Center.

87. Census Office, *Eleventh Census of the United States,* vol. 6, *Report on Manufacturing Industries,* pt. I, Totals for States and Industries.

88. Census Office, *Twelfth Census of the United States, 1900,* vol. 7, *Manufactures,* pt. I (Washington, D.C., U.S. Census Office, 1902).

89. Holcombe, *Patent Office Tax Stamps,* 355; copyright material, Prints and Photographs Division, Library of Congress; NJ 17307.

90. NJ 4840.

91. NJ 1178; Georgia Trade Marks Books, II.

92. Louis Fix copyright, Prints and Photographs Division, Library of Congress; Walter A. Taylor pamphlet, Atlanta, Special Collections, Woodruff Library, Emory Univ.; Tichenor bottle, in author's collection.

93. NJ 5781; Georgia Trade Marks Books, II.

94. *The Ladies Birthday Almanac,* 1907, Rare Books Division, Library of Congress; and 1976, author's collection.

95. *Taylor's Riddle Book,* Special Collections, Woodruff Library, Emory Univ.; Georgia Trade Marks Books, IV; Cherokee Chief bottle in author's collection, courtesy of Margaret Leake.

96. Georgia Trade Marks Books, III.

97. Ibid., II.

Selected Bibliography of
Writings on Southern Disease
and Southern Medicine

Beardsley, Edward H. *A History of Neglect: Health Care for Blacks and Mill Workers in the Twentieth-Century South.* Knoxville: Univ. of Tennessee Press, 1987.

Blanton, Wyndham B. *Medicine in Virginia in the 17th Century.* Richmond: William Byrd Press, 1930.

———. *Medicine in Virginia in the 18th Century.* Richmond: Garrett and Massie, 1931.

———. *Medicine in Virginia in the 19th Century.* Richmond: Garrett and Massie, 1933.

Boccaccio, Mary. "Ground Itch and Dew Poison: The Rockefeller Sanitary Commission, 1909–14." *Journal of the History of Medicine and Allied Sciences* 27 (1972), 30–53.

Breeden, James O. "States-Rights Medicine in the Old South." *Bulletin of the New York Academy of Medicine* 52 (1976), 348–72.

———. *Joseph Jones, M.D.: Scientist of the Old South.* Lexington: Univ. Press of Kentucky, 1975.

Carrigan, Jo Ann. "The Saffron Scourge: A History of Yellow Fever in Louisiana, 1796–1905." Ph.D. dissertation, Louisiana State University, 1961.

———. "Privilege, Prejudice, and the Strangers' Disease in Nineteenth-Century New Orleans." *Journal of Southern History* 36 (1970), 568–75.

Cassedy, James H. "The 'Germ of Laziness" in the South, 1900–1915: Charles Wardell Stiles and the Progressive Paradox." *Bulletin of the History of Medicine* 45 (1971), 159–69.

Cowdrey, Albert E. *This Land, This South: An Environmental History.* Lexington: Univ. Press of Kentucky, 1983.

Duffy, John. "A Note on Antebellum Southern Nationalism and Medical Practice." *Journal of Southern History* 34 (1968), 266–76.

———. "Sectional Conflict and Medical Education in Louisiana." *Journal of Southern History* 23 (1957), 289–306.

————. *Sword of Pestilence: The New Orleans Yellow Fever Epidemic of 1853.* Baton Rouge: Louisiana State Univ. Press, 1966.

————, ed. *The Rudolph Matas History of Medicine in Louisiana.* 2 vols. Baton Rouge: Louisiana State Univ. Press, 1962.

Ellis, John. "Business and Public Health in the Urban South During the Nineteenth Century: New Orleans, Memphis, and Atlanta." *Bulletin of the History of Medicine* 44 (1970), 197–212, 346–71.

Etheridge, Elizabeth. *The Butterfly Caste: A Social History of Pellagra in the South.* Westport, Conn.: Greenwood Press, 1972.

Ettling, John. *The Germ of Laziness: Rockefeller Philanthropy and Public Health in the New South.* Cambridge, Mass.: Harvard Univ. Press, 1981.

Galishoff, Stuart. "Germs Know No Color Line: Black Health and Public Policy in Atlanta, 1900–1918." *Journal of the History of Medicine and Allied Sciences* 40 (1985), 22–41.

Haller, John S. "The Negro and the Southern Physician: A Study of Medical and Racial Attitudes, 1800–1860." *Medical History* 16 (1972), 238–53.

Holley, Howard E. *A History of Medicine in Alabama.* Birmingham: Univ. of Alabama School of Medicine, 1982.

Jones, James H. *Bad Blood: The Tuskegee Syphilis Experiment.* New York: Free Press, 1981.

Kiple, Kenneth F., and Virginia Himmelsteib King. *Another Dimension to the Black Diaspora: Diet, Disease, and Racism.* Cambridge, England: Cambridge Univ. Press, 1981.

Kupperman, Karen Ordahl. "Fear of Hot Climates in the Anglo-American Colonial Experience." *William & Mary Quarterly,* 3d series, 16 (1984), 213–40.

Merrens, H. Roy, and George D. Terry. "Dying in Paradise: Malaria, Mortality, and the Perceptual Environment in Colonial South Carolina." *Journal of Southern History* 15 (1984), 533–50.

Numbers, Ronald L., and Todd L. Savitt, eds. *Science and Medicine in the Old South.* Baton Rouge: Louisiana State Univ. Press, forthcoming.

Postell, William Dosité. *The Health of Slaves on Southern Plantations.* Baton Rouge: Louisiana State Univ. Press, 1951.

Savitt, Todd L. *Medicine and Slavery: The Diseases and Health Care of Blacks in Antebellum Virginia.* Urbana: Univ. of Illinois Press, 1978.

————. "Filariasis in the United States." *Journal of the History of Medicine and Allied Sciences* 32 (1977), 140–50.

————. "The Use of Blacks for Medical Experimentation and Demonstration in the Old South." *Journal of Southern History* 48 (1982), 331–48.

Shryock, Richard H. "Medical Practice in the Old South." In *Medicine in America, Historical Essays,* 49–70. Baltimore: Johns Hopkins Univ. Press, 1966.

Steckel, Richard H. "A Dreadful Childhood: The Excess Mortality of American Slaves." *Social Science History* 10 (1986), 427–65.

———. "A Peculiar Population: The Nutrition, Health, and Mortality of American Slaves from Childhood to Maturity." *Journal of Economic History* 46 (1986), 721–41.

Tullos, Allen. "The Great Hookworm Crusade." *Southern Exposure* 6 (Summer 1978), 40–49.

Waring, Joseph I. *A History of Medicine in South Carolina, 1670–1825.* Columbia: South Carolina Medical Association, 1964.

———. *A History of Medicine in South Carolina, 1825–1900,* Columbia: South Carolina Medical Association, 1967.

Warner, John Harley. "The Idea of Southern Medical Distinctiveness: Medical Knowledge and Practice in the Old South." In *Sickness and Health in America,* edited by Judith Walzer Leavitt and Ronald L. Numbers, 2d ed., pp. 53–70. Madison: Univ. of Wisconsin Press, 1985.

———. "A Southern Medical Reform: The Meaning of the Antebellum Argument for Southern Medical Education." *Bulletin of the History of Medicine* 57 (1983), 364–81.

———. *The Therapeutic Perspective: Medical Practice, Knowledge, and Identity in America, 1820–1885.* Cambridge, Mass.: Harvard Univ. Press, 1986.

Warner, Margaret. "Local Control versus National Interest: The Debate Over Southern Public Health, 1878–1884." *Journal of Southern History* 50 (1984), 407–428.

Index

•